Introduction

The articles collected here are part of a public discussion on the continuity of communist strategy from 1848 to today, especially the political contributions of V.I. Lenin and the Bolshevik Party over the decade and a half prior to the October 1917 revolutionary victory in Russia.

The views of the leadership of the Socialist Workers Party in this debate were presented by Doug Jenness, editor of the biweekly newsmagazine *Intercontinental Press* at the time. Ernest Mandel, a leader of the Revolutionary Workers League, the section of the Fourth International in Belgium, presented a counterview.

The debate was sparked by Mandel's response to an article by Jenness in the November 1981 issue of the *International Socialist Review,* a monthly supplement to the *Militant*. The issue was celebrating the sixty-fourth anniversary of the October revolution; Jenness's article had been written to accompany Lenin's 1921 article "On the Fourth Anniversary of the Russian Revolution," which is reprinted here as the first item.

Mandel's article was published in the April 1982 *International Socialist Review,* and Jenness responded in the June 1982 issue. A rejoinder by Mandel then appeared in the August 8, 1983, issue of *Intercontinental Press.*

Of related interest is the book *Their Trotsky and Ours: Communist Continuity Today* by Jack Barnes, published by Pathfinder Press. It, as well as related books and pamphlets by Russian Bolshevik leaders V.I. Lenin and Leon Trotsky, can be ordered from www.pathfinderpress.com. See the ads at the back for some of these titles.

Steve Clark
NOVEMBER 2013

CELEBRATING THE OCTOBER REVOLUTION

On the Fourth Anniversary of the Russian Revolution

by V.I. Lenin

Reprinted below is an article by V.I. Lenin, central leader of the Russian Bolshevik Party. It was written on the occasion of the fourth anniversary of the Russian revolution, and first appeared in the October 18, 1921, edition of 'Pravda,' the Bolshevik newspaper.

The fourth anniversary of October 25 (November 7)[1] is approaching.

The farther that great day recedes from us, the more clearly we see the significance of the proletarian revolution in Russia, and the more deeply we reflect upon the practical experience of our work as a whole.

Very briefly and, of course, in very incomplete and rough outline, this significance and experience may be summed up as follows.

The direct and immediate object of the revolution in Russia was a bourgeois-democratic one, namely, to destroy the survivals of medievalism and sweep them away completely, to purge Russia of this barbarism, of this shame, and to remove this immense obstacle to all culture and progress in our country.

And we can justifiably pride ourselves on having carried out that purge with greater determination and much more rapidly, boldly and successfully, and, from the point of view of its effect on the masses, much more widely and deeply, than the great French Revolution over one hundred and twenty-five years ago.

Both the anarchists and the petty-bourgeois democrats (i.e., the Mensheviks[2] and the Socialist-Revolutionaries[3], who are the Russian counterparts of that international social type) have talked and are still talking an incredible lot of nonsense about the relation between the bourgeois-democratic revolution and the socialist (that is proletarian) revolution. The last four years have proved to the hilt that our interpretation of Marxism on this point, and our estimate of the experience of former revolutions were correct. We have consummated the bourgeois-democratic revolution as nobody had done before. We are advancing towards the socialist revolution consciously, firmly and unswervingly, knowing that it is not separated from the bourgeois-democratic revolution by a Chinese Wall, and knowing too that (in the last analysis) *struggle alone* will determine how far we shall advance, what part of this immense and lofty task we shall accomplish, and to what extent we shall succeed in consolidating our victories. Time will show. But we see even now that a tremendous amount—tremendous for this ruined, exhausted and backward country—has already been done towards the socialist transformation of society.

Let us, however, finish what we have to say about the bourgeois-democratic content of our revolution. Marxists must understand what that means. To explain, let us take a few striking examples.

The bourgeois-democratic content of the revolution means that the social relations (system, institutions) of the country are purged of medievalism, serfdom, feudalism.

What were the chief manifestations, survivals, remnants of serfdom in Russia up to 1917? The monarchy, the system of social estates, landed proprietorship and land tenure, the status of women, religion, and national oppression. Take any one of these Augean stables, which, incidentally, were

These two articles first appeared in the November 1981 *International Socialist Review,* monthly supplement to the *Militant.*

left largely uncleansed by all the more advanced states when they accomplished *their* bourgeois-democratic revolutions one hundred and twenty-five, two hundred and fifty and more years ago (1649 in England); take any one of these Augean stables, and you will see that we have cleansed them thoroughly. In a matter of *ten weeks*, from October 25 (November 7), 1917 to January 5, 1918, when the Constituent Assembly was dissolved, we accomplished a thousand times more in this respect than was accomplished by the bourgeois democrats and liberals (the Cadets[4]) and by the petty-bourgeois democrats (the Mensheviks and the Socialist-Revolutionaries) *during the eight months* they were in power.

Those poltroons, gas-bags, vainglorious Narcissuses and petty Hamlets brandished their wooden swords—but did not even destroy the monarchy! We cleansed out all that monarchist muck as nobody had ever done before. We left not a stone, not a brick of that ancient edifice, the social-estate system (even the most advanced countries, such as Britain, France and Germany, have not completely eliminated the survivals of that system to this day!), standing. We tore out the deep-seated roots of the social-estate system, namely, the remnants of feudalism and serfdom in the system of landownership, to the last. "One may argue" (there are plenty of quill-drivers, Cadets, Mensheviks and Socialist-Revolutionaries abroad to indulge in such arguments) as to what "in the long run" will be the outcome of the agrarian reform effected by the Great October Revolution. We have no desire at the moment to waste time on such controversies, for we are deciding this, as well as the mass of accompanying controversies, by struggle. But the fact cannot be denied that the petty-bourgeois democrats "compromised" with the landowners, the custodians of the traditions of serfdom, for eight months, while we completely swept the landowners and all their traditions from Russian soil in a few weeks.

Take religion, or the denial of rights to women, or the oppression and inequality of the non-Russian nationalities. These are all problems of the bourgeois-democratic revolution. The vulgar petty-bourgeois democrats talked about them for eight months. In not a *single* one of the most advanced countries in the world have *these* questions been *completely* settled on *bourgeois-democratic* lines. In our country they have been settled completely by the legislation of the October Revolution. We have fought and are fighting religion in earnest. We have granted *all* the non-Russian nationalities *their own* republics or autonomous regions. We in Russia no longer have the base, mean and infamous denial of rights to women or inequality of the sexes, that disgusting survival of feudalism and medievalism, which is being renovated by the avaricious bourgeoisie and the dull-witted and frightened petty bourgeoisie in every other country in the world without exception.

All this goes to make up the content of the bourgeois-democratic revolution. A hundred and fifty and two hundred and fifty years ago the progressive leaders of that revolution (or of those revolutions, if we consider each national variety of the one general type) promised to rid mankind of medieval privileges, of sex inequality, of state privileges for one religion or another (or "religious *ideas*", "the church" in general), and of national inequality. They promised, but did not keep their promises. They could not keep them, for they were hindered by their "respect"—for the "sacred right of private property". Our proletarian revolution was not afflicted with this accursed "respect" for this thrice-accursed medievalism and for the "sacred right of private property".

But in order to consolidate the achievements of the bourgeois-democratic revolution for the peoples of Russia, we were obliged to go farther; and we did go farther. We solved the problems of the bourgeois-democratic revolution in pass-

---

1. Under Czarism Russia used the old Byzantine calendar which was thirteen days behind the Gregorian calendar used by the rest of Europe. After the October revolution Russia went over to the more modern calendar.

2. Mensheviks—the minority faction of the Russian Social Democratic Labor Party after the split with the Bolsheviks in 1903. Believed that the working class must support the liberal bourgeoisie to overthrow Czarism and establish a democratic republic.

3. Social Revolutionary Party—formed in 1900 and emerged in 1902–03 as the political expression of all the earlier populist currents. It had the most influence among the peasantry before the 1917 revolution.

4. Cadets (Constitutional-Democratic Party)—the chief party of the liberal bourgeoisie in Russia.

ing, as a "by-product" of our main and genuinely *proletarian*-revolutionary, socialist activities. We have always said that reforms are a by-product of the revolutionary class struggle. We said—and proved it by deeds—that bourgeois-democratic reforms are a by-product of the proletarian, i.e., of the socialist revolution. Incidentally, the Kautskys, Hilferdings, Martovs, Chernovs, Hillquits, Longuets, MacDonalds, Turatis and other heroes of "Two-and-a-Half" Marxism[5] were incapable of understanding *this* relation between the bourgeois-democratic and the proletarian-socialist revolutions. The first develops into the second. The second, in passing, solves the problems of the first. The second consolidates the work of the first. Struggle, and struggle alone, decides how far the second succeeds in outgrowing the first.

The Soviet system is one of the most vivid proofs, or manifestations, of how the one revolution develops into the other. The Soviet system provides the maximum of democracy for the workers and peasants; at the same time, it marks a break with *bourgeois* democracy and the rise of a *new*, epoch-making *type* of democracy, namely, proletarian democracy, or the dictatorship of the proletariat.

Let the curs and swine of the moribund bourgeoisie, and of the petty-bourgeois democrats who trail behind them, heap imprecations, abuse and derision upon our heads for our reverses and mistakes in the work of building up *our* Soviet system. We do not forget for a moment that we have committed and are committing numerous mistakes and are suffering numerous reverses. How can reverses and mistakes be avoided in a matter so new in the history of the world as the building of an unprecedented *type* of state edifice! We shall work steadfastly to set our reverses and mistakes right and to improve our practical application of Soviet principles, which is still very, very far from being perfect. But we have a right to be and are proud that to us has fallen the good fortune to *begin* the building of a Soviet state, and thereby to *usher in* a new era in world history, the era of the rule of a *new* class, a class which is oppressed in every capitalist country, but which everywhere is marching forward towards a new life, towards victory over the bourgeoisie, towards the dictatorship of the proletariat, towards the emancipation of mankind from the yoke of capital and from imperialist wars.

The question of imperialist wars, of the international policy of finance capital which now dominates the whole world, a policy that must *inevitably* engender new imperialist wars, that must inevitably cause an extreme intensification of national oppression, pillage, brigandry and the strangulation of weak, backward and small nationalities by a handful of "advanced" powers—that question has been the keystone of all policy in all the countries of the globe since 1914. It is a question of life and death for millions upon millions of people. It is a question of whether 20,000,000 people (as compared with the 10,000,000 who were killed in the war of 1914–18 and in the supplementary "minor" wars that are still going on) are to be slaughtered in the next imperialist war, which the bourgeoisie are preparing, and which is growing out of capitalism before our very eyes. It is a question of whether in that future war, which is inevitable (if capitalism continues to exist), 60,000,000 people are to be maimed (compared with the 30,000,000 maimed in 1914–18). In this question, too, our October Revolution marked the beginning of a new era in world history. The lackeys of the bourgeoisie and its yes-men—the Socialist-Revolutionaries and the Mensheviks, and the petty-bourgeois, allegedly "socialist," democrats all over the world—derided our slogan "convert the imperialist war into a civil war." But that slogan proved to be the *truth*—it was the only truth, unpleasant, blunt, naked and brutal, but nevertheless the *truth*, as against the host of most refined jingoist and pacifist lies. Those lies are being dispelled. The Brest peace[6] has been exposed. And with every passing day the significance and consequences of a peace that is even worse than the Brest peace—the peace of Versailles—are being more relentlessly exposed. And the millions who are thinking about the causes of the recent war and

5. The Two-and-a-Half International—was founded in Vienna in 1921 at a conference of centrist parties and groups which, under pressure of the revolutionary-minded masses, temporarily seceded from the Second International and returned to it in 1923.

6. Brest peace—the peace treaty imposed on Russia by Germany in early 1918. It placed especially hard conditions on Russia.

of the approaching future war are more and more clearly realising the grim and inexorable truth that it is impossible to escape imperialist war, and imperialist peace (if the old orthography were still in use, I would have written the word *mir* in two ways, to give it both its meanings)[7] which inevitably engenders imperialist war, that it is impossible to escape that inferno, *except by a Bolshevik struggle and a Bolshevik revolution.*

Let the bourgeoisie and the pacifists, the generals and the petty bourgeoisie, the capitalists and the philistines, the pious Christians and the knights of the Second and the Two-and-a-Half Internationals vent their fury against that revolution. No torrents of abuse, calumnies and lies can enable them to conceal the historic fact that for the first time in hundreds and thousands of years the slaves have replied to a war between slave-owners by openly proclaiming the slogan: "Convert this war between slave-owners for the division of their loot into a war of the slaves of all nations against the slave-owners of all nations."

For the first time in hundreds and thousands of years that slogan has grown from a vague and helpless waiting into a clear and definite political programme, into an effective struggle waged by millions of oppressed people under the leadership of the proletariat; it has grown into the first victory of the proletariat, the first victory in the struggle to abolish war and to unite the workers of all countries against the united bourgeoisie of different nations, against the bourgeoisie that makes peace and war at the expense of the slaves of capital, the wage-workers, the peasants, the working people.

This first victory is *not yet the final victory,* and it was achieved by our October Revolution at the price of incredible difficulties and hardships, at the price of unprecedented suffering, accompanied by a series of serious reverses and mistakes on our part. How could a single backward people be expected to frustrate the imperialist wars of the most powerful and most developed countries of the world without sustaining reverses and without committing mistakes! We are not afraid to admit our mistakes and shall examine them dispassionately in order to learn how to correct them. But the fact remains that for the first time in hundreds and thousands of years the promise "to reply" to war between the slave-owners by a revolution of the slaves directed *against* all the slave-owners *has been completely fulfilled*—and is being fulfilled despite all difficulties.

We have made the start. When, at what date and time, and the proletarians of which nation will complete this process is not important. The important thing is that the ice has been broken; the road is open, the way has been shown.

Gentlemen, capitalists of all countries, keep up your hypocritical pretence of "defending the fatherland"—the Japanese fatherland against the American, the American against the Japanese, the French against the British, and so forth! Gentlemen, knights of the Second and Two-and-a-Half Internationals, pacifist petty bourgeoisie and philistines of the entire world, go on "evading" the question of how to combat imperialist wars by issuing new "Basle Manifestos" (on the model of the Basle Manifesto of 1912).[8] *The first Bolshevik revolution* has wrested *the first hundred million people* of this earth from the clutches of imperialist war and the imperialist world. Subsequent revolutions will deliver the rest of mankind from such wars and from such a world.

Our last, but most important and most difficult task, the one we have done least about, is economic development, the laying of economic foundations for the new, socialist edifice on the site of the demolished feudal edifice and the semi-demolished capitalist edifice. It is in this most important and most difficult task that we have sustained the greatest number of reverses and have made most mistakes. How could anyone expect that a task so new to the world could be begun without reverses and without mistakes! But we have begun it. We shall continue it. At this very moment we are, by our New Economic Policy,[9] correcting a number

7. In Russian, the word *mir* has two meanings (world and peace) and had two different spellings in the old way of spelling.

8. Basle Manifesto—the manifesto against imperialist war adopted unanimously by a congress of the Second International in Basle, Switzerland in 1912. When World War I broke out in 1914, the leaders of the Second International (Karl Kautsky, etc.) who had voted for the manifesto consigned it to oblivion and supported their own imperialist governments.

9. New Economic Policy—initiated at the Tenth Congress of the Russian Communist Party in 1921 to revive the economy

of our mistakes. We are learning how to continue erecting the socialist edifice in a small-peasant country without committing such mistakes.

The difficulties are immense. But we are accustomed to grappling with immense difficulties. Not for nothing do our enemies call us "stone-hard" and exponents of a "firm-line policy." But we have also learned, at least to some extent, another art that is essential in revolution, namely, flexibility, the ability to effect swift and sudden changes of tactics if changes in objective conditions demand them, and to choose another path for the achievement of our goal if the former path proves to be inexpedient or impossible at the given moment.

Borne along on the crest of the wave of enthusiasm, rousing first the political enthusiasm and then the military enthusiasm of the people, we expected to accomplish economic tasks just as great as the political and military tasks we had accomplished by relying directly on this enthusiasm. We expected—or perhaps it would be truer to say that we presumed without having given it adequate consideration—to be able to organise the state production and the state distribution of products on communist lines in a small-peasant country directly as ordered by the proletarian state. Experience has proved that we were wrong. It appears that a number of transitional stages were necessary—state capitalism and socialism—in order to *prepare*—to prepare by many years of effort—for the transition to communism. Not directly relying on enthusiasm, but aided by the enthusiasm engendered by the great revolution, and on the basis of personal interest, personal incentive and business principles, we must first set to work in this small-peasant country to build solid gangways to socialism by way of state capitalism. Otherwise we shall never get to communism, we shall never bring scores of millions of people to communism. That is what experience, the objective course of the development of the revolution, has taught us.

And we, who during these three or four years have learned a little to make abrupt changes of front (when abrupt changes of front are needed), have begun zealously, attentively and sedulously (although still not zealously, attentively and sedulously enough) to learn to make a new change of front, namely, the New Economic Policy. The proletarian state must become a cautious, assiduous and shrewd "businessman," a punctilious *wholesale merchant*—otherwise it will never succeed in putting this small-peasant country economically on its feet. Under existing conditions, living as we are side by side with the capitalist (for the time being capitalist) West, there is no other way of progressing to communism. A wholesale merchant seems to be an economic type as remote from communism as heaven from earth. But that is one of the contradictions which, in actual life, lead from a small-peasant economy via state capitalism to socialism. Personal incentive will step up production; we must increase production first and foremost and at all costs. Wholesale trade economically unites millions of small peasants: it gives them a personal incentive, links them up and leads them to the next step, namely, to various forms of association and alliance in the process of production itself. We have already started the necessary changes in our economic policy and already have some successes to our credit; true, they are small and partial, but nonetheless they are successes. In this new field of "tuition" we are already finishing our preparatory class. By persistent and assiduous study, by making practical experience the test of every step we take, by not fearing to alter over and over again what we have already begun, by correcting our mistakes and most carefully analysing their significance, we shall pass to the higher classes. We shall go through the whole "course," although the present state of world economics and world politics has made that course much longer and much more difficult than we would have liked. No matter at what cost, no matter how severe the hardships of the transition period may be—despite disaster, famine and ruin—we shall not flinch; we shall triumphantly carry our cause to its goal.

---

after the civil war. Was adopted as a temporary measure allowing a limited revival of free trade inside the Soviet Union and foreign concessions alongside the nationalized and state-controlled sectors of the economy.

How Lenin Saw the Russian Revolution

by Doug Jenness

In October 1917, the councils of workers and peasants of Russia, under the leadership of the Bolsheviks, took governmental power and began carrying out the greatest revolution of this century. In the nineteenth century, revolutionists admired and absorbed the lessons, and even the language, of the French Revolution of 1789. They compared and contrasted their own revolutions to that great historic watershed.

Similarly, for more than sixty years, revolutionists of our century have drawn inspiration and learned from the first successful proletarian revolution. We have turned to the Russian revolution to learn how to lead the working class to power in our countries. Where the masses have overturned capitalist rule in such countries as Cuba, Nicaragua, Grenada, and Vietnam, revolutionaries study how the Bolsheviks in power handled some of the problems they face.

World-wide, the working class is indebted to the Russian revolution in another way. The October victory altered the relationship of class forces between the imperialist rulers and the toiling masses in favor of the latter. The failure of the imperialist powers to overturn the basic social conquests of the Russian workers and reinstitute capitalism on Russian soil remains a fact of momentous historical importance.

It is precisely because of this change in the relationship of forces made possible by the Russian people that imperialism has not been able to crush the Chinese, Cuban, and Indochinese revolutions, which at crucial moments have received military and economic aid from the Soviet workers state.

On this sixty-fourth anniversary of the October revolution, we are publishing an article Lenin wrote in 1921 to celebrate the revolution's fourth anniversary.

Lenin was the central leader of the Bolshevik party and of the Soviet workers state in its early revolutionary years. The best place to learn the lessons of Bolshevism—to understand how the Bolshevik party was trained, carried through the October revolution, and led the organization of the world's first workers state—is Lenin's writings and speeches.

In this anniversary article. Lenin explains how the Russian revolution combined both the bourgeois-democratic and the socialist revolutions. He indicates that, with the workers and peasants wielding governmental power, the bourgeois-democratic revolution was carried through more thoroughly than in any country ever before. And that, to consolidate this achievement, they had to go further and begin the socialist revolution.

The relationship between the bourgeois-democratic and socialist revolutions in Russia had been debated among Russian Marxists since the turn of the century.

The program of the Russian Social Democratic Labor Party, adopted at its second congress in 1903, called for the overthrow of capitalism and explained, "A necessary condition for this social revolution is the dictatorship of the proletariat. . . ." It also indicated that "on the way to achieving" this "ultimate aim" the Social Democrats had to undertake certain immediate tasks. The most important of these was to overthrow the tsarist autocracy and convoke a constituent assembly, freely elected by the entire people.

At the 1903 congress, there were no fundamental differences on the program expressed by the two principal factions, the Bolsheviks and Mensheviks.

But the 1905 revolution in Russia revealed deep differences between the Bolsheviks and Mensheviks over the class forces that would carry through the bourgeois-democratic revolution and the relationship of this revolution to the socialist revolution.

Two Approaches

Reviewing the different approaches in a polemic with Karl Kautsky in November 1918, Lenin wrote:

"The Russian revolution is a bourgeois revolution, said all the Marxists of Russia before 1905. The Mensheviks, substituting liberalism for Marxism, drew the conclusion from this that, hence, the proletariat must not go beyond what was acceptable to the bourgeoisie and must pursue a policy of compromise with it. The Bolsheviks said that this was a bourgeois-liberal theory. The bourgeoisie, they said, was trying to bring about the reform of the state on bourgeois, *reformist*, not revolutionary lines, while preserving the monarchy, landlordism, etc., as far as possible. The proletariat must carry through the bourgeois-democratic revolution to the end, not allowing itself to be 'bound' by the reformism of the bourgeoisie. The Bolsheviks formulated the relation of *class* forces in the bourgeois revolution as follows: the proletariat, joining to itself the peasantry, will neutralize the liberal bourgeoisie and utterly destroy the monarchy, medievalism, and landlordism.

"The alliance between the proletariat and the peasantry *in general* reveals the bourgeois character of the revolution, for the peasantry in general are small producers who stand on the basis of commodity production. Further, the Bolsheviks then added, the proletariat will join to itself *the entire semi-proletariat* (all the toilers and exploited), will neutralize the middle peasantry and *overthrow* the bourgeoisie; this will be a Socialist revolution, as distinct from a bourgeois-democratic revolution (see my pamphlet *Two Tactics*, published in 1905 and reprinted in *Twelve Years*, St. Petersburg, 1907)." (*The Proletarian Revolution and the Renegade Kautsky*)

The course projected by the Bolsheviks gave an accurate portrayal of the line of march the Russian workers would follow and how the revolution would unfold. It armed them to participate effectively in the class struggle and to assume a leadership role in the revolution. In October 1917, the alliance between the proletariat and the peasantry *in general* overthrew the capitalist government and proceeded to smash all the remnants of the monarchy, medievalism, and landlordism. Governmental power gave the working class and the poor peasants an effective instrument to lead the revolution in their interests.

As Lenin explained in a report to the Eighth Congress of the Russian Communist Party in March 1919, ". . . our revolution was largely a *bourgeois* revolution until the Poor Peasants' Committees were set up, i.e., until the summer and even the autumn of 1918. We are not afraid to admit that. We accomplished the October Revolution so easily because the peasants as a whole supported us and fought the landowners for they saw that as far as they were concerned we would go the limit. . . . But from the moment the Poor Peasants' Committees began to be organized, our revolution became a *proletarian* revolution. . . . And only when the October revolution began to spread to the rural districts and was consummated, in the summer of 1918, did we acquire a real proletarian base; only then did our revolution *become a proletarian revolution in fact*, and not merely in our proclamations, promises and declarations." (*Speeches at Party Congresses: 1918–1922*)

The developments in the countryside that Lenin describes here coincided with the outbreak of the civil war, which saw the rich peasants and the capitalists going over to the counterrevolution. By the fall of 1918, virtually all industry had been nationalized.

Lenin explained that ". . . if the Bolshevik proletariat had tried at once, in October–November 1917, without waiting for the class differentiation in the rural districts, without being able to *prepare* for it and bring it about, to 'decree' a civil war or the 'introduction of Socialism' in the rural districts, had tried to do without a temporary bloc (alliance) with the peasants in general, without making a number of concessions to the middle peasants, etc., that would have been a Blanquist distortion of Marxism, an attempt of the minority to impose its will upon the majority; it would have been a theoretical absurdity, revealing a failure to understand that a general peasant revolution is *still* a bourgeois revolution, and that *without a series of transitions, of transitional stages,* it cannot be transformed into a Socialist revolution in a backward country." (*The Proletarian Revolution and the Renegade Kautsky*)

Lenin commented further on the nature of the Russian revolution in an April 15, 1919, article, "The Third International and Its Place in History." He wrote, "I have had occasion more than once to say that it was easier for the Russians than for the advanced countries *to begin* the great proletarian revolution, but that it will be more difficult for them *to continue* it and carry it to final victory, in the sense of the complete organization of a socialist society.

"It was easier for us to begin, firstly, because the unusual—for twentieth-century Europe—political backwardness of the tsarist monarchy gave unusual strength to the revolutionary onslaught of the masses. Secondly, Russia's backwardness merged in a peculiar way the proletarian revolution against the bourgeoisie with the peasant revolution against the landowners. That is what we started from in October 1917, and we would not have achieved victory so easily if we had not. As long ago as 1856, Marx spoke, in reference to Prussia, of the possibility of a peculiar combination of proletarian revolution and peasant war. From the beginning of 1905 the Bolsheviks advocated the idea of a revolutionary-democratic dictatorship of the proletariat and peasantry." (*Lenin Collected Works*, Vol. 29)

Revolutionary-Democratic Dictatorship

The 1905 revolution included both a massive upsurge of the working class and peasant uprisings. These powerful struggles posed for the first time the real possibility of overthrowing the monarchy and establishing a new government. This gave impulse to the debate among Russian socialists as to what kind of government should replace the autocracy. The Mensheviks argued that the Social Democrats should not participate in a provisional revolutionary government in the event the monarchy was overturned. For the party of the working class to raise the possibility of its participation in such a government, according to the Mensheviks, would pose the question of the socialist revolution, which was premature in Russia.

They argued that the Social Democrats should pressure the capitalist parties to take their rightful place as leaders of the bourgeois-democratic revolution.

Lenin rejected this approach as "tail-ending" the bourgeoisie. He countered by stating, "Marxism teaches the proletarian not to keep aloof from the bourgeois revolution, not to refuse to take part in it, not to allow the leadership of the revolution to be assumed by the bourgeoisie but, on the contrary, to take a most energetic part in it, to fight resolutely for consistent proletarian democracy, to fight to carry the revolution to its completion." (*Two Tactics of Social-Democracy in the Democratic Revolution*)

The class forces that the Bolsheviks saw could carry through the democratic revolution most resolutely were the working class in alliance with the revolutionary peasantry as a whole. Thus, they proposed that the monarchy be replaced with a *revolutionary* government to achieve the goals of the *bourgeois-democratic* revolution, in which the *workers* and *peasants* would exercise political power and repress their oppressors. This was the revolutionary-democratic dictatorship of the proletariat and peasantry.

Lenin wrote, "... such a victory will assume the form of a dictatorship, i.e. it is inevitably bound to rely on military force, on the arming of the masses, on an uprising, and not on institutions established by 'lawful' or 'peaceful' means. It can only be a dictatorship, for the introduction of the reforms which are urgently and absolutely necessary for the proletariat and the peasantry will call forth the desperate resistance of the landlords, the big bourgeoisie and tsarism. Without a dictatorship it will be impossible to break down that resistance and to repel the counterrevolutionary attempts. But of course it will be a democratic, not a socialist dictatorship." (*Two Tactics*)

Lenin described the revolution that would bring the revolutionary-democratic dictatorship into being as a "people's revolution." "Social Democracy," he said, "has justly fought and continues to fight against the bourgeois-democratic abuse of the word 'people.'" The revolutionary workers party, he explained, "must present to the whole of the people the tasks of a democratic revolution as widely and as boldly as possible." (*Two Tactics*)

The Bolsheviks also explained that a victory for

the democratic revolution in Russia was connected to the proletarian revolution in Europe. "Such a victory," Lenin wrote, "will enable us to rouse Europe, and the socialist proletariat of Europe will then throw off the yoke of the bourgeoisie and in turn help us to carry out a socialist revolution." (*Two Tactics*)

'Uninterrupted Revolution'

Lenin believed that the revolutionary-democratic dictatorship would create the most favorable circumstances for the working class to make the transition toward the socialist revolution. In an article, "Social Democracy's Attitude Toward the Peasant Movement," written two months after *Two Tactics*, Lenin explained:

". . . from the democratic revolution we shall at once, and precisely in accordance with the measure of our strength, the strength of the class-conscious and organized proletariat, begin to pass to the socialist revolution. We stand for uninterrupted revolution. We shall not stop half-way. If we do not now and immediately promise all sorts of 'socialization,' that is because we know the actual conditions for that task to be accomplished, and we do not gloss over the new class struggle burgeoning within the peasantry, but reveal that struggle. . . .

"To try to calculate *now* what the combination of forces will be within the peasantry 'on the day after' the revolution (the democratic revolution) is empty utopianism. . . . [W]e shall bend every effort to help the entire peasantry achieve the democratic revolution, *in order thereby to make it easier* for us, the party of the proletariat, to pass on as quickly as possible to the new and higher task—the socialist revolution." (*Collected Works*, Vol. 9, p. 237)

The formation of workers councils, called soviets, during the 1905 revolution gave a glimpse of how the revolutionary-democratic dictatorship might emerge.

Lenin, in an article, "Our Tasks and the Soviet of Workers' Deputies," written in November 1905, drew special attention to the soviets as "the embryo of a *provisional revolutionary government.*

"I think," he proposed, "the Soviet should proclaim itself the provisional revolutionary government of the whole of Russia as early as possible, or should *set up* a provisional revolutionary government (which would amount to the same thing, only in another form)." (*Collected Works*, Vol. 10)

Dual Power

In 1917, after the February insurrection, the Soviets were again established. The authority of these organizations among the masses led Lenin to characterize the situation as one of "dual power."

"What is this dual power?" he wrote in early April. "Alongside the Provisional Government, the government of the *bourgeoisie, another government* has arisen, so far weak and incipient, but undoubtedly a government that actually exists and is growing—the Soviets of Workers' and Soldiers' Deputies.

"What is the class composition of this other government? It consists of the proletariat and the peasants (in soldiers' uniforms). What is the political nature of this government? It is a revolutionary dictatorship, i.e., a power directly based on revolutionary seizure, on the direct initiative of the people from below, and *not on a law* enacted by a centralized state power." (*Collected Works*, Vol. 24)

Following the February 1917 revolution, many of the older Bolshevik leaders adapted to the Mensheviks who were carrying out a bourgeois-liberal line and supporting the Provisional Government. This put these "old Bolsheviks" in the position of giving *de facto* critical support to the capitalist provisional government.

Lenin fought this tendency toward opportunism. He opposed supporting the Provisional Government and called for the soviets to take power.

He explained:

"The revolutionary-democratic dictatorship of the proletariat and the peasantry has already been realized, but in a highly original manner, and with a number of extremely important modifications. . . .

"According to the old way of thinking, the rule of the bourgeoisie could and should be *followed* by the rule of the proletariat and the peasantry, by their dictatorship.

"In real life, however, things have *already* turned out *differently*; there has been an extremely original, novel and unprecedented *interlacing of the one with the other.* We have side by side, existing together, simultaneously, *both* the rule of the bourgeoisie (the government of Lvov and Guchkov) and a revolutionary-democratic dictatorship of the proletariat and the peasantry, which is *voluntarily* ceding power to the bourgeoisie, voluntarily making itself an appendage of the bourgeoisie." (*Collected Works*, Vol. 24, pp. 45–46)

Worker-Bolsheviks Were Ready

While many of the "old Bolsheviks" took opportunist positions, the majority of worker-Bolsheviks did not. It was this fact that made it possible for Lenin to win a majority for his line at the April 1917 party conference without a great deal of difficulty.

In the *History of the Russian Revolution,* Leon Trotsky explains:

"Already at the beginning of the war, when the government dealt the party a heavy blow by arresting the Bolshevik faction of the Duma, Lenin, speaking of the further revolutionary work, had demanded the education by the party 'of thousands of class-conscious workers, from among whom in spite of all difficulties a new staff of leaders will arise.'

"Although separated from these workers by two war fronts, and almost without communication, Lenin had never lost touch with them. 'Let the war, jails, Siberia, hard labor, shatter them twice, ten times, you cannot destroy that stratum. It is alive. It is imbued with revolutionism and anti-chauvinism.' " (p. 393)

This point helps underline the fact that Lenin approached the question of the Russian revolution from the standpoint of a party leader and builder. His writings reflect the collective experience and discussions of the Bolshevik party. They are stamped by the objective of arming the party to effectively participate in the class struggle and prepare for the revolution.

Transitional approach

At every stage, the Bolsheviks had to weigh their general conceptions of the revolution with the living reality of the struggle and determine the most effective slogans and arenas of party work.

The kind of party that Lenin sought to build was totally interconnected with his conception of the revolution. The Bolsheviks were a revolutionary workers party armed with the Marxist program. They participated in the mass organizations of the working class, in bourgeois elections, and other arenas, with the sole objective of preparing the working class to take power.

For example, Lenin explained that the work of party members in the trade unions was to educate the workers around the broad social and political issues. "It cannot be too strongly maintained," he wrote in 1902, ". . . that the Social Democrats' ideal should not be the trade union secretary, but *the tribune of the people,* who is able to react to every manifestation of tyranny and oppression, no matter where it appears, no matter what stratum or class of the people it affects; . . . who is able to take advantage of every event, however small, in order to set forth *before all* his socialist convictions and his democratic demands, in order to clarify for *all* and everyone the world-historic significance of the struggle for the emancipation of the proletariat." (*What Is to Be Done?*)

Lenin's writings on the relationship between the democratic and socialist revolutions in Russia also demonstrate how he applied a transitional approach. The Bolsheviks, starting from the objective needs of the working class, sought to develop slogans that would help bridge the struggle from one level of consciousness to the next and lead it along the road toward socialist revolution.

As Lenin points out in his fourth anniversary article, the Bolsheviks never saw the struggle for immediate and democratic demands as the struggle for "reforms." Rather, struggles around such demands were seen as part of preparing and mobilizing the masses to take political power and, after seizing power, to use it to lead the revolution forward.

The October revolution testifies that Lenin's view of the dynamics of the Russian revolution and the kind of vanguard party it required effectively armed the Bolsheviks to carry through their historic task.

THE DEBATE OVER THE CHARACTER AND GOALS OF THE RUSSIAN REVOLUTION

by Ernest Mandel

The November 1981 issue of *International Socialist Review* carried an article by Doug Jenness centered around the idea that in the 1905–1917 period, there had been two different concepts of the Russian revolution among Russian socialists. In the present article we defend the traditional analysis by Leon Trotsky and the Fourth International, according to which there were three—and not two—basically different strategies proposed by Russian socialists in that period.

Russian society entered a deep political and social crisis in the 1870s. The populists of *Narodnaya Volya* (People's Will) were organizing to overthrow tsarism. In 1882, they killed Tsar Alexander II who, twenty years earlier, had freed Russian peasants from serfdom, but burdened them in exchange with a terrible economic taxation.

The international workers movement, which was beginning to include some Russian emigre activists, took an interest in Russia and tried to obtain more information on the social conditions and political struggles of this far-away country. As a result, the movement was drawn into the debates on the nature of the coming Russian revolution—which revolutionaries considered inevitable—and the perspectives it would open up for Europe and the world.

The positions of Marx and Engels

Vera Zasulich, one of the main figures of Russian populism, invited Marx to take a stand on Russia's future. After some hesitation,[1] he arrived at an unambiguous position: Russia could "leap over the stage of capitalism."

In a March 8, 1881, letter to the Russian revolutionary, and again in the preface to the second Russian edition of *The Communist Manifesto*, published in 1882, Marx stated:

(a) That his thesis on the inevitable emergence of capitalism only applied to Western societies;

(b) That Russia had the possibility of avoiding "the terrible evils of capitalism" if its revolution could triumph in time;[2]

(c) That the starting point of the collectivist, noncapitalist evolution of Russian industrialization could be the collective property of the village community (the *obschina*);

(d) That this contingency would only be realized if the advance of private property and capitalism, which was under way since the abolition of serfdom in 1861, had not yet reached the stage of decisively dissolving the village community;

(e) That a second condition for the realization of this noncapitalist development in Russia was the victory of the revolution in the West, and the aid which the Western proletariat could thereby extend to the Russian masses in modernizing and industrializing Russia.

Through this analysis, Marx provided support to the revolutionaries of *Narodnaya Volya*. He believed that Plekhanov's group in Geneva, which originated in a split from the populists, had committed a mistake in attacking them. Engels maintained this position several years after Marx's death. He kept up a lively correspondence with populists like Nikolai Danielson and Lavrov, and showed a great deal of sympathy for them.[3]

Nevertheless, toward the end of the 1880s, and into the early 1890s, Engels changed his position; or, more accurately, he noted that history had now

---

This article first appeared in the April 1982 *International Socialist Review*.

answered Marx's question and had done so in the negative. The delay of the revolution had opened the way to a process of capitalist development in Russia, which was ruthlessly destroying the basis for the survival of the village community:

"Remember that our author [Marx] had said in his letter on Zhukovsky [the letter to the editorial board of *Oteshestvennie Zapiski* mentioned in footnote 2] that the peasant *obschina* was doomed if the evolution begun in 1861 continued. To my mind, this is exactly what is happening" (letter to N. Danielson, March 15, 1892).

Engels therefore believed that capitalist development had become inevitable in Russia and would lead to the emergence of a modern proletariat as the only fully revolutionary class, and the only class capable of introducing socialism in Russia. By the same token, he now gave his full support to the first nucleus of Russian Marxists around Plekhanov. All these positions were spelled out in his postscript to *Soziales aus Russland* (January 1894).

The polemic between the Russian populists and Marxists

Narodnaya Volya had given birth to several populist organizations, and then to the Social Revolutionary Party (SRP), which was clearly derived from populism. The SRP was to remain the largest and most influential organization in Russia until 1917.[4] It differed from the newly formed Russian social democracy, which was officially established as a party in 1898, on a series of analytical and political points.

The SRP believed capitalism could not develop extensively in Russia due to the narrowness of the domestic market. Consequently, it did not believe the proletariat would play a leading role in the coming Russian revolution, and instead attributed this role to the peasantry. It rejected the idea that the peasantry, which was now involved in petty commodity production and aspired to individual ownership of the land, could not form a social force fighting for a socialist society. Its platform therefore advocated the socialization of land and an immediate transition to an agrarian socialism (communism). However, under the pressure of its own peasant base, it gradually abandoned the last point and adopted a program for dividing up the land.

The Russian Marxists, backed up by the Western Marxists, launched a sustained polemic against these populist theses. They stated that capitalist development had become irreversible and prevalent in Russia. Along with capitalist development would come the development of the proletariat and its party, Russian social democracy, which was a part of international social democracy. Like its counterparts, Russian social democracy should struggle for the overthrow of capitalism through the dictatorship of the proletariat and collective ownership of the means of production.

With this goal in mind, the proletariat had to be organized completely independently of all other classes. Flowing from this analysis, the Russian Marxists viewed the populists, the SRP, as objectively bourgeois-democratic and nonproletarian because they lumped together working-class, peasant, semiproletarian plebeian, and urban petty-bourgeois forces.

Moreover, the populists opposed political support for the bourgeois liberal opposition movement, which they characterized as an internal quarrel within the ruling classes. By contrast, the Marxists favored critical support and even temporary agreements with bourgeois liberal opposition movements, while maintaining the political independence of the proletariat and warning the working masses that the liberal bourgeoisie was incapable of waging a consistent, radical, and

1. There are several successive drafts of the letter to Vera Zasulich in the *Collective Works of Marx and Engels*.

2. Earlier, in 1877, Marx had already written Mikailovsky, at that time the editor of the review *Oteshestvennie Zapiski* (Annals of the Fatherland), that Russia had the "greatest opportunity ever presented by history to any nation" to avoid the evils of capitalism.

3. See Marx's letter to Jenny Longuet of April 11, 1881. See also Engels's letter to Vera Zasulich of April 23, 1885.

4. We shouldn't forget that even after the October revolution, during the elections to the Constituent Assembly, the SRP still received an absolute majority of votes and seats. It is true that in the cities it was beaten by the Bolshevik Party, and its overall majority reflected mainly the overwhelming weight of the peasantry in Russia. It is also true that it had already split two ways: the right SRs ferociously opposing the seizure of power by the soviets, and the left SRs supporting and even joining, temporarily, a coalition government with the Bolsheviks. The coalition was broken by the left SRs when the Brest Litovsk peace treaty was signed.

thorough struggle against absolutism.

The Marxists drew this position from an estimate that can be seen in the following quote from the Russian Social Democratic Labor Party (RSDLP) program adopted at the Second Congress (1903) and drafted by Plekhanov and Lenin:

"On the way to achieving their common ultimate aim, which is conditioned by the dominance of the capitalist mode of production throughout the civilised world, the Social Democrats of the different countries are obliged to undertake different immediate tasks, both because this mode of production has not developed everywhere to the same degree and because its development in the different countries is coming to fruition under a variety of socio-political circumstances.

"In Russia, where capitalism has already become the dominent mode of production, there are still very many survivals from the old pre-capitalist order, which was based on the enslavement of the working masses by the landlords, the state or the sovereign. Hindering economic progress to a very considerable extent, these survivals inhibit an all-round development of the class struggle of the proletariat, and contribute to the maintenance and consolidation of the most barbarous forms of exploitation of the many millions of peasants by the state and the property-owning classes, and to keeping the entire people in ignorance and deprived of rights.

"The most important of all these survivals and the mightiest bulwark of all this barbarism is the Tsarist autocracy. By its very nature it is inimical to all social progress and cannot but be the most malevolent enemy of all the proletariat's strivings for freedom.

"Therefore, the Russian Social Democratic Labour Party takes as its most immediate political task the overthrow of the Tsarist autocracy and its replacement by a democratic republic."

In other words, the program of the RSDLP, the Russian Marxists, distinguished *two stages of the Russian revolution*:

- An immediate stage, which was the democratic (or bourgeois-democratic) revolution, whose goal was the overthrow of the tsarist autocracy and not of capitalism. In fact, the goal of the democratic revolution was to be *the unfettered development of capitalism*, and simultaneously the maximum development of the proletariat, the proletarian class struggle, and the proletarian party.
- A subsequent stage, that of the social revolution leading to the dictatorship of the proletariat, the overthrow of capitalism, and the construction of a socialist society.

The tasks of the first stage were democratic tasks—the bourgeois-democratic republic and the agrarian revolution. The tasks of the second stage were socialist tasks.

The great majority of Russian Marxists—especially Plekhanov, Lenin, Martov, Axelrod, and Trotsky—agreed on that distinction until 1904, despite their differences on the organizational question, which had divided them at the Second Congress of the RSDLP in 1903. This was clearly reflected in the political debates at the Second Congress, especially those on the agrarian question. Here are a few particularly telling interventions:

- *Lenin*: "We are pursuing in the countryside two aims which are different in kind: first, we want to secure freedom for bourgeois relations; secondly, we want to wage the proletarian struggle."
- *Trotsky*: "Our *general* minimum programme represents the maximum that we can demand of the capitalist order. Our *agrarian* programme calls for clearing feudal hindrances from the path of this capitalist order *as a whole. . . . We approach the Polish peasants with the general-democratic part of our programme, we approach the rural poor with our propaganda for socialism.*"
- *Lenin*: "Comrade Lieber has forgotten the difference between the democratic and the socialist parts of the programme. What he has taken for 'meagreness' is the absence of anything socialistic in the democratic programme. . . . Only the Socialist-Revolutionaries, with their characteristic lack of principle, are capable of confusing, and constantly do confuse, democratic and socialist demands. The Party of the proletariat, however, is in duty bound to separate and distinguish between them in the strictest fashion."
- *Plekhanov*: "Such a movement in favour of redistribution would certainly be a movement in the bourgeoisie's favour. We are, of course, not obliged actively to set forth a programme for the bourgeoisie, but if, in the struggle against survivals of serfdom relations, the peasantry should take

that path, then it would not be for us to hold back this progressive movement."[5]

The same clarity prevailed concerning the need to support the political struggle of the liberal bourgeoisie against the absolutist autocracy. The Second Congress of the RDSLP adopted two resolutions on this issue; the one submitted by Starover and endorsed by Trotsky stated:

"The party does not refuse to enter, and should the need arise will enter, through its central institutions, into temporary agreements with liberal or liberal-democratic trends."

The other, submitted by Plekhanov and endorsed by Lenin, stated:

"Social Democracy must support the bourgeoisie insofar as it is revolutionary or even merely oppositional in its struggle against tsardom."

Both resolutions stressed the limited and inadequate character of the bourgeois opposition.[6] The party program also included similar formulations.

At first, the differences between Bolsheviks and Mensheviks seemed limited to organizational problems; at the Second Congress of the RSDLP some Mensheviks even adopted a more "extremist" (in reality a half-economist, half-workerist) position toward the liberal bourgeoisie than the Bolsheviks.

The differences between Bolsheviks and Mensheviks after 1905

But it rapidly emerged that deep differences on *what tactic was appropriate for the Russian revolution* also divided Bolsheviks and Mensheviks. The Russian revolution of 1905, its aftermath, and the Unity Congress of the RSDLP in Stockholm, clarified the matter.

Both the Mensheviks and the Bolsheviks agreed on *the bourgeois nature of the coming Russian revolution* in a twofold sense:

- The immediate tasks of the revolution would be the overthrow of the tsarist autocracy and the elimination of semifeudal survivals in the countryside. These were obviously historical tasks of the bourgeois-democratic revolution and not of the socialist revolution;
- The victory of the Russian revolution would lead to an accelerated and unfettered development of capitalism in Russia, and not to the socialization of the economy.

But from these premises, the Mensheviks drew the conclusion that the revolution could succeed only under the leadership of the bourgeoisie. On the one hand, the party of the proletariat would have to drive the bourgeoisie forward with a sword to its back and force it to carry out the revolutionary work it hesitated to perform. In addition, the party of the proletariat would have to fight for the broadest political and economic reforms on behalf of the proletariat (the eight-hour day, compulsory education for all children with free lunches served in the schools, etc.). But this oppositional work would have to keep within the bounds of reason and moderation, lest the bourgeoisie prematurely desert the revolutionary camp and go over to the counterrevolution, which would doom the revolution to failure.

Lenin advocated a position diametrically counterposed to that of the Mensheviks. He reminded them that even the French revolution of 1789 had only been able to accomplish its historical tasks because the Jacobin petty bourgeoisie had successively driven out of power the various fractions of the bourgeoisie which, fearful of the people, had been prepared to capitulate to the counterrevolution or avoid the necessary radical measures. He recalled the revolution of 1848 in which the German bourgeoisie had behaved in an even more counterrevolutionary fashion, leading the revolution to defeat, which led Marx to note that the further east one went, the more cowardly the bourgeoisie became.

All this led to the conclusion that in Russia, where capitalism was far more developed in 1905 than in Germany in 1848, not to mention France in 1789, the bourgeoisie would be absolutely incapable of leading a radical democratic and agrarian revolution and moreover did not aspire to do so. This meant that under bourgeois leadership, the Russian revolution was doomed to fail. It could triumph only with the equivalent of a Jacobin leadership and a Jacobin dictatorship.

5. See the official record of the *Second Congress of the RSDLP*, translated from the Russian by Brian Pearce, English edition, London: New Park Publications, 1978, pp. 273, 254–255, 256–257, 267.

6. *Ibid.*, pp. 19–20.

In the context of Russian society in 1905, given the social classes existing in the country at that time, this could only mean an alliance between the proletariat and the peasantry: the democratic dictatorship of the workers and peasants.

Two key questions—the one strategic, the other tactical—crystallized the differences between the Bolsheviks and the Mensheviks on the nature and perspectives of the Russian revolution. The Mensheviks tended more and more to reduce the content of the democratic (bourgeois-democratic) revolution to strictly political questions: free elections, parliamentary representation, democratic freedoms, etc. By contrast, Lenin believed *the agrarian question* was the key question of the democratic revolution. Because the bourgeoisie feared a radical agrarian revolution—a generalized uprising of the peasantry, a revolutionary takeover of the land by the peasants—it refused to take up a determined struggle against the autocracy, the army, and the state apparatus, which in the last analysis were the guardians of *all* private property. Any conciliationist approach toward the liberal bourgeoisie necessarily involved *both* the rejection of a radical and persistent struggle for land *and* the rejection of a radical and persistent struggle for freedom.

Given their reductionist conception of the democratic revolution, the Mensheviks, after a few hesitations, began leaning more and more toward *a political bloc with the bourgeois parties.* Lenin rejected such a bloc with all his might, because he considered it would constitute an insurmountable obstacle to launching a successful agrarian revolution.

But Lenin and the Bolsheviks did not change their position on the perspective opened by a victory of the Russian revolution. For them, what was always involved was opening the way to the unfettered development of capitalism in Russia, and not initiating a socialized and collectivized economy (these days, we would say: not establishing a transitional society between capitalism and socialism). This appears clearly in Lenin's speech to the Fifth Congress (London) of the RSDLP on May 12, 1907:

"Speaking objectively, from the point of view not of our desires, but of the present economic development of Russia, the basic question of our revolution is whether it will secure the development of capitalism through the peasants' complete victory over the landowners or through the landowners' victory over the peasants. A bourgeois-democratic revolution in Russia's economy is absolutely inevitable. No power on earth can hinder it. But this revolution is possible in either of two ways: in the Prussian, if one might say so, or in the American way. This means the following; the landlords may win, may foist compensation payments or other petty concessions on the peasants, may unite with a handful of the wealthy, pauperise the masses, and convert their own farms into Junker-type, capitalist, farms. Such a revolution will be bourgeois-democratic but it will be to the least advantage of the peasants—to their least advantage from the angle of the rapidity of capitalist development. Or, on the contrary, the complete victory of the peasant uprising, the confiscation of all landed estates and their equal division will signify the most rapid development of capitalism, the form of bourgeois-democratic revolution most advantageous to the peasants" (*Collected Works* [C.W.], Vol. 12, p. 465).

The resolution is unambiguous: development of capitalism in the American way; the most rapid development of capitalism; it is clear and obvious. Many such quotations can be found in Lenin's writings between 1905 and 1916, especially in *Two Tactics of Social Democracy in the Democratic Revolution* (1905):

"It means that the democratic reforms in the political system, and the social and economic reforms that have become a necessity for Russia, do not in themselves imply the undermining of capitalism, the undermining of bourgeois rule; on the contrary, they will, for the first time, really clear the ground for a wide and rapid, European, and not Asiatic, development of capitalism; they will, for the first time, make it possible for the bourgeoisie to rule as a class" (C.W., Vol. 19, p. 48).

And in his January 3, 1911, letter to Gorky, he wrote:

"There is capitalism and capitalism. There is Black-Hundred-Octobrist capitalism and Narodnik ('realistic, democratic,' full of 'activity') capitalism. The more we expose capitalism before the workers for its 'greed and cruelty,' the more difficult is it for capitalism of the first order to persist, the more surely is it bound to pass into capitalism of the second order. And this just suits us, this just suits the proletariat. . . .

"There is practically no Octobrist capitalism left in Western Europe; practically all capitalism is democratic. Octobrist capitalism has gone from Britain and France to Russia and Asia. *The Russian revolution and the revolutions in Asia [are] the struggle for ousting Octobrist capitalism and replacing it by democratic capitalism.* And democratic capitalism [is] the last of its kind. It has no next stage to go on to. The next stage is its death" (*C.W.*, Vol. 34, pp. 438–439, emphasis added, E.M.).

The insurrection, the government, the state

Social democracy and revolutionary-bourgeois (i.e., peasant) democracy together must carry to the end the bourgeois revolution against the bourgeoisie, in order to allow the unfettered development of capitalism in Russia. That, in a few words, was the position of Lenin and the Bolsheviks in the 1905 Russian revolution and from then until after the February 1917 revolution, i.e., until the April Theses were formulated.

Unlike the Mensheviks, Lenin, in line with his own position, called for Social Democratic participation in a revolutionary insurrectional government, and even for an insurrectional process culminating in a revolutionary government under Social Democratic leadership:

"(1) that in order to complete the revolution, the urgent task now confronting the proletariat is, jointly with the revolutionary democrats, to help to unite the insurrection, and to set up an organ that will unite it, in the shape of a provisional revolutionary government. . ." (*C.W.*, Vol. 10, p. 155).

Did the idea of the seizure of power by a revolutionary government dominated by social democracy contradict the position on the bourgeois nature of the revolution and its tasks? Did it contradict Lenin's obstinate and frequent refusal to confuse, i.e., to *combine*, the democratic tasks and the socialist tasks, the minimum program and the maximum program?

In our opinion, there was no such contradiction in Lenin's mind, i.e., subjectively. This is why *all* these positions of Lenin are often stated *at the same time* in the same writing, the same article, the same report, the same brochure. Nor does the contradiction exist from the point of view of formal logic. One can be for the seizure of power by a *provisional* government and at the same time stress the fact that this government will be precisely . . . provisional, i.e. that it will have to give up or lose power later on, given the bourgeois character of the revolution.

This emerges from Lenin's analogy with the *Jacobins'* rule during the French revolution. In the Marxist tradition, the function of Danton, Marat, and Robespierre was to push the revolution forward to its ultimate, to push it to a point where the bourgeoisie neither wanted to nor could go. But after successfully carrying out this task, the *Jacobins* were condemned to lose power. What was on the historical agenda in France was the development of capitalism, not the development of an egalitarian society based on small private property, the utopia desired by the *Jacobins*, much less the construction of a socialist society.

This emerges even more clearly from the very formulas Lenin used in relation to the "democratic dictatorship of the workers and peasants," in which he stressed the transitional, provisional character of this dictatorship, of this government:

"In plain and simple Russian, an organ of power of the people which temporarily assumes the duties of a government that has collapsed is called a provisional revolutionary government. *Such a government is bound to be provisional, for its authority expires with the convocation of a constituent assembly representing the whole people.*" (*C.W.*, Vol. 10, p. 67, emphasis added).

This is obvious from Lenin's stress on the fact that the *political* counterrevolution, the "political restoration," would be inevitable unless the socialist revolution triumphs in the West. This is also obvious from Lenin's stress on the *bourgeois character* of the state that would emerge from the victory of the Russian revolution:

"A bourgeois revolution is a revolution which does not depart from the framework of the bourgeois, i.e. capitalist, socio-economic system. A bourgeois revolution expresses the needs of capitalist development, and, far from destroying the foundations of capitalism, it effects the contrary—it broadens and deepens them. . . . Since the rule of the bourgeoisie over the working class is inevitable under capitalism, it can well be said that a bourgeois revolution expresses the interests not so much of the proletariat as of the bourgeoisie.

"But it is quite absurd to think that a bourgeois revolution does not at all express proletarian interests. This absurd idea boils down either to the hoary Narodnik theory that . . . we do not need bourgeois political liberty; or to anarchism, which denies any participation of the proletariat in bourgeois politics, in a bourgeois revolution and in bourgeois parliamentarism." ("Two Tactics," *C.W.*, Vol. 9, p. 49).

Lenin insisted so strongly on this point that not only did he radically reject any notion of "revolutionary communes," any notion of a state (in contrast to an insurrection) based on soviets, but he went so far as to state:

"The real task the Commune had to perform was primarily the achievement of the democratic and not the socialist dictatorship, the implementation of our 'minimum programme' " (*C.W.*, Vol. 9, p. 141).

All these positions therefore were *logically* consistent. But were they consistent from the point of view of *the dialectic of social classes engaged in struggle*?

That is another question altogether, one which Trotsky (and history) basically answered in the negative.

Nevertheless, as we stress the contradictory aspect of Lenin's position, we must at the same time stress its contradictory *effects*, which were not all negative.

By educating his faction, and then his party, in the spirit of a clear-cut distinction between "minimum program" and "maximum program," in the spirit of limiting the "first stage" of the revolution to purely democratic tasks, in the spirit of Social Democratic participation in a provisional revolutionary government, Lenin facilitated the confusion in the first weeks of the February revolution, when *all* the Bolshevik leaders and *all* the Bolshevik cadres favored "critical" support to and even collaboration with the provisional coalition government and rejected as "utopian," "semi-anarchist," etc., any notion of a seizure of power by the working class, of a "workers government," let alone the dictatorship of the proletariat based on the soviets.

But, by educating his faction, and then his party, in the spirit of a *necessary seizure of power*, Lenin facilitated the "turn" towards a Soviet regime that was first made spontaneously by the vanguard working-class cadres, and later by the adoption by the party of the same turn to the dictatorship of the proletriat. The education in the spirit of strict class independence did the rest. The correct education given on these two points outweighed the erroneous dogma of the "two stages," of the separation between the "minimum program" and the "maximum program," of the counterposition of the "democratic dictatorship" to the dictatorship of the proletariat, of the soviets as "non-party" insurrectional organs in which the Social Democrats could be active but which could not be "substituted" for the "provisional" revolutionary government or the state emerging from the revolution. The soviets became organs of power, neither provisional nor bourgeois: organs of the dictatorship of the proletariat, the foundation of a new state, a non-bourgeois state, a workers state.

Trotsky's original position

Beginning in 1904, Trotsky developed an entirely new and original position on character and perspectives of the Russian revolution. He and his supporters alone defended that position against both the Mensheviks and Bolsheviks. The argument was presented in a small brochure published on the eve of the events of January 1905; then in *Results and Prospects*, published in 1906; in a less well-known article in the Polish social-democratic review *Przeglad Social-Demokratyczny* in 1908; and in his book *1905*, published in 1909. His position flowed from his discovery of the law of *uneven and combined development*, undoubtedly his fundamental contribution to Marxism.

Starting from the position shared by all Marxists that the Russian revolution had to solve the tasks of the bourgeois-democratic revolution, above all the conquest of political democracy and the conquest of the land, Trotsky immediately posed a question that Plekhanov and Lenin had either not, or only insufficiently, formulated: *In what concrete national and international social and economic context would this revolution unfold*? What would its main driving forces be? What would be the relationship of forces between the social classes involved in the revolution?

Trotsky answered: The particularities of uneven and combined development in Russia have caused the growth of the proletariat to considerably outdistance that of the Russian bourgeoisie because the proletariat is the product not only of the "organic" development of Russian capitalism, but also of the intervention of foreign capital and above all of the role of the state in stimulating industrialization. Paradoxically, because of its high degree of concentration in large industries, the Russian proletariat, which emerged in a "backward" country, was more militant and more advanced in many ways than the proletariat of far more-developed countries.

In the first place, this meant that insofar as the proletariat already had its own independent organizations and already acted as an independent force on the political scene, the bourgeoisie as a whole would go over to the counterrevolution, even more because of its fear of the proletariat than of peasant uprisings. Therefore no alliance with the bourgeoisie or with bourgeois parties could lead to the victory of the revolution. There were no differences between Lenin and Trotsky on this point.[7] Together, both opposed the Mensheviks.

Another consequence of Trotsky's analysis was the recognition that a revolutionary victory won under the leadership of the proletariat, at the head of all the oppressed classes of the nation, could not be confined to winning the goals of the bourgeois-democratic revolution alone. It was inconceivable a proletariat as centralized, as united, as conscious, as militant as the Russian proletariat, would accept being exploited by capitalist bosses *after having armed itself and taken power at the head of an insurrection* (there was of course no difference between Lenin and Trotsky on the necessity of such an insurrection).

The proletariat, having insured the victory of the agrarian revolution (the conquest of the land by the peasants), would move on to initiate the collectivization and confiscation of large capitalist property too, without interruption, without demobilization and without discontinuity.

In this sense, the revolution would be permanent, the conquest of the historical objectives of the bourgeois-democratic revolution *would, in real life, combine* with the conquest of the historical objectives of the socialist revolution without an intermediate period of capitalist development.

Would the Russian proletariat, being a small minority in a sea of peasant petty commodity producers, be able to keep power after having taken it? Trotsky answered no. It could remain in power only if the Russian revolution triggered a socialist revolution in the West. On this issue, and contrary to a longstanding myth, Trotsky's position *was not original* but was shared by Kautsky, Rosa Luxemburg, and Lenin. What is even more surprising, Lenin and the other leaders of the Marxist left stated that *even the bourgeois-democratic revolution was doomed to retreat* (that is, doomed to a *political* victory of reaction) if there were no socialist victory in the West:

"The only complete guarantee against restoration in Russia (after a victorious revolution in Russia) is a socialist revolution in the West. There is and can be no other guarantee. Thus, from this aspect, the question is: how can the bourgeois-democratic revolution in Russia facilitate, or accelerate, the socialist revolution in the West? The only conceivable answer to this is: if the miserable Manifesto of October 17 gave a powerful impetus to the working-class movement in Europe, then the *complete* victory of the bourgeois revolutions in Russia will almost inevitably (or at all events, in all probability) arouse a number of such political upheavals in Europe as will give a very powerful impetus to the socialist revolution" (C.W., Vol. 10, p. 334).

What political forms would the proletariat, at the head of the entire nation, have to use to accomplish the historical tasks of the bourgeois-democratic revolution in Russia? Since the bourgeoisie was doomed to go over to the camp of the counterrevolution, there were only two possibilities: either the alliance between a peasant political force (or political forces) and the party of the proletariat, or the conquest of power by the proletariat (led by its party) supported by the peasantry.

The first possibility was rejected by Trotsky because of the peasantry's inability to constitute an autonomous political force in the course of a

7. "It must be agreed that Trotsky's amendment is not Menshevik, that it expresses the 'very same', that is, Bolshevik, idea. But Trotsky has expressed this idea in a way that is scarcely better" ("Objections to Trotsky's Amendments to the Bolshevik Resolution on the Attitude Towards Bourgeois Parties," at the Fifth Congress of the RSDLP) (C.W., Vol. 12, p. 479).

revolution. Only the second variant remained: the Russian revolution could only succeed through the establishment of a dictatorship of the proletariat leading the peasantry. The law of uneven and combined development implied that the proletariat could take power in a backward country before it did so in the most advanced countries. Trotsky formulated this prediction as early as 1906. Subsequent events are well known.

The differences between Lenin and Trotsky

The differences between Lenin and Trotsky on the perspectives of the Russian revolution therefore basically concerned four points:

1. The impossibility for Russia, given the existing social and economic context, to undergo modernization and industrialization through a "rapid development of capitalism," and especially through "American-style" development of agriculture. To believe such an outcome possible, as Lenin persistently did until 1916, was to underestimate the weight of imperialism, of the world market (which left no room for a second America!), and of the agrarian crisis in Russia itself, which could no longer be solved in a capitalist framework.

We should draw attention to the fact that the only Marxist who took a few timid steps in the same direction and startled all the Russian Marxists, beginning with Lenin himself, was Kautsky.[8] In his balance sheet of the Russian revolution, Kautsky argued that, in order to resolve the agrarian question, the large industrial monopolies would have to be confiscated along with the large landed estates. But Lenin did not follow him on this road,[9] and Kautsky himself quickly took fright at his own boldness and from 1910 onward retreated to more traditional centrist positions.

2. The impossibility for the peasantry to constitute a political party or force that would be independent both of the bourgeoisie and the working class. Trotsky was certain that this was impossible. By contrast, Lenin was certain that the revolutionary peasantry had to *take political power*:

"But how can a peasant revolution win if the revolutionary peasantry does not seize power? Plekhanov has reduced his own arguments to absurdity. Having stepped on to a slope, he irresistably rolls down. First he denied that it was possible for the proletariat to seize power in the present revolution. Now he denies that it is possible for the revolutionary peasantry to seize power in the present revolution. But if *neither* the proletariat *nor* the revolutionary peasantry can seize power, then, logically, that power *must remain in the hands of the tsar and of Dubasov.* Or should the Cadets take power? But the Cadets do not want to seize power themselves, for they are in favour of retaining the monarchy, the standing army, the Upper Chamber and all the other delights" (*C.W.*, Vol. 10, p. 340–341).

To those who claimed there were no "revolutionary bourgeois democrats" in Russia to lead the revolution with the representatives of the proletariat, Lenin answered no less clearly:

"Unless the activities of the worker democrats and bourgeois democrats are co-ordinated, the bourgeois-democratic revolution cannot be successful. This is gospel truth. . . .

"It seems to you that there are no revolutionary bourgeois democrats in Russia, that the Cadets are the only, or at all events, the main force of bourgeois democracy in Russia. But it seems so to you only because you are short-sighted. . . . There are revolutionary bourgeois democrats in Russia, and there must be, so long as there is a revolutionary peasantry, which by thousands of millions of threads is also bound up with the poorer classes in the towns" (*C.W.*, Vol. 10, p. 260 and 263).

Moreover, Lenin tended to give concrete content to the algebraic formula "revolutionary bourgeois democrats" leading the peasantry; it meant the *Trudoviks* (Kerensky's party) and SRs. See the May 11, 1906, article "The Peasant, or 'Trudovik,' Group and the RSDLP":

"Today there is nothing more important for the success of the revolution than this organisation, education and political training of the revolutionary bourgeois democrats. The socialist proletariat,

8. Under the influence of the Russian revolution Kautsky adopted the most advanced positions of his career between 1906 and 1909, especially in his commentaries on the Russian revolution and in his work *Der Weg zur Macht*.

9. Kautsky, "The Motor Forces and Perspectives of the Russian Revolution," *Die Neue Zeit*, 1906. Lenin himself noted that this article went much further than even the most extreme Bolsheviks (*C.W.*, Vol. 11, p. 369). Kautsky excluded, however, any realization of the socialist program by the Russian revolution.

while ruthlessly exposing the instability of the Cadets, will do everything it can to promote this great work" (*C.W.*, Vol. 10, p. 413).

3. The capacity of the Russian proletariat *to begin* to resolve the socialist tasks of the revolution. For Trotsky, that capacity was obvious. It appeared in all the great workers' struggles (especially the mass strikes, the 1905 general strike, and the formation of soviets). For Lenin, that capacity did not exist:

"Finally, we will note that the resolution, by making implementation of the minimum programme the provisional revolutionary government's task, eliminates the absurd and semi-anarchist ideas of giving immediate effect to the maximum programme, and the conquest of power for a socialist revolution. The degree of Russia's economic development (an objective condition), and the degree of class-consciousness and organisation of the broad masses of the proletariat (a subjective condition inseparably bound up with the objective condition) make the immediate and complete emancipation of the working class impossible. Only the most ignorant people can close their eyes to the bourgeois nature of the democratic revolution which is now taking place; only the most naïve optimists can forget how little as yet the masses of the workers are informed about the aims of socialism and the methods of achieving it" (*C.W.*, Vol. 9, p. 28–29).

For Lenin, therefore, the "self-limitation of the proletariat," that is the refusal to move beyond the realization of the most radical bourgeois-democratic demands, even while the Social Democrats might participate in a revolutionary insurrectional government, correspond to an objective necessity. Only through prolonged experience with political democracy, through prolonged mass educational and organizational work that would coincide precisely with the "unfettered development of capitalism," could the proletariat acquire the capacity to accomplish the tasks of the socialist revolution.

4. Logically, Lenin's position led to *counterposing* the formula "democratic dictatorship of the proletariat and peasantry" to the formula "dictatorship of the proletariat." *The two formulas were not mere slogans but encapsulated the strategic perspectives of the revolution:* the character of the state and society that would emerge from the revolutionary victory:

"Without a dictatorship it is impossible to break down that resistance and repel counter-revolutionary attempts. But of course it will be democratic, not a socialist dictatorship. It will be unable (without a series of intermediary stages of revolutionary development) to affect the foundations of capitalism. At best, it may bring about a radical redistribution of landed property in favour of the peasantry, establish consistent and full democracy, including the formation of a republic, eradicate all the oppressive features of Asiatic bondage, not only in rural but also in factory life, lay the foundation for a thorough improvement in the conditions of the workers and for a rise in their standard of living, and—last but not least—carry the revolutionary conflagration into Europe. Such a victory will not yet by any means transform our bourgeois revolution into a socialist revolution; the democratic revolution will not immediately overstep the bounds of bourgeois social and economic relationships; nevertheless, the significance of such a victory for the future development of Russia and of the whole world will be immense" (*C.W.*, Vol. 9, p. 56–57).

And even more sharply and precisely:

"This means: not the socialist dictatorship of the proletariat, but the democratic dictatorship of the proletariat and the peasantry" (*C.W.*, Vol. 11, p. 374).

Clearly then the Russian Marxists were divided between *three*, not *two*, conceptions of the Russian revolution, its perspectives, and the strategic tasks it implied.[10]

The verdict of the 1917 revolution

Lenin explicitly changed his position on three of these four issues in his April Thesis of 1917; and now in fact stood for the same positions Trotsky had defended since 1904–1906:

1. Contrary to what he previously contended, he now argued that the experience of all modern revolutions had demonstrated the peasantry's inability to form a political force independent of the bourgeoisie and the proletariat. All illusions about

10. Comrade Trotsky admirably summarized his position on the existence of *three*, not *two*, conceptions of the Russian revolution in his document, "Three Conceptions of the Russian Revolution," appended to his book, *Stalin*.

an independent role of the *Trudoviks* (Kerensky!) or the SRs disappeared. These parties emerged as tail-enders of the bourgeoisie, just as incapable of carrying out a radical agrarian revolution as the bourgeois liberals. Insofar as one wing of the SRs participated in the revolutionary victory, it did so under the leadership of the Bolsheviks and the proletariat, not as a force wielding equal power alongside the proletariat, and even less as the major force involved:

"We know from our own experience—and revolutions all over the world confirm it if we take the modern epoch of, say, a hundred and fifty years—that the result has always been the same everywhere: the petty bourgeoisie in general, and the peasants in particular, have failed in all their attempts to realise their strength, and to direct economics and politics their own way. They have had to follow the leadership either of the proletariat, or the capitalists—there is no middle way open to them. Anyone who thinks of a middle way is an empty dreamer" ("Speech to the Congress of Transport Workers," March 27, 1921. *C.W.*, Vol. 32, p. 277–278).

2. Contrary to what he previously contended, the socialist revolution was fully on the agenda even before the agrarian revolution was accomplished. Let us not forget that Lenin began his speech to the Second Congress of the soviets, the very congress which took power, with these words: "We will now proceed to the construction of socialism." The fact that in the beginning, the revolutionary government was content to establish workers control over industry rather than nationalize it, no longer had anything to do with any belief in the "socialist immaturity" of the proletariat. It had to do only with scheduling the socialist tasks of the revolution in a chronologically and economically rational way.

Many more quotations could be produced. It is enough to note that in a March 7, 1918, document (*C.W.*, Vol. 27, p. 89–90), Lenin explicitly characterized the October revolution as a socialist revolution.

3. Contrary to what he previously contended, the state that issued from the revolution was now clearly presented as a workers state, as the dictatorship of the proletariat, and not as a bourgeois state. This is why all Lenin's writings after the polemics around the April Theses and, understandably, all references to the October revolution after its victory, never mention the "democratic dictatorship of the workers and peasants" but always speak of "the dictatorship of the proletariat." The same applies to the documents of the Communist International on the Russian revolution.

In his report on the Russian revolution of 1905, delivered in January 1917, Lenin still stated that this revolution: "was a *bourgeois-democratic* revolution in its social content, but a *proletarian* revolution in its methods of struggle. It was a bourgeois-democratic revolution since its immediate aim, which it could achieve directly and with its own forces, was a democratic republic, the eight-hour day and confiscation of the immense estates of the nobility" (*C.W.*, Vol. 23, p. 238–239).

But a few weeks later, in his "Letters from Afar," he already saw in the soviets the *"embryo* of a *workers government*," and proclaimed the necessity for a state like that of the Paris Commune, that is for a workers state (*C.W.*, Vol. 23, 295–342). While he still maintained in that text that this would not yet be the dictatorship of the proletriat but the "democratic dictatorship of the workers and peasants," he abandoned the formula in the April Theses and "codified" the dictatorship of the proletariat in *State and Revolution.*

It is clear that in Lenin's mind, as well as Trotsky's, "democratic dictatorship of the workers and peasants" and "dictatorship of the proletariat" were antithetical formulas and mutually exclusive. The one implied a bourgeois state, the other a workers state. By April 1917, Lenin had decided in favor of the workers state.

On March 8, 1918, Lenin characterized the Russian state as issuing from a revolution in the course of which "the workers created their own state" (*C.W.*, Vol. 27, p. 126). On March 9 of the same year, he formulated his position even more clearly:

"The Revolution of October 25 (November 7), 1917 in Russia brought about the dictatorship of the proletariat, which has been supported by the poor peasants or semi-proletarians" (*C.W.*, Vol. 27, p. 153).

The only issue on which Lenin did not take a stand after April 1917 was the objective impossibility of a long period of capitalist economic growth in Russia "on the European and not the Asiatic model." But here too, everything he had written about imperialism, about the First World War, about its objective consequences, and especially *The Imminent Catastrophe and the Means to Conjure It*, clearly indicate the direction in which he was heading. At any rate, the "unfettered development" of capitalism occurred neither between 1906 and 1914, nor between February and October 1917, much less after October 1917.

It was the dictatorship of the proletariat supported by the peasantry that made it possible to carry out the agrarian revolution, the main task of the bourgeois-democratic revolution in Russia. This was the verdict of history. Only if one reduces, in Menshevik fashion, the tasks of that revolution solely to the overthrow of absolutism (and not even to the complete conquest of freedom since the standing army still stood and there was no Constituent Assembly and no emancipation of the oppressed nationalities) can one claim that the "democratic stage" was realized in February 1917.

In reality, the tasks of the democratic revolution were accomplished only after the establishment of the dictatorship of the proletariat, *after* the conquest of power by the soviets, *after* the creation of a workers state. And they were accomplished in the closest combination with a whole series of tasks (not all, of course) that were already socialist in nature.

January 1, 1982

OUR POLITICAL CONTINUITY WITH BOLSHEVISM

by Doug Jenness

Our November 1981 issue celebrated the 64th anniversary of the Russian revolution by featuring Lenin's complete 1921 article, "Fourth Anniversary of the October Revolution." This was the first time it had been run in the *Militant* or *International Socialist Review.* We accompanied Lenin's article with a brief description of the Bolsheviks' political strategy of the Russian revolution, around which the party was built, which made possible the victory in October.

In the April 1982 issue of the *ISR*, Ernest Mandel takes issue with our description. Mandel offers his own interpretation of Lenin's strategy, counterposing it positively to the pre-1917 positions of the Mensheviks and negatively to the pre-1917 views of Leon Trotsky.

The result is an erroneous presentation of the Bolshevik strategy and a distorted picture of the differences in the Russian workers movement leading up to the 1917 revolution.

This remains an important question today. It cannot be dismissed merely as history, since it bears directly on the question: What is the *revolutionary continuity* of Marxist strategy that has guided communists since 1847? Does it remain valid today? Arriving at correct answers to these questions is indispensable if the international workers' movement is to lead its allies in overturning the old ruling classes, abolishing capitalist exploitation and all the forms of oppression bred and perpetuated by it, and preventing the imperialists from blowing up the world in pursuit of profits.

What is the historic line of march of the working class in its struggle for the world socialist revolution? That question is necessarily posed by any discussion of Lenin's strategy, since it was the Bolshevik Party that led the workers and peasants in the first successful socialist revolution in world history.

Russia at the turn of the century was a country, as Lenin put it, "where modern capitalist imperialism is enmeshed . . . in a particularly close network of precapitalist relations." A feudal monarchy still governed the country, and many remnants of serfdom and medievalism existed in the countryside. The peasantry remained a large majority of the population, while the working class, concentrated in cities such as St. Petersburg and Moscow, was a small minority. (*Imperialism, the Highest Stage of Capitalism*, an Education for Socialists publication, (Pathfinder Press, 2002), p. 38, [2021 printing]. Also in *Collected Works of Lenin [CW]*, Vol. 22, 1916, p. 259).

The central question facing Russian Marxists was how to chart a course toward a revolution of the toilers that would bring down the tsar, abolish semifeudal oppression of the peasant masses, help to impel the socialist revolution in Western Europe, and culminate in the expropriation of the capitalist exploiters. In other words, in a country where most tasks of the bourgeois revolution were still unfulfilled, what strategy and what class alliances were necessary to build a bridge to the socialist revolution? Solving that problem, both in theory and practice, was what Russian Marxists set out to do.

Russian opponents of tsarist autocracy had been grappling with how to make a revolution there for several decades before the Bolsheviks and Mensheviks, as separately defined currents, appeared on the scene. There was an especially important debate between the narodniks (the Russian term

---

This article first appeared in the June 1982 *International Socialist Review.*

for populists) and the Marxists. From Mandel's description of this debate, however, one might draw the incorrect impression that Marx and Engels, in the 1870s and 1880s, adapted to populism. It is important to be clear on this, since Lenin consciously and explicitly rooted himself in the continuity of Marx and Engels's writings.

Mandel asserts that "after some hesitation," Marx—in correspondence with populist leader Vera Zasulich in 1881—"arrived at an unambiguous position: Russia could 'leap over the stage of capitalism.'" "Through this analysis," Mandel says, "Marx provided support" to the narodniks against a current evolving away from populist positions. In the late 1880s and early 1890s, following Marx's death, Engels drew the conclusion that history was not bearing out Marx's 1881 hypothesis. Only then did Engels finally throw in his lot with the first nucleus of Russian Marxists. This, in a nutshell, is Mandel's account.

The record shows that Marx and Engels's views on the development of Russian society and their relations with the emerging revolutionary movement there were quite a bit richer and more complex. In fact, they provide a model both of a materialist analysis of a concrete social and economic situation and of how proletarian revolutionists approach fighters struggling against oppression who show potential to evolve toward scientific communism.

Did Marx and Engels adapt to populism?

Throughout their political lives in the nineteenth century, Marx and Engels regarded tsarist Russia as the bastion of reaction in Europe. Moreover, until the Crimean War of 1853–56, they considered revolutionary prospects in Russia to be quite far off. As a result of the tsarist regime's defeat in that war and worsening economic and social conditions, however, the Russian peasants stepped up their struggles. Despite efforts by the tsar in the 1860s to contain these struggles, including a decree of "emancipation" from serfdom that in reality preserved the peasants' bondage to the landlords, the unrest in the countryside could not be permanently quelled. By the 1870s a revolutionary democratic movement—the populists—had arisen in Russia, aiming to overthrow the tsarist autocracy.

Marx and Engels welcomed these revolutionary developments in Russia, recognizing in them a potentially powerful ally of the workers and peasants of Western Europe, whose struggles had always occurred in the menacing shadow of the tsarist armies.

"There is another great power which, ten years ago, most powerfully checked the revolutionary current [throughout Europe]," Marx wrote in 1858. "We mean Russia. This time, combustible matter has accumulated under her own feet, which a strong blast from the West may set on fire" (*CW*, vol. 15, p. 568).

Not only did Marx greet the development of the populist movement in the 1870s as a breach in "the deathly quiet of Russia at home," but many populists also became interested in socialism and were influenced by Marx and Engels's writings. They organized the translation of a number of them into Russian, including *Capital.*

Industrialization in Russia at this time was only in its infancy, and the working class was very small. No organized working-class movement had yet emerged. Many populists developed the idea that the peasantry could be the social basis for a transition to socialism. They pointed to the communal ownership of land, still existing in the rural areas throughout Russia, as the basis for "peasant socialism."

Since Marx and Engels recognized the international significance of the developing Russian revolutionary movement, they took a special interest in the issues it was discussing. Both learned the Russian language in order to read the literature and correspond with Russian revolutionary democrats. Their goal was to influence and win a generation of revolutionary fighters to scientific socialism.

In 1879 the principal populist organization, Land and Liberty (*Zemlya i Volya*), split in two; the majority formed the People's Will (*Narodnaya Volya*), the minority the General Redistribution (*Chernyi Peredel*). All attempts to reunify the two populist factions failed. The principal leadership of the latter group—Georgi Plekhanov, Vera Zasulich, and Pavel Axelrod—subsequently evolved toward Marxism, and in 1883, the year Marx died, established Russia's first Marxist organization, the Emancipation of Labor group.

Marx had no opportunity to learn first hand

about the evolution of the political views of the General Redistribution. Based on the information he did have, he sharply reproached it for its initial anarchist-leaning opinions. Recognizing the centrality of the revolutionary democratic tasks of the Russian revolution, Marx criticized the General Redistribution for being "against all political-revolutionary action" and instead proposing that Russia somehow "somersault into the anarchist-communist-atheist millenium." He considered its decision to establish its base of operations in Geneva—a stronghold of Bakunin's anarchism—to be a retreat from revolutionary activity inside Russia. (*Marx and Engels Selected Correspondence,* Progress Publishers, 1880, p. 313).

Marx and Engels respected the courage and dedication of many of the fighters in the People's Will group, but they disagreed with its conspiratorial methods and utopian conceptions of the revolution.

Despite these differences, Marx and Engels kept up their correspondence and meetings with leaders of both groups. Following Marx's death, Plekhanov's group continued its political evolution, coming over to scientific socialism. Engels greeted their development with enthusiasm in an April 1885 letter to Vera Zasulich. "I am proud to know that there is a party among the youth of Russia which frankly and without equivocation accepts the great economic and historical theories of Marx," he wrote, "and has definitely broken with all the anarchist and also the few existing Slavophil traditions of its predecessors. . . . It is an advance which will be of great importance for the revolutionary development of Russia" (*Marx and Engels Selected Correspondence*, p. 361).

At the same time, Engels never gave up trying to influence figures in the populist movement; he continued to meet and correspond with them for the rest of his life.

The peasant communes

In the 1870s and early 1880s, Marx and Engels considered the prospect of a revolution in Russia to be very possible. Unlike the narodniks, however, they approached this prospect from the standpoint of proletarian revolutionists. And they made their views known to figures in the populist movement.

Marx and Engels noted the uneven economic development between Western Europe, where industrial capitalism was far more advanced, and Russia, where communal landholdings still existed on a national scale and modern capitalist development was just beginning to get under way. If a proletarian revolution in Europe could make the more developed productive forces of the West available to the peasants of Russia, then it was possible that communal property, instead of being carved up into privately-owned plots as capitalist relations penetrated the countryside, could instead be used by a revolutionary government in Russia to develop the economy in the interests of the exploited producers. Only under these circumstances, Marx and Engels said, could Russia move toward socialism, bypassing the type of capitalist development (and attendant ills) that had occurred in Western Europe. Given these conditions, the remnants of communal property could enable progress on the basis of collective labor, the highest form of social organization.

In 1875, Engels, in a polemic with Pyotr Tkachov, a Russian populist, wrote:

"It is clear that communal ownership in Russia is long past its period of florescence and to all appearances is moving towards its disintegration. Nevertheless, the possibility undeniably exists of raising this form of society to a higher one, if it should last until circumstances are ripe for that, and if it shows itself capable of development in such manner that the peasants no longer cultivate the land separately, but collectively; of raising it to this higher form without it being necessary for the Russian peasants to go through the intermediate stage of bourgeois small holdings.

"This, however, can only happen if, before the complete break-up of communal ownership, a proletarian revolution is successfully carried out in Western Europe, creating for the Russian peasant the preconditions requisite for such a transition, particularly the material conditions which he needs if only to carry through the revolution necessarily connected therewith of his whole agricultural system."

To make crystal clear that his point of departure was entirely different from that of the narodniks, Engels explained that, "It is, therefore, sheer bounce for Mr. Tkachov to say that the Russian peasants, although 'owners,' are 'nearer to socialism' than the propertyless workers of Western Europe. Quite the opposite. If anything can still save Russian communal ownership and give it a chance of growing into a new, really viable form, it is a proletarian revolution in Western Europe" ("On Social Relations in Russia," *Marx and Engels Selected Works* (*MESW*), Vol. 2, p. 395).

Marx detailed the same position in a letter the same year to *Otechestvenniye Zapiski*, a populist journal, and in the 1881 letter to Zasulich, mentioned above.

Marx and Engels concisely summarized their views on this question in their jointly-authored preface to the 1882 Russian edition of the *Communist Manifesto*. "If the Russian Revolution becomes the signal for a proletarian revolution in the West, *so that both complement each other*," they wrote, "the present Russian common ownership of land may serve as the starting-point for a communist development (emphasis added)" (*MESW*, Vol. 1, p. 100–101).

Neither a Russian revolution nor a proletarian revolution in the West occurred at that time, however. So, as Marx and Engels had foreseen under such circumstances, the destruction of communal property continued under the onslaught of capitalist economic development in Russia.

Until his death in 1895, Engels continued to follow the evolution of the economic and class structure in Russia—the structure that a popular revolution would inherit. In an 1894 postscript to his article, "On Social Relations in Russia," he noted that "the development of capitalism and the dissolution of the village community in Russia have both taken enormous strides forward."

"There continues this accelerated transformation of Russia," he wrote, "into an industrial capitalist state, the proletarianization of a large part of her peasantry, and the destruction of the old communist community." Engels wasn't sure "whether this community is still sufficiently intact to become, when the occasion arises, and in combination with a revolution in Western Europe, the starting point for communist development as Marx and I had still hoped in 1882.

"This much, however, is certain," he said. "If anything of this community is to be salvaged, the first requirement is the overthrow of the tsarist despotism, a revolution in Russia. The Russian revolution will not only wrest the greater part of the nation, the peasants, from their isolation in the villages, constituting their *mir*, their universe; it will not only lead the peasants out into the large arena, where they will come to know the outside world and with it their own selves, their own condition, and the means of escape from their present misery—the Russian revolution will also give a fresh impulse to the labor movement in the West, creating for it new and better conditions for struggle and thereby advancing the victory of the modern industrial proletariat, a victory without which present-day Russia, whether on the basis of the community or of capitalism, cannot achieve a socialist transformation of society" (*MESW*, Vol. 2, p. 407–410)

Mandel states that in this 1894 postscript Engels had changed his earlier opinion and come to the conclusion "that capitalist development had become inevitable in Russia." This is misleading, as the above passage from that article makes clear. Engels had not fundamentally altered the point of view that he and Marx had expressed 12 years earlier. As they had foreseen at that time, in the absence of a successful revolution, the forward march of capitalist relations in Russia had continued, and Engels, in the closing decade of the nineteenth century, took this fact into account in pointing to the most likely course of development.

These statements by Marx and Engels on the peasant communes in Russia were continually referred to and quoted by both sides in the debates between the populists and the Marxists.

Alexi Voden, a Russian socialist who visited with Engels in 1893, wrote that Engels had told him that he expected Voden to raise "the 'usual' question on the idea of Marx's letter to *Otechestvenniye Zapiski* and wondered what was not clear in that letter, since Marx had clearly stated his own and Engels's conviction that it was important that the achievement of power by Social-Democracy in the West should coincide with the political and agrarian revolution in Russia."

According to Voden's account, Engels added that he "wished that the Russians—and not only the Russians—would not pick quotations from Marx or from him, Engels, but would think as Marx would have thought in their place, and that it was only in that sense that the word 'Marxist' had any *raison d'etre.* . . ."

Engels also told Voden that "the most necessary thing of all for the Russian Social-Democrats was to work seriously on agrarian problems in Russia" (*Reminiscences of Marx and Engels*, Foreign Language Publishers, p. 328–329).

So, Mandel's account turns out to be misleading on several counts: 1) what changed over the 1880s and 1890s were not Marx and Engels's basic views but their judgment on the degree of expansion of capitalism in Russia and dormancy of the European revolution, which they had taken into account from the outset as key factors in determining the direction of Russian social and economic development; 2) Marx and Engels's analysis did not "provide support" to the populists against proletarian communism, no matter how some populists tried to misuse it; 3) Marx's initial circumspection about the General Redistribution was based not on his adaptation to the populists, but on the group's initial anarchist tendency to downplay the political struggle in Russia and its revolutionary-democratic axis; and 4) Engels welcomed their evolution to communist positions only shortly after Marx's death, while continuing his efforts to influence Russian revolutionists still in the camp of the populists.

A post-1917 aside

As an aside, it should be noted that a development to a certain extent analogous to what Marx and Engels suggested as a possibility for Russia at the end of the 1880s occurred following the 1917 proletarian revolution. Some of the former tsarist colonies on Russia's eastern border were overwhelmingly peasant in composition and dominated by precapitalist economic and political relations—medievalism and landlordism. While communal property did not predominate, they were extremely backward, even more backward than Afghanistan today, and there was virtually no working class or capitalist industry. They established peasant soviet republics that developed close links with the Russian workers state and became part of the Union of Soviet Socialist Republics in 1922. They did not go through capitalist development, and will not unless a counterrevolution overthrows state property in the USSR.

This experience, along with the new rise of the colonial revolution inspired by the Russian revolution, led Lenin to draw some further conclusions about prospects for the road forward in economically backward countries throughout the world. In reporting to the Second Congress of the Communist International in 1920 on the "Draft Theses on the National and Colonial Questions," he stated:

". . . are we to consider as correct the assertion that the capitalist stage of economic development is inevitable for backward nations now on the road to emancipation and among whom a certain advance towards progress is to be seen since the war? We replied in the negative. If the victorious revolutionary proletariat conducts systematic propaganda among them, and the Soviet governments come to their aid with all the means at their disposal—in that event it will be mistaken to assume that the backward peoples must inevitably go through the capitalist stage of development.

"Not only should we create independent contingents of fighters and party organizations in the colonies and the backward countries, not only at once launch propaganda for the organization of peasants' Soviets and strive to adapt them to the precapitalist conditions," Lenin said, "but the Communist International should advance the proposition, with the appropriate theoretical grounding, that with the aid of the proletariat of the advanced countries, backward countries can go over to the Soviet system and, through certain states of development, to communism, without having to pass through the capitalist stage" (*The National Liberation Movement in the East,* Lenin, Progress Publishers, p. 287).

Lenin, like Marx and Engels before him, recognized that unevenness in economic development could lead to unanticipated and particular combinations of social relations as society advanced on a world scale. And this was, if anything, becoming more accentuated by imperialism.

Where Mandel says Lenin went wrong

Mandel says Lenin's strategy was wrong on many points. He claims that Lenin dumped these erroneous positions in favor of correct ones following the February 1917 revolution. Lenin's alleged errors are:

- The "erroneous dogma" of dividing the Russian revolution into two distinct stages. The first was the democratic revolution aimed at overthrowing tsarist autocracy and eliminating semifeudal survivals in the countryside. "The goal of the democratic revolution was to be the *unfettered development of capitalism,*" Mandel says, "and simultaneously the maximum development of the proletariat, the proletarian class struggle, and the proletarian party." [Note: Throughout this article all emphases in quotes are those of the person quoted, unless otherwise indicated.]

The second stage was "that of the social revolution leading to the dictatorship of the proletariat, the overthrow of capitalism, and the construction of a socialist society."

- The Bolsheviks were educated in "the spirit of limiting the 'first stage' of the revolution to purely democratic tasks." Lenin favored the "self-limitation of the proletariat, that is the refusal to move beyond the realization of the most radical bourgeois-democratic demands."

He favored seizure of power by a provisional revolutionary government and participation of the revolutionary workers party in this government; but this government would be "provisional, i.e., that it will have to give up or lose power later on, given the bourgeois character of the revolution."

- "Lenin's obstinate and frequent refusal to confuse, i.e., to *combine,* the democratic tasks and the socialist tasks, the minimum program and the maximum program."
- Lenin radically rejected "any notion of 'revolutionary communes,' any notion of a state (in contrast to an insurrection) based on soviets."
- Lenin "had either not, or insufficiently" dealt with the "main driving forces" of the revolution and "the relationship of forces between the social classes involved in the revolution."
- Lenin held an exaggerated view of the role that the peasantry would play in the revolution. He was "certain that the revolutionary peasantry had to *take political power,*" that it would establish its own political party, and that it would wield "equal power alongside the proletariat."
- Lenin erroneously counterposed the revolutionary democratic dictatorship of the proletariat and peasantry to the dictatorship of the proletariat.
- Lenin "had either not, or only insufficiently," dealt with the "concrete national and international social and economic context" in which the democratic revolution would unfold in Russia.
- By "persistently" believing that Russia would go through a rapid growth of capitalism, and especially through American-style development of agriculture, Lenin underestimated "the weight of imperialism, of the world market (which left no room for a second America!), and of the agrarian crisis in Russia itself. . . ."
- Lenin's "erroneous dogma" disarmed the Bolshevik party following the February revolution, "when *all* the Bolshevik leaders and *all* the Bolshevik cadres favored 'critical support' to and even collaboration with the provisional coalition government."
- For Lenin, "The capacity of the Russian proletariat *to begin* to resolve the socialist tasks of the revolution . . . did not exist."

That's quite a list! If the reader did not know the outcome of the October 1917 revolution, he or she could quite justifiably conclude, part way through Mandel's article, that the Bolsheviks, allegedly educated in an "erroneous dogma" for at least a dozen years, were going to make a mess of it, that the whole affair would end in disaster.

But that is not what happened. The Bolshevik party *did* lead the Russian revolution, *did* establish a workers and peasants government, which *did* carry through the democratic revolution and *did* complete the transition to a workers state. How could a party so mistrained on such fundamental questions reorient itself so quickly? How could it lead this revolution to victory? Was it really all with the efforts of a single person, Lenin, who fortunately came to his senses in the clutch?

The answer requires examining the Bolsheviks' true positions, the positions that made possible the October Revolution, which are not the ones Mandel claims the Bolsheviks held.

Importance of the democratic revolution

When Lenin became a Marxist in the early 1890s, he did precisely as Engels had suggested to Voden. He approached the strategy for the Russian revolution by thinking "as Marx would have thought," applying that method to the concrete reality of social relations in Russia. And he began "to work seriously on agrarian problems in Russia," doing an exhaustive study of the question.

Lenin's first major works included *What the Friends of the People Are* (1894) and the *Development of Capitalism in Russia* (1899). From a standpoint converging with Plekhanov's Emancipation of Labor group, Lenin described the expansion of capitalism in the cities and countryside, as well as the corresponding growth of the working class as growing layers of the peasantry began to be proletarianized.

Unlike the populists, for whom the peasantry was the principal force for a socialist revolution, Lenin's point of departure was the need to build an independent Marxist workers party capable of leading the working class in the fight for democracy and socialism in Russia.

From the beginning, Lenin emphasized the enormous importance of the fight for democracy—above all, the agrarian question—and its relationship to the struggle against capitalism.

"In Russia, the relics of medieval, semifeudal institutions," he wrote in 1894, "are still so enormously strong (as compared with Western Europe), they are such an oppressive yoke upon the proletariat and the people generally, retarding the growth of political thought in all estates and classes, that one cannot but insist on the tremendous importance which the struggle against all feudal institutions, absolutism, the social-estate system, and the bureaucracy has for the workers.

"The workers must be shown in the greatest detail what a terribly reactionary force these institutions are, how they intensify the oppression of labor by capital, what a degrading pressure they exert on the working people, how they keep capital in its medieval forms, which, while not falling short of the modern, industrial forms in respect of the exploitation of labor, add to this exploitation by placing terrible difficulties in the way of the fight for emancipation. The workers must know that unless these pillars of reaction are overthrown, it will be utterly impossible for them to wage a successful struggle against the bourgeoisie. . . ."

Lenin went on to explain that it was "the direct duty of the working class to fight side by side with the radical democracy [peasantry] against absolutism and the reactionary social estates and institutions—a duty which the Social-Democrats must impress upon the workers, while not for a moment ceasing also to impress upon them that the struggle against all these institutions is necessary only as a means of facilitating the struggle against the bourgeoisie, that the worker needs the achievement of the general democratic demands only to clear the road to victory over the working people's chief enemy, over an institution that is purely democratic by nature, *capital,* which here in Russia is particularly inclined to sacrifice its democracy and to enter into alliance with the reactionaries in order to suppress the workers, to still further impede the emergence of a working-class movement" ("What the Friends of the People Are," *CW,* Vol. 1, 1894 p. 290–292).

And in Lenin's article, "Tasks of the Russian Social Democrats," published four years later in 1898, he wrote:

"The object of the practical activities of the Social-Democrats is, as is well known, to lead the class struggle of the proletariat and to organize that struggle in both its manifestations: socialist (the fight against the capitalist class aimed at destroying the class system and organizing socialist society), and democratic (the fight against absolutism aimed at winning political liberty in Russia and democratizing the political and social system of Russia).

"We said *as is well known,*" Lenin continued. "And indeed, from the very moment they appeared as a separate social-revolutionary trend, the Russian Social-Democrats have always definitely indicated this object of their activities, have always emphasized the dual manifestation and content of the class struggle of the proletariat and have always insisted on the inseparable connection between their socialist and democratic tasks . . ." (*CW,* Vol. 2, 1898, p. 328).

These extensive quotations from Lenin's early works present the general framework in which he was to view the combined tasks of the working class in the Russian revolution through the October 1917 revolution. This outline acquired more flesh as the Russian toilers, and the Marxist movement along with them, went through the experiences of the Russo-Japanese war, the 1905 revolution, and the first worldwide imperialist war. But the central elements were already there in the 1890s: combining the democratic and socialist tasks of the working class; the alliance of the working class with the revolutionary peasantry; the necessity for proletarian leadership; and the irreversible tendency for bourgeois political forces to ally with the autocracy against the peasantry and proletariat.

A prolonged capitalist stage?

In Mandel's opinion, Lenin saw the "goal of the democratic revolution" in Russia to be a "prolonged" period of "unfettered capitalist development." And the author of *Imperialism* didn't even know that there was "no room for a second America" in the world! This is dead wrong.

In order to illustrate Lenin's "unambiguous" support of a prolonged capitalist stage, Mandel offers several quotations from the Bolshevik leader. He quotes Lenin speaking before the delegates at the Fifth Congress of the Russian Social Democratic Labor Party (RSDLP) in May 1907.

". . . the basic question of our revolution is whether it will secure the development of capitalism through the peasants' complete victory over the landowners or through the landowners' victory over the peasants. A bourgeois-democratic revolution . . . is possible in either of two ways: in the Prussian, if one might say so, or in the American way.

"This means the following; the landlords may win, may foist compensation payments or other petty concessions on the peasants, may unite with a handful of the wealthy, pauperise the masses and convert their own farms into Junker-type, capitalist, farms. Such a revolution will be bourgeois-democratic but it will be to the least advantage of the peasants—to their least advantage from the angle of the rapidity of capitalist development.

"Or, on the contrary, the complete victory of the peasant uprising, the confiscation of all landed estates and their equal division will signify the most rapid development of capitalism, the form of bourgeois-democratic revolution most advantageous to the peasants" (*CW*, Vol. 12, 1907, p. 465).

Lenin's point was as simple as it is correct. The complete elimination of the remnants of medievalism and serfdom, together with the overturn of the autocracy, would create the best conditions for the development of capitalism, especially in agriculture. That is a basic precept of historical materialism, nothing more.

By the "American way," Lenin was making an historical analogy to the policy in the United States in the nineteenth century whereby the government distributed millions of acres of public land to homesteaders. This facilitated the rapid development of capitalist agriculture in the United States, which in turn fostered a large internal market and the optimum conditions for industrial development, as well.

In Russia, Lenin argued, nationalizing the land and confiscating the landed estates would create the best conditions for free farmers upon a free soil.

Contrary to Mandel, however, Lenin's recognition of the ABCs of the laws of development of human history did *not* mean that he either proposed or expected a "prolonged" stage of rule by the bourgeoisie, or that the Bolsheviks were proved wrong on this score in 1917. Lenin, in fact, drew the opposite conclusion in a November 1918 polemic with Karl Kautsky, the prominent leader of the Second International who took a centrist position at the outbreak of World War I and attacked the Soviet government in Russia. This is what Lenin had to say (remember, this is a *full year after* the October 1917 revolution):

". . . already the 1905 Revolution revealed that the vast majority of the peasants in Russia, members of village communes as well as homestead peasants, were in favor of nationalization of all the land. The 1917 Revolution confirmed this, and after the assumption of power by the proletariat this was done.

"The Bolsheviks remained loyal to Marxism," Lenin said, "and never tried (in spite of Kautsky, who, without a scrap of evidence, accuses us of doing so) to 'skip' the bourgeois-democratic revolution. The Bolsheviks, first of all, helped the most radical, most revolutionary of the bourgeois-democratic ideologists of the peasants, those who stood closest to the proletariat, namely, the Left Socialist-Revolutionaries, to carry out what was in effect nationalization of the land. On October 26, 1917, i.e., on the very first day of the proletarian, socialist revolution, private ownership of land was abolished in Russia.

"This laid the foundation, the most perfect from the point of view of the development of capitalism (Kautsky cannot deny this without breaking with

Marx), and at the same time created an agrarian system which is the *most flexible* from the point of view of the transition to socialism" ("Proletarian Revolution and the Renegade Kautsky," *CW*, Vol. 28, 1918, p. 314–315).

The October Revolution, Lenin says, created the foundation for "the most perfect" development of capitalism in the countryside. (Mandel cannot deny this without breaking with Marx *and* Lenin.) That's what the Bolsheviks, for years, had been pointing out would be possible if the workers and peasants could overthrow the autocracy and establish a revolutionary dictatorship, a workers and peasants government.

The fact that the Russian revolution would be a bourgeois-democratic revolution neither meant that the bourgeoisie would lead it or support it, nor that the government issuing from it would put the bourgeoisie in power. Lenin pointed out before 1905, and it became even clearer during World War I, that the bourgeoisie would actively oppose a decisive victory of the democratic revolution. He pointed out repeatedly that the *bourgeois revolution* in Russia was of a particular variety, that is, it was a *peasant revolution.* Only the peasantry, with the support and leadership of the working class, which at the same time was waging its own struggle against the capitalists, could carry this revolution through in the most complete way.

"Marxism teaches the proletarian not to keep aloof from the bourgeois revolution," Lenin wrote in 1905, "not to be indifferent to it, not to allow the leadership of the revolution to be assumed by the bourgeoisie but, on the contrary, to take a most energetic part in it, to fight most resolutely for consistent proletarian democratism, for the revolution to be carried to its conclusion" (*CW*, Vol. 9, 1905, p. 52).

Lenin correctly insisted on drawing a distinction between the peasant democratic revolution and the proletarian socialist revolution, since this was necessary to determine how the revolutionary workers party should participate in the class struggle, what slogans it should advance, and what alliances it should build at different junctures in the revolutionary struggle.

Lenin defended this fundamental Bolshevik proposition, too, in his 1918 polemic against the centrist Kautsky.

"It was the Bolsheviks who strictly differentiated between the bourgeois-democratic revolution and the socialist revolution: by carrying the former through, they opened the door for the transition to the latter. This was the only policy that was revolutionary and Marxist" (*CW*, Vol. 28, 1918, p. 312).

Peasant revolution in Russia

To dissolve the peasant revolution into the socialist revolution, Lenin argued, would mean not recognizing the necessity of establishing a worker-peasant alliance, thus missing the opportunity to forge the class alliance required for victory.

Lenin had studied closely Marx and Engels's analysis of the German revolution of 1848 and the conclusions they had drawn from that experience. Lenin referred to this in an article on Karl Marx written for the *Granat Encyclopedia* in 1913. Pointing to Marx's assessment of how the German bourgeoisie had betrayed both the proletariat and the peasantry in the 1848 revolution, Lenin quoted Marx's appraisal eight years later of how the German revolution could triumph next time.

"The whole thing in Germany will depend on the possibility of backing the proletarian revolution by some second edition of the Peasant War," Marx had written to Engels in an 1856 letter (*CW*, Vol. 21, 1913, p. 77).

This was precisely the course that the 1905 revolution had shown for Russia: the combination of a proletarian revolution and a peasant war. Based on this experience, the Bolsheviks confirmed the strategy they had developed even prior to the 1905 upheaval and developed it further.

The revolution to bring down the tsar and wipe out feudal remnants in the countryside, Lenin pointed out time and again, would unite broad sectors of the population; this included sectors which do not have identical class interests, such as the workers and poor peasants, and even some who have conflicting class interests, such as the rich exploiting peasants and the exploited toilers of town and country.

In his principal work on the class relations in the Russian revolution, *Two Tactics of Social Democracy in the Democratic Revolution*, written in July–August 1905 as a polemic against Menshevik (and later Stalinist) leader A.S. Martynov, Lenin stated:

"The absence of unity on questions of socialism

and in the struggle for socialism does not preclude singleness of will on questions of democracy and the struggle for a republic. To forget this would be tantamount to forgetting the logical and historical differences between a democratic revolution and a socialist revolution. To forget this would be tantamount to forgetting the character of the democratic revolution as one of the *whole* people . . ." (*Two Tactics,* Progress Publishers, p. 70).

The most favorable relation of class forces carrying through the democratic revolution, Lenin said, would be a "revolutionary-democratic dictatorship of the proletariat and peasantry." This, he said, would create the best possible conditions for completing the democratic revolution in the most thorough fashion and for opening the road for the socialist revolution. Such a revolutionary dictatorship pushes forward the democratic revolution "and strives to give it forms most advantageous to the proletariat; consequently, it strives to make the utmost of the democratic revolution to order to attain the greatest success in the proletariat's further struggle for socialism" (*Two Tactics,* p. 73).

This was contrary to the Menshevik view, which didn't see the bourgeois revolution in Russia as a peasant revolution, but as a revolution that would put the bourgeoisie in power, that would establish a period of capitalist rule. For the Mensheviks, the role of the working class was to help put the bourgeoisie in power. The role of the peasants was to help the workers do this.

Since the bourgeoisie must lead the revolution, the Mensheviks argued, the proletariat must temper its militancy and subordinate the fight for its own class interests and those of the rural poor, since this would frighten the bourgeoisie and cause them to recoil from their necessary revolutionary role.

"One side says: advance the revolution to its consummation despite resistance or passivity on the part of the inconsistent bourgeoisie," Lenin wrote in *Two Tactics,* referring to the Bolshevik position.

"The other side says: do not think of independently advancing the revolution to completion, for if you do, the inconsistent bourgeoisie will recoil from it.

"Are these not two diametrically opposite paths? Is it not obvious that one set of tactics absolutely excludes the other, that the first tactics is the only correct tactics of revolutionary Social-Democracy? . . ." (*Two Tactics,* p. 87).

'Self-limitation' of the working class

Mandel argues that the Bolsheviks' distinction between the democratic and socialist revolutions, between the peasant and proletarian revolutions, led Lenin to advocate that the working class limit its objectives and not attempt to carry through the socialist revolution. According to Mandel, Lenin insisted that if, indeed, the workers assumed the leadership of a revolutionary government, they would "have to give up or lose power later on, given the bourgeois character of the revolution." Mandel puts "self-limitation of the proletariat" between quotation marks, as if this were something that Lenin actually said.

This is pure invention. In fact, it is totally contrary to the entire thrust of what Lenin wrote throughout his political life. Lenin always stressed that, as the revolution unfolded, the working class should go as far as it could in pushing the democratic revolution through to its completion and beginning the socialist revolution. Not only did he place no *limits* on the struggle to do this, but the object of Bolshevik strategy was precisely to prepare the workers to accomplish as much as possible.

Lenin did not place any arbitrary time schedule on the transition from the democratic to the socialist revolution. He did not refer to a prolonged, protracted, or lengthy transition. Neither did he talk about the working class limiting, self-limiting, or restraining itself.

Lenin didn't view the transition from the standpoint of predicting clock time or calendar time (as Mandel might have us think), but according to political time, i.e., the class relationship of forces, the strength and resoluteness of the revolutionary workers party, the organization and independence of the rural poor, and the thoroughness of the democratic revolution.

Here are just a few of many statements reflecting this:

- "The more complete, determined, and consistent the bourgeois revolution, the more assured will the proletariat's struggle be against the bourgeoisie and for socialism" (*Two Tactics,* p. 37).
- "The working class and its class-conscious representatives are marching forward and car-

rying this struggle forward, not only unafraid of bringing it to completion, but striving to go far beyond the uttermost limits of the democratic revolution" (*Two Tactics*, p. 107).

• The revolutionary workers party says to the working class, "you must strive to extend the framework and the content of your class struggle so as to make it *include* not only *all* the aims of the present democratic Russian revolution of the whole people, but the aims of the subsequent socialist revolution as well" (*Two Tactics*, p. 104).

• "The revolution must be taken *very much further* than its direct, immediate and already fully-matured bourgeois aims, if *those* aims are really to be achieved, and if even minimum bourgeois conquests are to be irreversibly consolidated" (*CW*, Vol. 15, 1908, p. 59).

• ". . . the bourgeoisie as a whole is incapable of waging a determined struggle against the autocracy; it fears to lose in this struggle its property which binds it to the existing order; it fears an all-too revolutionary action of the workers, who will not stop at the democratic revolution but will aspire to the socialist revolution . . ." (*CW*, Vol. 8, 1905, p. 511).

Of course Lenin correctly recognized, as Grenada's Prime Minister Maurice Bishop has put it, that making the socialist revolution is not like making a cup of instant coffee. How quickly the workers could move toward measures to expropriate the capitalists would depend on the concrete conditions and relationship of class forces at the time of the revolution. (And unlike today, Lenin was writing at a time when no socialist revolution had yet triumphed anywhere in the world, or could depend on support from an existing workers state.)

The Bolsheviks urged the proletariat and rural poor to organize themselves independently, in order to be in the best position to take advantage of whatever situation they might face to advance their own class interests. The Bolsheviks also sought to steel the vanguard workers against anarchist or ultraleft political currents that ignored this reality of the class struggle in Russia; it seems to be this latter aspect of Bolshevik policy that Mandel refers to as "self-limitation."

Lenin himself faced somewhat similar arguments, and he answered them in *Two Tactics*. "Replying to the anarchists' objection that we are putting off the socialist revolution, we say: we are not putting it off, but are taking the first step towards it in the only possible way, along the only correct path, namely, the path of a democratic republic" (*Two Tactics*, p. 16).

So, the proletarian party must know how to *lead* the workers and their exploited allies in deepening the revolution, advancing their class consciousness and self-confidence, and crossing the bridge from the democratic to the socialist revolution at whatever pace the class struggle allows.

Lenin explained this point very clearly in his 1905 article, "Social Democracy's Attitude Toward the Peasant Movement":

". . . from the democratic revolution we shall pass at once, and precisely in accordance with the measure of our strength, the strength of the class conscious and organized proletariat, begin to pass to the socialist revolution. We stand for uninterrupted revolution. We shall not stop half-way.

"If we do not now and immediately promise all sorts of 'socialization'," Lenin said, "that is because we know the actual conditions for that task to be accomplished, and do not gloss over the new class struggle burgeoning within the peasantry, but reveal that struggle. . . .

"To try to calculate *now* what the combination of forces will be within the peasantry 'on the day after' the revolution (the democratic revolution) is empty utopianism. . . . We shall bend every effort to help the entire peasantry achieve the democratic revolution, *in order thereby to make it easier* for us, the party of the proletariat, to pass on as quickly as possible to the new and higher task—the socialist revolution" (*CW*, Vol. 9, 1905, p. 237).

Who confuses what

As we've seen, Mandel also comments on "Lenin's obstinate and frequent refusal to confuse, i.e., to *combine*, the democratic tasks and the socialist tasks. . . ."

But it's Mandel who is confused, not Lenin. A baker who didn't know how to combine flour and eggs couldn't make a cake, that's true. But the baker wouldn't have any better luck by thinking that eggs and flour are the same thing!

The Bolsheviks did obstinately refuse *to confuse* the democratic and socialist tasks of the revolution, correctly so. To have done otherwise would have been to confuse the key strategic class alliance necessary, first, to bring down the tsarist regime and landlordism and, then, to lead the revolution forward toward expropriating the capitalists. This is what Lenin explained in the very last paragraph of *Two Tactics:*

"At the head of the whole people, and particularly of the peasantry—for complete freedom, for a consistent democratic revolution, for a republic! At the head of all the toilers and the exploited—for socialism! Such in practice must be the policy of the revolutionary proletariat, such is the class slogan which must permeate and determine the solution of every tactical problem, every practical step of the workers' party during the revolution" (*Two Tactics*, p. 97).

But this did not mean that Lenin, who Mandel will admit had some acquaintance with the dialectical method, erected a wall between the democratic and socialist revolutions. Just the opposite, Lenin saw the democratic and socialist tasks as being intertwined.

"Like everything else in the world," he wrote, "the revolutionary-democratic dictatorship of the proletariat and peasantry has a past and a future. Its past is autocracy, serfdom, monarchy, and privilege. In the struggle against this past, in the struggle against counter-revolution, a 'single will' of the proletariat and the peasantry is possible, for here there is unity of interests.

"Its future is the struggle against private property, the struggle of the wage-worker against the employer, the struggle for socialism. Here singleness of will is impossible. Here the path before us lies not from autocracy to a republic, but from a petty-bourgeois democratic republic to socialism.

"Of course, in actual historical circumstances, the elements of the past become interwoven with those of the future; the two paths cross. Wage-labor with its struggle against private property exists under autocracy as well; it arises even under serfdom. But this does not in the least prevent us from logically and historically distinguishing between the major stages of development.

"We all contrapose bourgeois revolution and socialist revolution; we all insist on the absolute necessity of strictly distinguishing between them; however, can it be denied that in the course of history individual, *particular* elements of the two revolutions become interwoven?" (*Two Tactics*, p. 71).

So much for Lenin's "obstinate" refusal to recognize that the democratic and socialist tasks are combined!

Weight of the agrarian question

Mandel contends that Lenin exaggerated the independent role of the peasantry in the revolution by predicting that it would wield "equal power alongside the proletariat."

What are the facts?

Lenin was always clear that the working class had to assume the vanguard role in the democratic and socialist revolutions in Russia.

But in a country where the working class was a small minority and the peasantry a big majority, it was absolutely essential for the working class to forge an alliance with the peasantry. Lenin and the Bolsheviks charted a course to do this, developing and enriching their position with each new experience of the class struggle.

In 1899, in a draft program for the Russian Social Democratic Labor Party, Lenin explained that "a working-class party cannot, without violating the basic tenets of Marxism and without committing a tremendous political mistake, *overlook* the revolutionary elements that exist among the peasantry and not afford those elements support. . . ."

"Two basic forms of the class struggle are today intertwined in the Russian countryside: 1) the struggle of the peasantry against the privileged landed proprietors and against the remnants of serfdom; 2) struggle of the emergent rural proletariat against the rural bourgeoisie. For Social-Democrats the second struggle, of course, is of greater importance; but they must also indispensably support the first struggle *to the extent that it does not contradict* the interests of social development.

"It is no accident that the peasant question has always occupied and continues to occupy such a prominent place in Russian society and in the Russian revolutionary movement; this fact is a reflection of the great significance still retained by the first of the two forms of struggle" (*CW*, Vol. 4, 1899, p. 251–252).

The differences on the agrarian question between the Bolsheviks and all the opportunist and conciliationist currents in the workers movement were at the center of the divergent strategies they projected for the Russian revolution.

This was apparent by 1903 at the time of the Social Democratic Party's second congress, where the split between the Bolsheviks and Mensheviks occurred. Mandel states that "At first, the differences . . . seemed limited to organizational problems." He quotes extensively from the discussion on the agrarian question at the congress to show the broad political agreement by "the great majority of Russian Marxists."

It may have seemed to many participants at the congress that the differences were limited to organizational questions—and it may seem so to some today—but that's not how Lenin saw it.

Writing about the congress six months later, Lenin answered the Menshevik leader Martov, who was attempting to paper over the political differences at the congress. Lenin stated:

"The inconsistency of principle of the anti-*Iskra*ists and the 'Centre' was also clearly brought out by the debate on the agrarian program, which took up so much time at the congress . . . and raised quite a number of extremely interesting points. As was to be expected, the campaign against the program was launched by Comrade Martynov . . ."[1]

The opposition to the agrarian program that Lenin helped draft was one of the more substantial, representing 40 percent of the congress. The heart of the disagreement was over the proposal defended by Lenin that the working class ally with the peasantry *as a whole* in the struggle against the autocracy and the remnants of serfdom. The opposition argued that agricultural workers and poor peasants would not join with rich farmers in the fight against their common enemy—landlordism, medievalism, and autocracy. They reduced the agrarian program of the workers party to the class struggle of farm workers against capitalist farmers.

Lenin noted that "their failure to grasp the importance of the peasant movement, their failure to grasp that it was not overestimation, but, on the contrary, underestimation of its importance (and a lack of forces to utilize it) that was the weak side of our Social-Democrats at the time of the first famous peasant revolts [1902]: ("One Step Forward, Two Steps Backward," *CW*, Vol. 7, 1904, p. 231–232).

In the debate at the congress itself, Lenin argued: "We are pursuing two qualitatively different aims in the countryside: firstly, we want to achieve freedom [from feudal and semi-feudal restrictions] for bourgeois relations; secondly, we want to conduct the proletarian struggle. . . . [I]t is our task to show the peasants where the revolutionary proletarian task of the peasant proletariat begins. . . ."

Lenin disagreed with the opportunist opposition's concentration on the backwardness of the peasantry. "In 1852 Marx said that the peasants had judgement as well as prejudices," Lenin pointed out. "And now, when we point out to the poor peasants the cause of their poverty, we may count on success" (*CW*, Vol. 6, 1903, p. 495).

The program adopted at the 1903 congress called for the convocation of peasant committees to struggle for the abolition of all remnants of serfdom. Just before the congress, Lenin wrote that the peasants "will unavoidably and inescapably remain miserable slaves until they take their destiny into their own hands, until they take their first and most important step and achieve the establishment of *peasant committees* for real and not sham emancipation of the peasantry" (*CW*, Vol. 6, 1903, p. 349).

While the Mensheviks abandoned this demand, it remained a part of the Bolsheviks' program through the October 1917 revolution. Committees of the poor peasants, which the Bolsheviks helped launch, were a crucial instrument beginning in the

---

1. The delegates at the 1903 Congress included supporters of *Iskra* edited by Plekhanov, Martov, and Lenin; anti-Iskraists primarily around the economist newspaper *Rabocheye Dyelo*, of which Martynov was one of the editors; and a middle group—the centre—that wavered between the other two groups.

On most questions of program, including the agrarian program, most Iskraists voted together. However, on decisive votes on the nature of the party, the Iskraists divided; the majority becoming the Bolsheviks and the minority blocking with the anti-Iskraists and the Centre to become the Mensheviks. After the Congress the Menshevik Iskraists openly retreated from the program they had voted for at the Congress.

Trotsky was an Iskraist who at first went with the Mensheviks and broke with them in 1904 over their political direction. Lenin, while criticizing Trotsky's support to the Mensheviks at the Congress, praised his arguments in the debate on the agrarian question ("One Step Forward, Two Steps Backward," *CW*, Vol. 7, 1904, p. 238).

summer and fall of 1918 for the struggle against exploitation, and for deepening the class struggle in the countryside and the socialist course of the revolution in general.

It was only a matter of months following the 1903 congress that many Mensheviks like Axelrod and L. Martov, who had voted with the Bolsheviks on the overall program, including the section on the agrarian question, openly adopted or conciliated with the opportunist views of those who had opposed the program at the congress. These differences became even more clear during the 1905 revolution and its aftermath.

Lessons of 1905 revolution

The 1905 revolution combined the largest proletarian uprising since the Paris Commune in 1871 with the most massive peasant revolt in Russia in 130 years. This experience offered an unprecedented opportunity to test in real life the role that different social forces would play in the Russian revolution and to see the forms the struggle might take.

The 1905 revolution underlined for Lenin the correctness of the Bolsheviks' emphasis on the democratic struggle and the weight of the peasantry in the Russian revolution. In a 1909 article he observed that "the alliance of proletarian and peasant forces" was "a characteristic feature of the whole of the first period of the Russian revolution, of all the great events of 1905–07" (*CW*, Vol. 15, 1909, p. 333).

In the aftermath of this experience Lenin wrote or completed four book-size works, as well as many articles, speeches, and resolutions, on the agrarian question.

Lenin's political strategy started from the unshakeable conviction that only working-class leadership could carry the democratic revolution and the worker-peasant alliance to victory.

"Our Party," he wrote in 1909, "holds firmly to the view that the role of the proletariat is the *role of leader* in the bourgeois-democratic revolution; that *joint actions* of the proletariat and the peasantry are essential to carry it through to victory; that unless *political power is won* by the revolutionary classes, victory is impossible" (*CW*, Vol. 15, 1909, p. 379).

This statement captures the essence of the class alignment that Lenin proposed for the Russian revolution.

He explained that the independent policy of the working class was necessary "to split the peasantry away from the liberals, rid it of their influence, rally the peasantry behind it in the struggle and thus bring about an 'alliance' *de facto*—one that emerges and becomes effective, when and to the extent that the peasantry are conducting a revolutionary fight" (*CW*, Vol. 15, 1908, p. 58).

To pursue any other policy, Lenin insisted, was to give up the fight for proletarian leadership of the democratic revolution, abandoning the peasantry to the bourgeois betrayers and thereby abandoning any perspective of a thoroughgoing revolution.

"In a word," Lenin wrote in *Two Tactics*, "to avoid finding itself with its hands tied in the struggle against the inconsistent bourgeois democracy, the proletariat must be class-conscious and strong enough to rouse the peasantry to revolutionary consciousness, guide its assault, and thereby independently pursue the line of consistent proletarian democraticism."

Lenin continued: "Only the proletariat can be a consistent fighter for democracy. It can become a victorious fighter for democracy only if the peasant masses join its revolutionary struggle. If the proletariat is not strong enough for this the bourgeoisie will be at the head of the democratic revolution and will impart an inconsistent and self-seeking nature to it." To ignore the centrality of the alliance with the peasantry is "playing into the hands of the bourgeois democrats," he said (*Two Tactics*, p. 47).

Thus, while Lenin always recognized the indispensable need for the proletariat's *political* leadership in the revolution, he correctly did not attempt to assign some *a priori* weight—one quarter, equal, or three-quarters—to the peasantry's role in the worker-peasant alliance in order to insure its *victory*. He did not exclude, however, the possibility that the social composition of the workers and peasant dictatorship would "lead to the participation, or even predominance, within it of the most heterogeneous representatives of revolutionary democracy" (*CW*, Vol. 8, 1905, p. 291).

Lenin's view was that the peasantry's relative weight in the worker-peasant alliance would be determined by the class struggle. He had no blueprint detailing every feature of the revolution. His was a strategic approach designed to arm the revolutionary workers party to vigorously pursue the fight for a worker-peasant alliance and use it as a battering ram to bring down tsarism and open the road to the socialist revolution. Toward this goal the Bolsheviks aimed to bring to bear the greatest possible mobilization of the revolutionary peasantry.

Lenin and the Bolsheviks used many formulations to describe the relationship between the proletariat and the peasantry, including the proletariat "allies to itself," "leads," or carries out "joint actions" with the mass of the peasantry.

Mandel insists that Lenin's position necessarily assumed that the peasantry had to build its own "independent" party and play an "independent" role. This Mandel considers to be unrealizable.

Lenin took up this very argument in a 1908 polemic with Martov and Trotsky.

"A 'coalition' of classes *does not at all* presuppose *either* the existence of any particular powerful party, *or* parties in general. This is only confusing classes with parties. A 'coalition' of the specified classes *does not in the least* imply *either* that one of the existing bourgeois parties will establish its sway over the peasantry *or* that the peasants should form a powerful independent party! Theoretically this is clear because, first, the peasants do not lend themselves very well to party organization; and because, secondly, the formation of peasant parties is an extremely difficult and lengthy process in a bourgeois revolution, so that a 'powerful independent' party may emerge only towards the end of the revolution."

Then Lenin went on to explain that "The experience of the Russian revolution shows that 'coalitions' of the proletariat and the peasantry were formed *scores and hundreds of times,* in the most diverse forms, without any 'powerful independent party' of the peasantry. Such a coalition was formed when there was 'joint action,' between, say, a Soviet of Workers' Deputies and a Soviet of Soldiers' Deputies, or a Railwaymen's Strike Committee, or Peasants' Deputies, etc. All these organizations were mainly *nonparty*; nevertheless, every joint action between them undoubtedly represented a 'coalition' of *classes.*

"In the course of this," Lenin continued, "a peasant party took shape as an idea, in germ, coming into being in the form of the Peasant Union of 1905 or the Trudovik group of 1906—and *as* such a party grew, developed and constituted itself, the coalition of *classes* assumed different forms, from the vague and unofficial to definite and official political agreements."

Lenin added that three calls for insurrection issued during the revolution were signed by workers' parties, unions, and the peasant organizations. "That was a fully constituted political coalition of parties and non-party organizations!" he said. "That was the 'dictatorship of the proletariat and the peasantry' *proclaimed* in the form of a threat to tsarism, in the form of a call to the whole people, but not yet realized!" (*CW*, Vol. 15, 1909, p. 371–372).

Mandel charges Lenin with "illusions about an independent role of the *Trudoviks* (Kerensky!) or the SRs [Socialist-Revolutionaries]."

This is false. Lenin's approach was not based on the possible evolution—either positive or negative—of the particular parties or their leaders. It was based on the living experience of the class struggle. On that basis, Lenin concluded that the peasantry would establish its own organizations or find some organizational expression to fight for its revolutionary demands. In 1905 this took the form of the Soviets of Peasant Deputies, the Trudoviks, and the Peasant Union. In 1917 it took the form of the Soviets of Soldiers Deputies, the Congresses of Peasant Deputies, and the left-wing of the Socialist Revolutionary Party.

That's what happened. So Mandel's argument is not with Lenin, it's with the *facts.*

Lenin, however, never believed that the peasantry could offer an *independent class program* for the Russian revolution. Only the Marxist program of the Russian working class could ensure the completion of the democratic revolution and its growing over to the socialist revolution.

Nor did Lenin have any illusions about the petty-bourgeois misleaders of the peasant organizations or their program. He observed in 1907 that:

"No one at this stage can tell what forms bourgeois democracy in Russia will assume in the future. Possibly, the bankruptcy of the Cadets may lead to the formation of a peasant democratic party, a truly mass party, and not an organization of terrorists such as the Socialist-Revolutionaries have been and still are. It is also possible that the objective difficulties of achieving political unity among the petty bourgeoisie will prevent such a party from being formed and, for a long time to come, will keep the peasant democracy in its present state as a loose, amorphous, jelly-like Trudovik mass."

So much for "illusions" in the Trudoviks!

Lenin continued, "In either case our line is one: to hammer out the democratic forces by merciless criticism of all vacillations, by uncompromising struggle against the democrats joining the liberals, who have proved their counterrevolutionariness" (*CW*, Vol. 13, 1907, p. 121–122).

Does Mandel agree with this line? The problem is not Lenin's alleged "illusions" in the Trudoviks, but Mandel's lightminded dismissal of the strategic and tactical problems that a revolutionary workers party had to confront in Russia in order to lead the workers and peasants to victory.

This was a life-or-death question for the Russian revolution, however. It was a very practical question for the Bolsheviks in the Duma, for example. When it was possible and served the interests of advancing the class struggle, the Bolsheviks correctly established blocs with the Trudoviks to get candidates elected, and they formed voting blocs in the Duma on particular measures.

Lenin, who followed the speeches and votes in the Duma closely, wrote many articles showing that, in spite of differences, the Trudovik peasant deputies were closer to the Bolsheviks than to the liberal Cadets, or even the Trudovik intellectuals (Kerensky!), on the agrarian questions.

The Mensheviks, who formed a bloc with the liberal bourgeoisie, repudiated this policy of "left-blocs" pursued by the Bolsheviks following the defeat of the 1905 revolution. During that period of reaction and repression, many opponents of tsarism, including the Mensheviks, contended that the peasants had become too disillusioned to be counted on in the next revolution. Lenin noted that on their faces "a contemptuous grimace appears whenever someone talks about some peasant democracy or other, but [that their] mouths water at the mere sight of the "'enlightened' liberals."

The Bolsheviks, in marked contrast, developed their strategy on the premise that the peasantry would again emerge as a major revolutionary force, as it had during the 1905 revolution. "We must know," Lenin wrote, "that the certain sign of a genuinely widespread rise in the social tide, of a genuinely approaching revolutionary crisis, will inevitably be, in Russia of today, a movement among the peasantry" (*CW*, Vol. 15, 1908, p. 275).

This was vindicated many times over by the 1917 revolution, and the Bolsheviks codified these lessons on the centrality of the worker-peasant alliance at the Second and Fourth congresses of the Communist International. Far from Lenin having an exaggerated view of the role of the peasantry, it is Mandel who downgrades the revolutionary continuity of Marxism on this key question of revolutionary strategy.

Soviets as an 'embryo' of revolutionary gov't

One of Mandel's more amazing claims is that, before the February 1917 revolution, Lenin "radically" rejected "any notion of a state (in contrast to an insurrection) based on the Soviets."

The facts show otherwise. Not only did Lenin not "radically" reject this proposition, he did not reject it at all. In fact, he returned many times to the experience of 1905 to show how the soviets had been an embryonic revolutionary government.

In November 1905, a month after the workers formed the first soviet in Russia, Lenin wrote his first major article on the soviets. "I believe", he wrote, "that politically the Soviets of Workers' Deputies should be regarded as the embryo of a provisional revolutionary government."

It "must proclaim itself the provisional revolutionary government, or form such a government, and must by all means enlist to this end the participation of new deputies not only from the workers, but, first of all, from the sailors and soldiers, who are everywhere seeking freedom; secondly from the revolutionary peasantry, and thirdly from the revolutionary bourgeois intelligentsia" (*CW*, Vol. 10, 1905, p. 21–23).

Lenin, in fact, polemicized against the Mensheviks, who *did* deny that the soviets had this potential. In a 1906 polemic, for example, he wrote, "The organs of authority that we have described [Soviets of Workers', Soldiers', Railwaymen's and Peasants' Deputies] represented a dictatorship in embryo, for they recognized *no* other authority, *no* law and *no* standards, no matter by whom established" (*CW*, Vol. 10, 1906, p. 244).

In the same article he noted that the Bolsheviks regarded the soviets "as embryonic organs of revolutionary state power that united the proletariat with the revolutionary democrats" (*CW*, Vol. 10, 1906, p. 252).

A revolutionary dictatorship—or state power—based on the soviets, which united the working class and peasantry. That, Lenin said, would be the revolutionary-democratic dictatorship of the proletariat and peasantry.

In 1907 Lenin wrote, "In all the embryonic organs of revolutionary power (the Soviets of Workers' Deputies, the Soviets of Peasants' and Soldiers' Deputies, etc.) representatives of the proletariat were the main participants, followed by the most advanced of the insurgent peasantry" (*CW*, Vol. 12, 1907, p. 459).

Lenin returned to this theme once again in January 1917, just one month before the outbreak of the Russian revolution, in a speech to Swiss socialists looking back on the lessons of the 1905 revolution. He explained that "In several cities these *Soviets of Workers' Deputies* began more and more to play the part of a provisional revolutionary government, the part of organs and leaders of the uprising. Attempts were made to organize Soviets of Soldiers' and Sailors' Deputies and to combine them with the Soviets of Workers' Deputies.

"For a time several cities in Russia became something in the nature of small local 'republics.' The government authorities were deposed and the Soviet of Workers' Deputies actually functioned as the new government. Unfortunately, these periods were all too brief, the 'victories' were too weak, too isolated" (*CW*, Vol. 23, 1917, p. 248).

Finally, referring back to the debate between the Bolsheviks and Mensheviks in 1905, Lenin pointed out in 1920 that:

". . . the Bolsheviks emphasized that the Soviets of Workers' Deputies were *'actually an embryo of a new revolutionary power'*, as was literally said in the draft of the Bolshevik resolution (p. 92 of my *Report*). The Mensheviks acknowledged the importance of the Soviets; they were in favor of 'helping to organize' them, etc., but they did not regard them as embryos of revolutionary power, did not in general say anything about a 'new revolutionary power' of this or some similar type, and flatly rejected the slogan of dictatorship" (*CW*, Vol. 31, 1920, p. 343).

How could Mandel have overlooked Lenin's unambiguous statements that the soviets could become the basis of a revolutionary dictatorship of the exploited classes, of a new state power? It makes no sense, unless you accept Mandel's erroneous view that Lenin somehow thought that the workers and peasants would make the revolution—with soviets if they were available—but that in a historic act of "self-limitation," the workers would have "to give up or lose power [to the liberal bourgeoisie] later on," in order to make way for the stage of prolonged capitalist development.

This view turns Lenin into a Menshevik. But that, according to Mandel's version, is Lenin's position.

Evidently anticipating that this assertion will strike many readers as outlandish, Mandel assures us that there is no contradiction either "in Lenin's mind" or "from the point of view of formal logic." Mandel's "formal logic" is hard to follow, and none of us will ever know what was "in Lenin's mind." But we do know about Lenin's *writings* and *actions*, and these *are* in contradiction with Mandel's rendering of Bolshevism on this question.

International context

Following up the lead left by Marx and Engels, Lenin saw—well before 1905—that the Russian revolution could be the prologue to the socialist revolution in Western Europe. At the same time, he took note after the 1905 revolution of how that uprising had inspired a series of democratic revolutions in the East—Persia, China, and Turkey. Even before World War I, Lenin was describing the overall international situation as an era of proletarian and democratic revolutions and explaining the interconnectedness of this world revolutionary process. He saw the Russian revolution in this context.

Yet Mandel claims that Lenin "had either not, or only insufficiently" dealt with the "concrete national and international social and economic context" of the revolution.

Mandel makes no effort to bolster this assertion, he simply states it, lumping Lenin together with Plekhanov on this score.

In particular, Mandel makes no reference to Lenin's views during the period when the international situation had the greatest repercussions for the Russian revolution—World War I.

While the Bolsheviks' strategic approach to the Russian revolution didn't change during World War I, concrete shifts in the class struggle inside Russia and worldwide—which Mandel says Lenin "underestimated"—did influence how the Bolsheviks assessed the prospects for revolution in Russia and their international ramifications.

"The imperialist war," Lenin pointed out, "has *linked up* the Russian revolutionary crisis, which stems from a bourgeois-democratic revolution, with the growing crisis of the proletarian socialist revolution in the West. This link is so direct that no individual solution of revolutionary problems is possible in any single country—the Russian bourgeois-democratic revolution is now not only a prologue to, but an indivisible and integral part of, the socialist revolution in the West.

"In 1905, it was the proletariat's task to consummate the bourgeois revolution in Russia so as to kindle the proletarian revolution in the West. In 1915, the second part of this task has acquired an urgency that puts it on a level with the first part" (*CW,* Vol. 21, 1915, p. 379).

The war divided the revolutionary movement in Russia between the "chauvinist revolutionaries," who desired revolution the better to defeat Germany, and the "proletarian revolutionaries," who wanted a revolution in Russia for the sake of the proletarian revolution in the West.

The Russian liberals, who gave their full and unconditional support to the imperialist war, were clearly shown to have taken the path of counterrevolution. "The facts have shattered the view held by our opportunists that Russian liberalism is still a motive force of a revolution in Russia," Lenin concluded (*CW,* Vol. 21, 1915, p. 318).

Lenin noted that "The war crisis has *strengthened* the economic and political factors that are impelling the petty bourgeoisie, including the peasantry, to the left. Herein, lies the objective foundation of the full possibility of victory for the democratic revolution in Russia" (*CW,* Vol. 21, 1915, p. 418).

He pointed out that the deepening differentiation of the peasantry had enhanced the class struggle in the countryside, as well. The antagonism between the peasants and the landlords was becoming more acute, and the rural poor were drawing closer to the urban workers. All these factors pointed to an even closer relationship between the peasants and the workers and an even greater intertwining of the democratic and proletarian revolutions.

Acknowledging the initial patriotism of the peasant masses, Lenin was confident that "With the return of the soldiers from the field of slaughter . . . sentiment in the rural areas will undoubtedly turn against the tsarist monarchy" (*CW,* Vol. 21, 1915, p. 318).

In March 1917, one week after the tsar had been toppled by the workers' uprising, Lenin wrote:

"It was natural that the revolutionary crisis should have broken out *first of all* in tsarist Russia, where the disorganization was most appalling and the proletariat most revolutionary (not by virtue of any special qualities, but because of the living traditions of 1905).

"This crisis was precipitated by the series of extremely severe defeats sustained by Russia and her allies," Lenin wrote. "They shook up the old machinery of government and the old order and roused the anger of *all* classes of the population against them; they embittered the army, wiped out a very large part of the old commanding personnel, composed of diehard aristocrats and exceptionally corrupt bureaucratic elements, and replaced it by a young, fresh, mainly bourgeois, commoner, petty-bourgeois personnel.

"Those who, grovelling to the bourgeoisie or simply lacking backbone, howled and wailed about 'defeatism,'" Lenin said, "are now faced by the fact of the historical connection between the defeat of the most backward and barbarous tsarist monarchy and the *beginning* of the revolutionary conflagration" (*CW,* Vol. 23, 1917, p. 300–301).

Lenin pointed out that both World War I and the Balkan Wars (1912–1913) that preceded it had intensified the imperialist pressure on oppressed nations, as well, creating an explosive situation. This was of decisive importance in the Russian empire, where the majority of the population were part of nations oppressed by the tsar's regime. Lenin recognized the revolutionary significance of the struggle of the oppressed nations and defended the Marxist program of the right to self-determination, including the right to separation.

In several theses drawn up in October 1915, Lenin reiterated the Bolsheviks' position that it was permissible for Social Democrats to participate in a provisional revolutionary government with the democratic petty bourgeoisie. But "not with the revolutionary chauvinists," he stated unequivocally.

"If the revolutionary chauvinists won in Russia," he said, "we would be opposed to a defence of *their* 'fatherland' in the present war. Our slogan is: against the chauvinists, even if they are revolutionary and republican. . . ."

Then he answered the question as to what the revolutionary workers party would do if the revolution placed power in its hands during the war. Contrary to Mandel's assertions, Lenin did not say: self-limit yourself, turn it over to the bourgeoisie to govern during an extended stage of capitalist development.

Lenin's answer was: "We would propose peace to *all* the belligerents on the condition that freedom is given to the colonies and *all* peoples that are dependent, oppressed and deprived of rights. Under the present governments, neither Germany, nor Britain and France would accept this condition. In that case, we would have to prepare for and wage a revolutionary war, i.e., not only resolutely carry out the whole of our minimum program, but work systematically to bring about an uprising among all peoples now oppressed by the Great Russians, all colonies and dependent countries in Asia (India, China, Persia, etc.), and also, and first and foremost, we would raise up the socialist proletariat of Europe for an insurrection against their governments and despite the social-chauvinists. There is no doubt that a victory of the proletariat in Russia would create extraordinarily favorable conditions for the development of the revolution in both Asia and Europe. *Even* 1905 proved that" (*CW*, Vol. 21, 1915, p. 403).

This is the same answer the Bolsheviks gave two years later when they won the majority in the soviets and led the workers and peasants to power.

Yet Mandel would have us believe that "until after the February 1917 revolution, i.e., until the April Theses were formulated," the Bolsheviks were committed to a strategy that the revolutionary dictatorship "will have to give up or lose power later on, given the bourgeois character of the revolution"!

That wasn't Lenin's position—in 1905, 1915, *or* 1917.

Did Lenin dump his perspectives in 1917?

Mandel claims that after the February 1917 revolution, Lenin dumped the strategy of the revolutionary democratic dictatorship of the proletariat and peasantry and rearmed the Bolshevik party with a new strategy. Only this, Mandel says, made the October Revolution possible.

But an obvious question is posed: Where did Lenin write that he was dumping the Bolsheviks' pre-1917 strategy? Where did he ever say that the party had held an incorrect orientation for more than two decades?

Since Mandel offers no evidence that Lenin ever made any such statements, the reader can only assume that the old position just faded away without comment, that Lenin dropped the Bolsheviks' strategy for the Russian revolution without explaining why. Perhaps Lenin was embarrassed, or trying to cover his tracks, or just didn't think the change was important. Maybe it took minds more acute than Lenin's following his death to even ascertain the change. Maybe Lenin maneuvered and deceived the party and the working class for the only time in his life.

None of these possible explanations hold up very well. All are highly uncharacteristic of Lenin, who was very frank when correcting errors and adopting new policies, and considered it important to be so.

Any reader who is inspired—and many will be—to go back to Lenin's writings in 1917 and after can check for themselves what he had to say. They will discover that Mandel chose to ignore what Lenin actually wrote.

Lenin's response to the February revolution and his proposals for what the working class should do are outlined clearly in a series of letters, articles, and resolutions written in March and April 1917. The major documents are: "Letters from Afar," "The Tasks of the Proletariat in the Present Revolution (April Theses)," "The Dual Power," "Letters on Tactics," and "The Tasks of the Proletariat in our Revolution (Draft Platform for the Proletarian Party)".

In the first of the "Letters on Tactics," which was written a few days *after* the April Theses, Lenin explained his approach in some detail. He defined the situation as "a period of *transition* from the first stage of the revolution to the second. . . ."

"What, then, is the first stage?

"It is the passing of state power to the bourgeoisie. Before the February–March revolution of 1917, state power in Russia was in the hands of one old class, namely, the feudal landed nobility, headed by Nicholas Romanov.

"After the revolution, the power is in the hands of a *different* class, . . . namely, the *bourgeoisie.*

"The passing of state power from one class to another is the first, the principal, the basic sign of a *revolution,* both in the strictly scientific and in the practical political meaning of that term.

"To this extent, the bourgeois, or the bourgeois-democratic, revolution in Russia is *completed.*

"But at this point we hear a clamour of protest from people who readily call themselves 'Old Bolsheviks' [the letter was a polemic against Bolshevik leader Kamenev and his supporters]. Didn't we always maintain, they say, that the bourgeois-democratic revolution is completed only by the 'revolutionary-democratic dictatorship of the proletariat and the peasantry'? Is the agrarian revolution, which is also a bourgeois-democratic revolution completed? Is it not a fact, on the contrary, that it has *not even* started?

"My answer is: the Bolshevik slogans and ideas *on the whole* have been confirmed by history; but *concretely* things have worked out *differently;* they are more original, more peculiar, more variegated than anyone could have expected."

The war, as Lenin had explained in his first "Letter from Afar," had accelerated the revolutionary process in Russia and shaped its contours somewhat differently than could have been anticipated a decade earlier. Nonetheless, the Bolsheviks' strategic orientation, while algebraic as all strategies and programs must be, was generally confirmed and it served as the indispensable guide for determining what to do in 1917.

Lenin's "Letter on Tactics" continued by criticizing "those 'Old Bolsheviks' who more than once already have played so regrettable a role in the history of our Party by reiterating formulas senselessly *learned by rote* instead of *studying* the specific features of the new and living reality.

"'The revolutionary-democratic dictatorship of the proletariat and peasantry' has *already* become a reality [here Lenin added a footnote: "In a certain form and to a certain extent"] in the Russian revolution, for this 'formula' envisages only a *relation of classes,* and not a *concrete political institution implementing* this relation, this co-operation. 'The Soviet of Workers' and Soldiers' Deputies'—there you have the 'revolutionary-democratic dictatorship of the proletariat and peasantry' already accomplished in reality.

"This formula is already antiquated. Events have moved it from the realm of formulas into the realm of reality, clothed it with flesh and bone, concretized it and thereby modified it."

Note that Lenin does not say the Bolsheviks' formula of the revolutionary-democratic dictatorship of the proletariat and peasantry was proven wrong or was unconfirmed. No, Lenin says it has been "accomplished in reality."

Mandel may disagree with Lenin's conclusion. That's certainly his right. But it would be outrageous to conclude that Lenin did not mean what he said.

Lenin went on to say that, "A new and different task now faces us: to effect a split *within* this dictatorship between the proletarian elements (the anti-defencist, internationalist, 'Communist' elements, who stand for a transition to the commune) and the *small-proprietor* or *petty-bourgeois* elements (Chkheidze, Tsereteli, Steklov, the Socialist-Revolutionaries and the other revolutionary defencists who are opposed to moving towards the commune and are in favor of 'supporting' the bourgeoisie and the bourgeois government).

"The person who *now* speaks only of a "revolutionary-democratic dictatorship of the proletariat and the peasantry' is behind the times, consequently, he has in effect *gone over* to the petty bourgeoisie against the proletarian class struggle; that person should be consigned to the archive of 'Bolshevik' pre-revolutionary antiques (it may be called the archive of 'Old Bolsheviks'). . . .

"For the present, it is essential to grasp the incontestable truth that a Marxist must take cognizance of real life, of the true facts of *reality* and not cling to a theory of yesterday, which, like all theories, at best only outlines the main and the general, only *comes near* to embracing life in all its complexity."

Lenin put the old formulation in the archives not because it had been proven wrong, but precisely because it had been realized. The *general* formulation has been replaced by a *concrete* political institution—the workers' and peasants' soviets—which expressed it "in a certain form and to a certain extent." Lenin discontinued using the more general, algebraic formula in favor of the new, more concrete demand for a government of the Workers', Soldiers' and Peasants' Soviets.

"According to the old way of thinking," Lenin continued, "the rule of the bourgeoisie could and should be *followed* by the rule of the proletariat and the peasantry, by their dictatorship.

"In real life, however, things have *already* turned out *differently*; there has been an extremely original, novel and unprecedented *interlacing of the one with the other.* We have side by side, existing together, simultaneously *both* the rule of the bourgeoisie (the government of Lvov and Guchkov) and a revolutionary-democratic dictatorship of the proletariat and peasantry, which is *voluntarily* ceding power to the bourgeoisie, voluntarily making itself an appendage of the bourgeoisie" (*CW*, Vol. 24, April 1917, p. 43–46).

The capitalist provisional government was continuing the imperialist war effort—in the name of defending the revolution. And the Menshevik-SR leadership of the Soviets was strongly supporting this policy. Lenin's and the Bolsheviks' position since 1914 had been to oppose the imperialist war effort and to argue that a defeat of the Russian imperialists was a lesser evil for the working class of Russia.

The dual power

A key characterization of the situation in Russia following the February revolution was the coming into existence of what the bourgeois press, with regret, first termed "dual power." Lenin had begun explaining the significance of this situation with his first "Letter from Afar." In "The Dual Power," written in mid-April about the same time as the "Letters on Tactics," Lenin pointed out that "The highly remarkable feature of our revolution is that it has brought about a *dual power.* This fact must be grasped first and foremost: unless it is understood, we cannot advance" (*CW*, Vol. 24, April 1917, p. 38).

How would this dual power be resolved? In the tasks adopted by the April Bolshevik congress, which Lenin drafted, he explained that "The dual power merely expresses a *transitional* phase in the revolution's development, when it has gone further than the ordinary bourgeois-democratic revolution, *but has not yet reached* a 'pure' dictatorship of the proletariat and peasantry" (*CW*, Vol. 24, April 1917, p. 61).

In the "Letters on Tactics," Lenin had posed the question: ". . . are we not in danger of falling into subjectivism, of wanting to arrive at the socialist revolution by 'skipping' the bourgeois-democratic revolution—which is not yet completed and has not yet exhausted the peasant movement?"

He answered, "I might be incurring this danger if I said: 'No tsar, but a *workers* government.' But I did *not* say that, I said something else. I said that there *can be no* government (barring a bourgeois government) in Russia *other than* that of the Soviets of Workers', Agricultural Laborers', Soldiers' and Peasants' Deputies. I said that power in Russia now can pass from Guchkov and Lvov *only* to these Soviets. And in these Soviets, as it happens, it is the peasants, the soldiers, i.e., petty bourgeoisie, who predominate, to use a scientific, Marxist term, a class characterization, and not a common, man-in-the-street, professional characterization" (*CW*, Vol. 24, April 1917, p. 48).

In other words, a soviet government would be one in which the peasants preponderated. But this, Mandel has informed us, is impossible, which even Lenin had come to realize by April 1917. Yet here is Lenin continuing to advocate a provisional revolutionary government in which the representatives of the peasantry would initially hold the majority.

During the entire eight months of preparation for the October insurrection, Lenin continually emphasized that the Bolsheviks were not proposing the immediate institution of socialism. Rather, they proposed implementing a far-reaching agrarian program, including nationalization of the land; taking over the banks; and imposing workers control over the industrial and commercial capitalists.

These measures, Lenin explained in the April

Theses, "do not in any way constitute the 'introduction' of socialism. . . ." They were "steps toward socialism" (*CW*, Vol. 24, April 1917, p. 74).

Were the Bolsheviks disarmed?

Mandel asserts that as a result of their longstanding strategic orientation, the Bolsheviks were unprepared for and politically disarmed during and immediately following the February 1917 revolution. Fortunately, in the first three weeks after Lenin's return to Russia, the Bolsheviks were able to make a rapid turnabout.

If this were actually true, it would have been quite astonishing. The Bolsheviks—disoriented on the place of the democratic tasks in the revolution, on the weight and role of the peasantry, on the perspective of establishing a worker-peasant alliance on the governmental level—turned on a dime and scrapped what they had supported, voted for, and campaigned around for a decade and a half.

As has already been shown, however, the Bolsheviks didn't abandon their strategy, but saw it confirmed and realized by the unfolding revolution.

What about Mandel's charge that "*all* the Bolshevik leaders and *all* the Bolshevik cadres favored 'critical' support to and even collaboration with the provisional coalition government" and rejected "any notion of a seizure of power by the working class"? Mandel says this alleged universal confusion flowed inevitably from Lenin's "erroneous dogma" on the revolutionary democratic dictatorship of the proletariat and peasantry.

Once again, the facts reveal something quite different. They show that: 1) the Bolsheviks were *not* unanimous in their approach to the capitalist provisional government; and 2) these differences inside the party revealed a current, based in the working class, that strongly opposed the Provisional Government and its imperialist war policy and another current that favored conciliation with the Mensheviks, particularly on the decisive war question.

When the February revolution began, all the central Bolshevik leaders were in exile or prison. Thus, how to respond inside Russia was initially up to younger and less experienced leaders. Before the Provisional Government was established, the leaders on the spot issued a manifesto that was published in *Izvestia,* the organ of the soviets.

It called on the workers and soldiers to organize around the Soviet of Workers' Deputies "to create a 'provisional revolutionary government.'" This government would, among other things, "enter into negotiations with the proletariat of the belligerent countries against their oppressors and enslavers . . . and for the termination of the bloody human slaughter which has been imposed on the enslaved peoples" (*The Bolshevik Revolution,* Vol. 1, 1917–1923, Carr, Penguin Books, p. 83).

When Lenin, still in Switzerland, learned of this manifesto from an abridged version in a German newspaper, he immediately sent a telegram hailing it to the Bolshevik paper *Pravda* in Petrograd. In his "Letters from Afar," Lenin singled out for special praise the statement's position against the imperialist war.

The main leaders in Petrograd—Shlyapnikov, Zalutsky, and Molotov—started to republish *Pravda* on March 5. According to historian E.H. Carr, "The views expressed in the first seven numbers of the new *Pravda* were broadly those of the party manifesto. It denounced the existing Provisional Government as 'a government of capitalists and landowners', and thought that the Soviet should convene a constituent assembly to establish a 'democratic republic.' On the issue of the war, it published on 10 March 1917 a resolution of the bureau [of the Bolshevik Central Committee] advocating a transformation of the imperialist war into a civil war for the liberation of the peoples from the yoke of the ruling classes, though it still refrained from the explicit advocacy of national defeatism" (*The Bolshevik Revolution*, Vol. 1, 1917–1923, Carr, p. 84).

Then, in mid-March, older party leaders—Kamenev, Stalin, and Muranov—returned and took over the reins of *Pravda.* The line toward the coalition government and the war immediately changed. Criticism of the class-collaborationist leadership of the soviets and of the liberal leadership of the Provisional Government was dropped.

A prowar proclamation issued by the Petrograd Soviet under the leadership of the Mensheviks and SRs was published on the front page of *Pravda.* It announced that "we should stoutly defend our own liberty" and that "the Russian revolution will not flinch before the bayonets of the aggressors."

This was followed by a whole-hearted endorsement of national defense by Kamenev. He stated in a signed article that "When army faces army, it would be the most insane policy to suggest to one of these armies to lay down its arms and go home. This would not be a policy of peace but a policy of slavery, which would be rejected with disgust by a free people" (Carr, p. 86).

Kamenev and Stalin also favored pursuing discussions aimed at unification with the Mensheviks.

This radical shift in line hardly received a unanimous response among Bolsheviks in Petrograd. Marcel Leibman, in *Leninism Under Lenin,* quotes from Shlyapnikov's memoirs:

"'The whole of the Tauride Palace, from the members of the Committee of the Duma to the Executive Committee [of the Soviets], the heart of revolutionary democracy (i.e., the moderate majority in the Soviets, M.L.) was full of the news—the victory of the moderate, reasonable Bolsheviks over the extremists.'

"On the other hand," Leibman says, "some of the Bolshevik militants were indignant at the tone adopted by the editors of *Pravda.* The Petersburg section even called for Kamenev's expulsion, and in the Vyborg quarter [strongest fraction of worker-Bolsheviks] Stalin's expulsion was demanded as well."

Leibman includes a footnote indicating that "What was published in *Pravda* was extremely interesting, but of no less importance was what was *not* published there. When Alexandra Kollontai brought to Petrograd, in the last days of March, the first two of Lenin's *Letters from Afar,* . . . the editorial board hesitated for several days before publishing only one of them—and then suppressed the passages in which Lenin opposed any agreement with the Mensheviks" (*Leninism Under Lenin,* Marcel Leibman, Merlin Press, 1975, p. 123).

During this period, Iakov Sverdlov, who was to play a key role in organizing the Bolshevik party from April 1917 until his death from influenza in March 1919, also opposed the capitalist Provisional Government. In an unpublished manuscript *Iakov M. Sverdlov and the Organization of the Russian Revolution* (1978), Prof. Charles Duval reports that when Sverdlov was freed from internment in Siberia in March, he spent a few days in Krasnoiarsk, where he participated in party and soviet meetings. On March 22 in the Krasnoiarsk Soviet, dominated by conciliatory Social-Democrats, Sverdlov, according to Duval:

". . . accused the Mensheviks and SRs of promising everything to the people and delivering nothing and predicted that they would eventually turn against the revolution. He argued that the Menshevik and SR idea of 'civil peace' retarded the development of the revolution. He supported instead the soviets as the key to a victorious proletarian revolution and the only organs acceptable to the Bolsheviks as legitimate sources of power. The majority in the Krasnoiarsk Soviet remained unmoved by his appeal, however, and endorsed the new government with the standard socialist formula: 'in so far as it follows a course satisfying the demands of the working class and the revolutionary peasantry.'"

Kamenev, Stalin, et al. did not deduce their concilialionist line from traditional Bolshevik formulations such as the revolutionary democratic dictatorship of the proletariat and peasantry. Rather, they cloaked their conciliationist line in these and other revolutionary formulations, as centrists always do.

In fact, their line had nothing in common with the positions adopted by the Bolshevik Party congresses and carried in its press since 1903. In particular, it would be hard to find any questions that the Bolsheviks were better armed against than conciliationism toward the Mensheviks and opposition to defending the imperialist government's war. This was the opposite of the Mensheviks' line, which was followed out to its logical capitulationist conclusion in February 1917. Moreover, as already indicated, Lenin had explained explicitly in 1915 that the Bolsheviks would give no support whatever to any provisional government of the social chauvinists.

The fact that some Bolshevik leaders accepted a conciliationist course and abandoned the Bolshevik line on the war testifies to the profound pressures on the party, especially on those sectors most removed from the working class.

It is true that many of the Bolsheviks who were attempting to apply the party's revolutionary Marxist positions did not see the unfolding events and way forward as clearly as Lenin. They were open to the explanations he offered when he returned, however, *because of,* not *in spite of,* their absorption of the Bolshevik strategy. Lenin helped clarify and give leadership to a struggle that was already taking place inside the party. If this had not been the case, there is no way that the proletarian wing could have won a majority in the party in the first three weeks after Lenin's return.

The program of the Bolsheviks, hammered out and tested by experience for nearly two decades, prepared the majority of the party to orient itself correctly to the events of 1917. Any other explanation borders on attributing supernatural qualities to Lenin as a leader—the better to differentiate oneself from the line of march and strategic orientation that he had imbued the Bolsheviks with for a decade and a half.

From October 1917 to October 1918

In October 1917 the workers and peasants resolved the question of dual power through their soviets by establishing a revolutionary dictatorship, the dictatorship of the proletariat and poor peasantry, a workers and farmers government. This government immediately called "for a just, democratic peace," began to implement a radical agrarian program, and took the first steps toward expropriating the bourgeoisie and establishing a workers state.

Mandel says that the dictatorship of the proletariat, i.e., a workers state, was established with the October Revolution. To back up this opinion, he presents statements by Lenin describing the October Revolution as "socialist" and the new government as "the dictatorship of the proletariat supported by the poor peasants."

Lenin and other Bolsheviks at this time used many different formulations to characterize the soviet government: "workers and peasants government," "socialist republic of soviets," "dictatorship of the proletariat," "dictatorship of the proletariat and poor peasantry," "people's government," and so on.

The name officially adopted on October 26 for the Council of Peoples' Commissars, on Lenin's proposal, was the Provisional Workers and Peasants Government; in January the "provisional" was dropped by the Third All-Russian Congress of Soviets following the dispersal of the Constituent Assembly.

But the label, while important, is not the main point. What's key is the class composition and direction of the government, the tasks before it, and the transitional struggle necessary to accomplish those tasks.

The new government established in October 1917 was independent of the capitalist class, but at the same time stood on the capitalist economic foundations it inherited. That's not only what the Provisional Workers and Peasants Government inherited, but what it stood on to begin with and for some months after coming to power. The capitalist class still owned most of the means of production, and the class struggle in the countryside between the capitalist farmers and the great mass of poor peasants, semiproletarians, and rural workers had only begun.

Using this governmental power, the workers and peasants carried out a struggle to wrest control of the economy from the capitalists and to consolidate their power in the countryside. This involved nationalizing the banks, abolishing commercial secrecy, countering capitalist sabotage, and establishing workers' control over production. These measures prepared the way for expropriating the capitalists and beginning to institute workers management of industry.

By the end of the first year of the revolution, a monopoly of foreign trade had been established, most capitalist industry had been expropriated, and big strides had been made in the development of workers control.

Workers control: schedules vs. class struggle

Mandel contends that "The fact that in the beginning, the revolutionary government was content ["content" is a strange choice of words to describe the transitional struggle of the working class] to establish workers control over industry rather than nationalize it, no longer had anything to do with the belief in the 'socialist immaturity' of the proletariat. It had to do only with scheduling the socialist tasks of the revolution in a chronologically and economically rational way."

Contentedly "scheduling tasks" in neat chronological order totally abstracts the transition of a capitalist state to a workers state from the living class struggle. Workers control is a *necessary* form of *struggle* by the working class—not a state of contentedness or "rational" scheduling. It is necessary not primarily because of the "socialist immaturity" of the workers, but to strengthen their hand against the capitalist class and prepare the way for expropriation and workers management. It is a key way that workers increasingly curb the prerogatives of the capitalists, while simultaneously building their own self-confidence and political class consciousness.

Lenin put it this way in the report to the November 1918 Soviet congress: "We did not decree socialism immediately throughout industry, because socialism can only take shape and be consolidated when the working class has learnt how to run the economy and when the authority of the working people has been firmly established. Socialism is mere wishful thinking without that. That is why we introduced workers' control, appreciating that it was a contradictory and incomplete measure, but an essential one so that workers themselves might tackle the momentous tasks of building up industry in a vast country without and opposed to exploiters. And comrades, everyone who took a direct, or even indirect, part in this work, everyone who lived through all the oppression and brutality of the old capitalist regime, learned a great deal" (*On Workers' Control and the Nationalization of Industry*, Progress Publishers, Lenin, 1918, p. 198).

Notice that Lenin talks about living through "oppression and brutality" and "learning" and "establishing authority," *not* about "scheduling tasks."

A transition also took place in the countryside. In looking back over the first year of the revolution, Lenin wrote that "The victorious Bolshevik revolution meant the end of vacillation, meant the complete destruction of the monarchy and of the landlord system (which had *not* been destroyed before the October Revolution). We carried the *bourgeois* revolution *to its conclusion.* The peasants supported us *as a whole.* Their antagonism to the socialist proletariat could not reveal itself all at once. The Soviets united the peasants *in general.* The class divisions among the peasants had not yet matured, had not yet come into the open.

"*That* process took place in the summer and autumn of 1918. The Czech counter-revolutionary mutiny roused the Kulaks. A wave of kulak revolts swept over Russia. The poor peasants learned, not from books or newspapers, *but from life itself,* that their interests were irreconcilably antagonistic to those of the kulaks, the rich, the rural bourgeoisie. Like every other petty-bourgeois party, the 'Left Socialist-Revolutionaries' reflected the vacillation of the people, and in the summer of 1918 they split: one section joined forces with the Czechs . . . while the other section . . . remained with the Bolsheviks."

Lenin went on to say that ". . . it is only now, in the summer and autumn, of 1918, that the rural districts *themselves* are passing through the *October* (i.e., proletarian) Revolution. Things are beginning to change. The wave of kulak revolts is giving way to a rise of the poor, to a growth of the 'Poor Peasants Committees.'"

So the dictatorship of the proletariat—that is, if it is defined to mean the establishment of a state based on state property rather than capitalist private property—was not accomplished in one fell swoop in October 1917. It was a process, a transition, that required a massive struggle by the working class and the poor peasantry.

"If the Bolshevik proletariat had tried at once, in October–November 1917," Lenin wrote, "without waiting for the class differentiation in the rural districts, without being able to *prepare* it and bring it about, to 'decree' a civil war or the 'introduction of socialism' in the rural districts, had tried to do without a temporary bloc [alliance] with the peasantry in general, without making a number of concessions to the middle peasants, etc., that would have been a *Blanquist* distortion of Marxism, an attempt by the *minority* to impose its will upon the majority; it would have been a theoretical absurdity, revealing a failure to understand that a general peasant revolution is *still* a bourgeois revolution, and that without *a series of transitions, of transitional stages,* it cannot be transformed into a socialist revolution in a backward country" ("The Proletarian Revolution and the Renegade Kautsky," *CW*, Vol. 28, 1918, p. 302–305).

Echoing the concluding paragraph of *Two Tactics* written 13 years earlier, Lenin added that, "With all the peasants right through to the end of the bourgeois-democratic revolution; and with the poor, the proletarian and semi-proletarian section of the peasants, forward to the socialist revolution! This has been the policy of the Bolsheviks, and it is the only Marxist policy" (Ibid., p. 311).

Fifteen years later, Leon Trotsky explained in a similar way how the transition to a workers state in Russia took place. Looking back at the experience of the 1917–1918 revolution, he wrote in 1933:

"Not only up to the Brest-Litovsk peace [March 1918] but even up to autumn of 1918, the social content of the revolution was restricted to a petty-bourgeois agrarian overturn and workers' control over production. This means that the revolution in its actions had not yet passed the boundaries of bourgeois society. During this first period, soldiers' soviets ruled side by side with the workers' soviets and often elbowed them aside.

"Only toward the autumn of 1918," Trotsky wrote, "did the petty-bourgeois soldier-agrarian elemental wave recede a little to its shores, and the workers went forward with the nationalization of the means of production. Only from this time can one speak of the inception of a real dictatorship of the proletariat. But even here it is necessary to make certain large reservations. During those initial years, the dictatorship was geographically confined to the old Moscow principality and was compelled to wage a three-years' war along all the radii from Moscow to the periphery. This means that up to 1921, precisely up to the NEP [New Economic Policy], that is, what went on was still the struggle to establish the dictatorship of the proletariat upon the national scale" ("The Class Nature of the Soviet State," *Writings of Leon Trotsky 1933–34* (Pathfinder Press, 1972, 1995), p. 140 [2011 printing]).

Thus, Mandel creates a tangle of confusion in the concluding paragraph of his article when he asserts:

"In reality, the tasks of the democratic revolution were accomplished only after the establishment of the dictatorship of the proletariat, *after* the conquest of power by the soviets, *after* the creation of a workers state. And they were accomplished in the closest combination with a whole series of tasks (not all, of course) that were already socialist in nature."

Let's look at this paragraph more closely, starting from the bottom and working our way up.

1) Mandel says that the tasks of the democratic revolution were accomplished in combination with beginning to carry out the socialist tasks. Correct. The Bolsheviks had foreseen both the primacy of the democratic tasks in the first stage of the revolution and their intertwining with socialist tasks as the class struggle deepened. The concrete form that this process would take was given, as it could only have been, by the concrete combination of domestic and international class relations that determined the framework of the revolution during its first years.

2) The democratic tasks were completed only "*after* the creation of a workers state." Wrong. At least using the scientific criteria for a workers state that Marxists have used since the 1930s, based on our analysis of the bureaucratic degeneration of the Soviet workers state—criteria we learned with the aid of Trotsky. According to those criteria—state property, economic planning, and a monopoly of foreign trade—a workers state did not come into existence in Russia until at least the autumn of 1918, as Trotsky explained in the 1933 article. This was well after the major tasks of the revolution had been accomplished.

3) The democratic tasks were accomplished only "*after* the conquest of power by the soviets." Yes and no. As Lenin explained in his April 1917 "Letter on Tactics," the toppling of the tsar in February and consequent "passing of state power to the bourgeoisie" meant that "To this extent, the bourgeois, or the bourgeois-democratic, revolution in Russia is *completed.*" But the central democratic tasks, such as the agrarian reform and self-determination of the nations oppressed by Russia, were not and could not have been completed until after the conquest of power by the soviets. (We'll see what Lenin had to say about this question on the fourth anniversary of the October Revolution a little bit later in this article.)

4) The democratic tasks were completed only "after the establishment of the dictatorship of the proletariat." That depends. If by the "dictatorship of the proletariat" Mandel means a workers state, which is how our movement has used the term since the 1930s, then the answer is provided by point 2) above; if he means by it the conquest of power of the soviets in October 1917, which is how the term was often used prior to the 1930s, then the answer is provided in point 3) above.

So Mandel's concluding flourish doesn't tell us much. It certainly doesn't throw into question the fundamental revolutionary continuity of Bolshevik strategy before, during, and after 1917, and the fact that this leadership and strategy were responsible for the October victory.

Peasant representation in the government

How were the peasants represented in the new revolutionary government that came to power in October? Did they play any independent role?

By the time of the October insurrection, the Bolsheviks were a majority in the All-Russian Soviets of Workers and Soldiers Deputies, but not in the peasants' soviets where the Socialist Revolutionaries (SRs) still dominated.

At the All-Russian Soviet Congress meeting on October 25, the Bolsheviks expressed agreement with a proposal to form a government that would include not only the Bolsheviks, but also the Mensheviks, Socialist Revolutionaries, and Left Socialist Revolutionaries. The Mensheviks and SRs, however, with the exception of the Left SRs, rejected this proposal and walked out of the soviets. For the Bolshevik leaders, this final act of betrayal and display of allegiance to the exploiters shut the door to any coalition with the right Menshevik and SR leaders.

The new Central Executive Committee elected by the October Congress of the Soviets included 62 Bolsheviks, 19 Left SRs, 6 Menshevik-Internationalists, and 4 independent socialists.

About three weeks later the All-Russian Congress of Peasants Deputies was held. All attempts by the Right SRs to prevent the congress from meeting and the peasant delegates from coming into contact with the Bolsheviks failed. The Bolsheviks successfully established a coalition with the Left SRs who held a majority at the congress. Without this coalition, the Bolsheviks had only 11 percent of the delegates. A union was established between the Central Executive Committee and the Peasants Congress, and the CEC was expanded to include 100 delegates from the Peasants Congress. This even included some Right SRs and Mensheviks.

At this point, the Left SRs agreed to serve on the Council of People's Commissars. Several were appointed to head up Commissariats and more to other governmental posts, thus establishing a Bolshevik-Left SR coalition government. The third Congress of Soviets in January elected a Central Executive Committee that included 160 Bolsheviks and 125 Left SRs.

The Left SR commissars resigned in March 1918 over opposition to the Brest-Litovsk pact that ended the war with Germany, as well as disagreements flowing from the developing class struggle and social differentiations in the countryside. The SRs remained on the CEC until July, however, when several Left SR leaders participated in the assassination of the German ambassador and an attempted coup. The Committees of Poor Peasants were being established in the countryside at the Bolsheviks' initiative during this same period, and the Bolsheviks were gaining a growing base among the poor peasants and even layers of the middle peasants.

So, at least through the first phase of the revolution, the coalition between the working class and the peasantry existed both as a coalition of soviets and of parties. This runs contrary to Mandel's unqualified assertion that the peasants would not be able to exercise any independent, organized role in a revolutionary government.

Moreover, the Bolsheviks' efforts to forge a coalition with the Left SRs played a *crucial role* in the first months of the revolution, when the Bolsheviks remained a small minority among the peasants. It bought the proletariat time to win the support of more and more poor peasants, and at least a wait-and-see attitude among many middle peasants, through the revolutionary government's policies of ending the war and carrying through the agrarian reform.

What happened subsequently also followed the general pattern anticipated by the Bolshevik strategy. As the class struggle deepened and the socialist course of the revolution advanced, the peasantry polarized between the poor and landless layers and the kulaks who exploited labor, with the middle peasants pulled in both directions. On the political and organizational level, these class differentiations were reflected by the desertion of growing numbers of SR leaders to the camp of the capitalist counterrevolution, while those most firmly based on the rural poor remained with the government and eventually joined the Communist Party of their own free will and political conviction.

The solidity of the worker-peasant alliance that

resulted from this course by the Bolsheviks remained the bedrock of the survival of the soviet regime.

Verdict of history

Mandel argues that the Bolsheviks' positions on the relationship between the democratic and socialist revolutions, and the role of the peasantry in them, were proven wrong by history, and that Lenin recognized this just in the nick of time in early 1917.

But Mandel, as we've already seen in several cases, ignores and contradicts what Lenin himself said about this in retrospect. Let's look at a few more examples.

In 1918 Karl Kautsky, a prominent leader of the Second International who pursued a centrist course during World War I, wrote a book entitled, *The Dictatorship of the Proletariat*, attacking the Russian revolution and the Bolsheviks' policies. He rehashed positions that had been debated before 1917 by the Mensheviks and Bolsheviks.

Lenin responded with the pamphlet, "The Proletarian Revolution and the Renegade Kautsky," which has been referred to previously in this article. Lenin wrote:

"The Russian revolution is a bourgeois revolution, said all the Marxists of Russia before 1905. The Mensheviks, substituting liberalism for Marxism, drew the following conclusion from this: the proletariat therefore must not go beyond what is acceptable to the bourgeoisie and must pursue a policy of compromise with them. The Bolsheviks said this was a bourgeois-liberal theory. The bourgeoisie were trying to bring about the reform of the state on bourgeois, *reformist*, not revolutionary lines, while preserving the monarchy, the landlord system, etc., as far as possible.

"The proletariat must carry through the bourgeois-democratic revolution to the end, not allowing itself to be 'bound' by the reformism of the bourgeoisie," Lenin said. "The Bolsheviks formulated the alignment of *class* forces in the bourgeois revolution as follows: the proletariat, winning over the peasants, will neutralize the liberal bourgeoisie and utterly destroy the monarchy, medievalism and the landlord system.

"It is the alliance between the proletariat and the peasants *in general* that reveals the bourgeois character of the revolution," Lenin emphasized, "for the peasants in general are small producers who exist on the basis of commodity production. Further, the Bolsheviks then added, the proletariat will win over *the entire semi-proletariat* (all the working and exploited people), will neutralize the middle peasants and *overthrow* the bourgeoisie; this will be a socialist revolution, as distinct from a bourgeois-democratic revolution (See my pamphlet *Two Tactics*, published in 1905 and reprinted in *Twelve Years*, St. Petersburg, 1907)" (*CW*, Vol. 28, 1918, p. 295).

Notice that Lenin says nothing here about the Bolsheviks' pre-1917 positions having been wrong. To the contrary, he uses essentially the same formulations to defend those positions, and he explicitly urges people to read *Two Tactics*, which contains the most complete presentation of these positions. "The question which Kautsky has so tangled up was fully explained by the Bolsheviks as far back as 1905," Lenin continued. "Yes, our revolution is a bourgeois revolution *as long* as we march *with* the peasants *as a whole*. This has been as clear as clear can be to us; we have said it hundreds and thousands of times since 1905, and we have never attempted to skip this necessary stage of the historical process or abolish it by decrees. . . .

"Beginning with *April* 1917, however, long before the October Revolution, that is long before we assumed power, we publicly declared and explained to the people: the revolution cannot now stop at this stage, for the country has marched forward, capitalism has advanced, ruin has reached fantastic dimensions, which (whether one likes it or not) *will demand* steps forward, *to socialism*. For there is *no* other way of advancing, of saving the war-weary country and of *alleviating* the sufferings of the working and exploited people.

"Things have turned out just as we said they would," Lenin said. "The course taken by the revolution has confirmed the correctness of our reasoning. *First*, with the 'whole' of the peasants against the monarchy, against the landowners, against medievalism (and to that extent the revolution remains bourgeois, bourgeois-democratic). *Then*, with the poor peasants, with the semi-proletarians, with all the exploited, *against capitalism*, including the rural rich, the kulaks, the profiteers, and to that extent the revolution becomes a *socialist* one. To attempt to raise an artificial Chinese Wall between the first and second, to separate them *by anything else* than the degree of preparedness of the proletariat and the degree of its unity with the poor peasants, means to distort Marxism dreadfully, to vulgarise it, to substitute liberalism in its place" (*CW*, Vol. 28, 1918, p. 300–301).

(Note the striking parallel to the following passage from *Two Tactics* written 13 years earlier: "The proletariat must carry the democratic revolution to completion, allying to itself the mass of the peasantry in order to crush the autocracy's resistance by force and paralyze the bourgeoisie's instability. The proletariat must accomplish the socialist revolution, allying to itself the mass of the semi-proletarian elements of the population, so as to crush the bourgeoisie's resistance by force and paralyze the instability of the peasantry and the petty bourgeoisie" (*Two Tactics*, 1905, p. 85).

Contrary to Mandel, Lenin says in 1918 that "Things have turned out just as [the Bolsheviks] said they would." The revolution "confirmed the correctness of our reasoning." And Lenin, correctly, never changed his mind as to this judgment.

The social crisis and economic ruin caused by the imperialist war, the development of capitalism in Russia over the dozen years since 1905, the relations among the various classes and political forces in the aftermath of the February revolution—by April 1917 these concrete factors had filled in the variables in the Bolsheviks' "algebraic" strategy, and in October the equation was led to a solution in struggle. A workers and farmers government was established, and a whole new stage of the revolution was opened, leading toward the expropriation of the capitalists and the struggle to deepen, defend, and extend the socialist revolution.

Lenin commented further on the experience of the Russian revolution in an April 1919 article, "The Third International and Its Place in History."

He wrote, "... Russia's backwardness merged in a peculiar way the proletarian revolution against the bourgeoisie with the peasant revolution against the landowners. That is what we started from in October 1917, and we would not have achieved victory so easily then if we had not. As long ago as 1856, Marx spoke, in reference to Prussia, of the possibility of a peculiar combination of proletarian revolution and peasant war. From the beginning of 1905 the Bolsheviks advocated the idea of a revolutionary-democratic dictatorship of the proletariat and peasantry" (*CW*, Vol. 29, 1919, p. 310).

Of all the wonders to behold! Lenin harks back to the very formula that Mandel says "facilitated the confusion" of the Bolsheviks in the first weeks after February, a formula Mandel tells us Lenin had thrown on the scrap heap in April 1917, the formula encapsulizing Lenin's "erroneous dogma." But here, two years later, this same formula turns up again in an article by Lenin. And Lenin clearly refers to it as an affirmation of the Bolsheviks' strategic line on the relationship of the peasant and proletarian revolutions, that is, the democratic and socialist revolutions.

In a 1920 article on "A Contribution to the History of the Question of the Dictatorship" (*CW*, 1920, Vol. 31, p. 340), Lenin again refers back with approval to *Two Tactics* and other pre-1917 writings of the Bolsheviks.

Finally, in 1921, on the fourth anniversary of the revolution, Lenin summarized the experience of the October Revolution. He explained that the Mensheviks and SRs "have talked and are still talking an incredible lot of nonsense about the relation between the bourgeois-democratic revolution and the socialist (that is proletarian) revolution. The last four years have proved to the hilt that our interpretation of Marxism on this point, and our estimate of the experience of former revolutions were correct.

"We have *consummated* the bourgeois-democratic revolution as nobody had done before," Lenin said. "We are *advancing* towards the socialist revolution consciously, firmly and unswervingly, knowing that it is not separated from the bourgeois-democratic revolution by a Chinese Wall, and knowing too that (in the last analysis) *struggle alone* will determine how far we shall advance . . ." (*CW*, Vol. 33, 1921, p. 51).

The Bolsheviks' communist strategy was "proved to the hilt." That's how Lenin saw the verdict of history.

Trotsky's position

Mandel not only argues that Lenin scrapped the Bolsheviks' "erroneous dogma" in 1917, but that in doing so he came over to "the same positions

Trotsky had defended since 1904–1906." According to Mandel, it was these "entirely new and original" positions of Trotsky that the judgment of history upheld against Lenin's pre-1917 strategy (and as we have seen his post-April 1917 judgment on this strategy.)

What were Trotsky's positions? How did they differ from those of Lenin and the Bolsheviks?

Trotsky was in basic agreement with the Bolsheviks on the question of what approach the working class should take toward the liberal bourgeoisie. He agreed with the Bolsheviks that the bourgeoisie would cling ever more closely to the old order as the revolution advanced, and that the working class should not look to it for leadership or view it as a reliable or strategic ally. The working class must assume the vanguard political role in the Russian revolution.

Trotsky had initially lined up with the Mensheviks following the split in the Russian Social Democracy at the 1903 RSDLP Congress, but he broke with them over this question one year later in 1904. This was a key dividing line between class struggle and class collaboration, between reform and revolution in the Russian workers' movement. Trotsky placed himself in the camp of the revolution and remained there, despite serious errors and vacillations, through 1917, when he came over all the way to Bolshevism.

Trotsky's pre-1917 differences with the Bolsheviks were fundamental, however. He had broken with the Bolsheviks at the 1903 Congress, and he maintained a centrist position in the social democracy throughout the next 14 years.

Mandel lists what he considers to be four of Trotsky's differences with the Bolsheviks during these years. On all of them, Mandel says, Trotsky was right against Lenin.

- Trotsky disagreed with what Mandel claims to be the Bolsheviks' view of a prolonged capitalist stage during which Russia would undergo modernization and industrialization through a "rapid development of capitalism."
- Trotsky recognized "the capacity of the Russian proletariat *to begin* to resolve the socialist tasks of the revolution," while "for Lenin, that capacity did not exist."
- Trotsky defended "the impossibility for the peasantry to constitute a political party or force that would be independent both of the bourgeoisie and the working class," while Lenin "was certain that the revolutionary peasantry had to *take political power.*"
- Trotsky counterposed the formula of the "dictatorship of the proletariat" to the Bolsheviks' "revolutionary-democratic dictatorship of the proletariat and peasantry." *"The two formulas,"* Mandel writes, *"were not mere slogans but encapsulated the strategic perspectives of the revolution."*

The first two differences pointed to by Mandel simply repeat his erroneous view of Lenin's positions. As this article has already established, the Bolsheviks recognized that the completion of the bourgeois-democratic revolution was an essential task of the proletariat and would create the best conditions for the development of capitalism, but they were not fighting in order to open a prolonged stage of capitalist development and rule.

Lenin's transitional strategy—following the course originally proposed by Marx and Engels in the *Communist Manifesto*—was aimed at mobilizing the working class and peasants to carry the democratic revolution as far as they could. This included, from the outset of the revolution, taking up tasks that would open the road to the socialist revolution. It was through the revolutionary struggle to complete the democratic revolution, the Bolsheviks argued, that the working class would develop its capacity to carry out the socialist revolution.

There was no decisive difference between Trotsky and the Bolsheviks over these points. Instead, the difference was over the relationship between the democratic-peasant revolution and the proletarian-socialist revolution, and the alignment of classes necessary to connect and carry through these revolutions. This difference over fundamental strategy was reflected in the disagreement between Trotsky and the Bolsheviks on the role and weight of the peasantry in the revolution. On this decisive question, Mandel takes the side of Trotsky against Lenin and argues that Trotsky was proven right in 1917.

This article has already described where the peasants fit into the Bolshevik strategy for the revolution and how this orientation was confirmed in 1917. Let's now examine Trotsky's position.

The major presentation of Trotsky's orientation

appears in *Results and Prospects*, which was published in 1906. This was Trotsky's balance sheet on the political lessons of the 1905 revolution, in which he had played a leadership role in Petrograd.

There, like the Bolsheviks, Trotsky explained that the working class must assume the leadership of the revolution and chart a course independent of and in opposition to the liberal bourgeoisie. He agreed with the Bolsheviks that the working class must have the support of the peasantry if the revolution were to succeed. He also recognized the differentiations within the peasantry that would, as the revolution advanced, impel the most exploited layers to move closer to the working class. And he correctly recognized that the international extension of the Russian revolution would be decisive to its consolidation and survival.

Where Trotsky differed with the Bolsheviks was on his insistence that the peasants had no independent role of any sort to play in the revolution, as well as his assessment of the slim prospects for any durable worker-peasant alliance.

Lenin recognized that class differentiations within the peasantry, as well as its vacillations between the proletariat and bourgeoisie conditioned by its intermediate position in society, made the formation of mass peasant organizations and an independent movement of peasants difficult. He recognized that the peasantry would ultimately either look to the historic solutions of the proletariat or to those of the bourgeoisie for a road forward out of the dead-end of tsarist society.

From Lenin's perspective of building a vanguard working-class party capable of leading the toilers in a successful revolution, however, all this only underlined the importance of the working class charting a course toward the peasantry that could maximize support from the broadest possible layers in the countryside and maximize the possibility of welding and preserving a worker-peasant alliance. That was the aim of Bolshevik strategy.

Trotsky, however, concentrated primarily on the backwardness of the peasants, downplaying the prospective role they would play in the revolution and emphasizing the limits and problems involved in political organization in the countryside. Unlike the Bolsheviks, he did not propose an active policy for the working class and its vanguard party aimed at attempting to surmount these obstacles in order to forge an alliance with the peasants.

While the Bolsheviks' policy was always to fight for the leadership of the peasantry as the only way to carry the revolution through to the end, they did not exclude that the peasantry through its own organizations would play a major or even dominant role in the initial stage of a revolutionary government. If such a situation did develop, the Bolsheviks argued that it would be permissible, depending on the circumstances, for the revolutionary workers party to participate in it "for the purpose of waging a relentless struggle against all counter-revolutionary attempts and of defending the independent interests of the working class" (*CW*, Vol. 8, 1905, p. 397).

Trotsky argued, however, that while "revolutionary representatives of non-proletarian social groups" should be in the government, "the whole problem consists in this: *who will determine the content of the government's policy, who will form within it a solid majority*?"

He added that "the participation of the proletariat in a government is also objectively most probable, and permissible in principle, only as a *dominating and leading participation*. One may, of course, describe such a government as the dictatorship of the proletariat and peasantry, a dictatorship of the proletariat, peasantry, and intelligentsia, or even a coalition government of the working class and the petty bourgeoisie, but the question nevertheless remains: who is to wield the hegemony in the government itself, and through it in the country? And when we speak of a workers' government, by this we reply that the hegemony should belong to the working class."

This means, Trotsky said, "that the representative body of the nation, convened under the leadership of the proletariat, which has secured the support of the peasantry, will be nothing else than a democratic dress for the rule of the proletariat."

A government that was only "democratic dress" for the rule of the proletariat was not what the Bolsheviks were fighting for. The proletariat had to fight for the leadership of the peasantry and for a revolutionary government with other exploited producers to carry out the democratic revolution and begin the socialist revolution.

Continuing with Trotsky's *Results and Prospects*: "But is it not possible that the peasantry may push the proletariat aside and take its place? This is impossible. All historical experience protests against this assumption. Historical experience shows that the peasantry are absolutely incapable of taking up an *independent* political role."

Yes, historical experience shows that the peasantry can't "push the proletariat aside and take its place." Whereas the Bolsheviks paid close attention to every expression of independent organization and mobilization by the peasants, however, Trotsky belittled them on the grounds that historically the peasants are incapable of playing an independent role. While it is true, as Lenin recognized, that the peasantry has no historic program independent of the bourgeoisie or the working class, it does not at all follow—as Trotsky suggests—that the peasantry cannot form independent organizations and that the peasant revolution plays no independent role in modern revolutions. History shows the opposite.

Trotsky asks in *Results and Prospects,* "Does the fact of the rise and development first of the peasant union and then of the Group of Toil (Trudoviki) in the Duma run counter to these and subsequent arguments?" He answers, "Not in the least."

"The radicalism and formlessness of the Group of Toil was the expression of the contradictoriness in the revolutionary aspirations of the peasantry. During the period of constitutional illusions it helplessly followed the 'Cadets' (Constitutional Democrats). At the moment of the dissolution of the Duma it came naturally under the guidance of the Social-Democratic Group. The lack of independence on the part of the peasant representatives will show itself with particular clearness at the moment when it becomes necessary to show firm initiative, that is, at the time when power has to pass into the hands of the revolutionaries."

For Trotsky, the lack of "firm initiative," the lack of "independence," and the "formlessness" of the peasant organizations thrust forward by the 1905 revolution is simply proof that the peasantry cannot play any independent or decisive role in the revolution.

Trotsky, unlike Lenin, did not see the revolutionary possibilities inherent in the peasant organizations created in 1905, for example. He did not treat them as embryos of a possible mass peasant party or mass organization, as the Bolsheviks did. Trotsky, unlike the Bolsheviks, did not chart a course toward seeking out joint actions with the peasant organizations and struggling in that way to divide them from the liberal capitalist parties. Trotsky did acknowledge that "The Russian bourgeoisie will . . . have to surrender the revolutionary hegemony over the peasants. In such a situation, created by the transference of power to the proletariat, nothing remains for the peasantry to do but to rally to the regime of workers' democracy."

But then, expressing his usual estimation of the peasants' role in the revolution, he commented that, "It will not matter much even if the peasantry does this with a degree of consciousness not larger than that with which it usually rallies to the bourgeois regime."

Continuing, Trotsky stated, "From what we have said above, it will be clear how we regard the idea of a 'proletarian and peasant dictatorship.' It is not really a matter of whether we regard it as admissible in principle, whether 'we do or do not desire' such a form of political cooperation. We simply think that it is unrealisable—at least in a direct immediate sense.

"Indeed, such a coalition presupposes either that one of the existing bourgeois parties commands influence over the peasantry or that the peasantry will have created a powerful independent party of its own, but we have attempted to show that neither the one nor the other is possible" ("Results and Prospects," in *The Permanent Revolution* (Pathfinder Press, 1931, 1969), pp. 55–60 [2001 printing]).

But the Bolsheviks proved that this course was not only "admissible in principle," but even more important, that it was "realisable." That was the basis of their strategic line of march that successfully led to taking power. It was the basis of their decision on the eve of the insurrection in 1917 to adopt the Socialist Revolutionary Party's agrarian program. It was at the heart of their decision to sign the peace agreement at Brest-Litovsk in 1918, ending, as quickly as possible, the slaughter of Russian soldiers, the majority of whom were from the peasantry. It remained the backbone of their policy through the formation of the Committees of Poor Peasants, the civil war, the launching of the New Economic Policy, and the generalization of all these experiences by the Communist International.

Lenin's response

Lenin strongly disagreed with Trotsky's approach to the peasantry. In a 1909 polemic with Menshevik leader Martov, Lenin wrote,

". . . the most fallacious of Trotsky's opinions that Comrade Martov quotes and considers to be 'just' is . . .: 'even if they [the peasantry] do this [support the regime of working class democracy] with no more political understanding than they usually support a bourgeois regime.'

"The proletariat cannot count on the ignorance and prejudices of the peasantry as the powers that be under a bourgeois regime count and depend on them," Lenin said, "nor can it assume that in time of revolution the peasantry will remain in their usual state of political ignorance and passivity. The history of the Russian revolution shows that the very first wave of the upsurge at the end of 1905, at once stimulated the peasantry to form a political organization (the All-Russian Peasant Union) which was undoubtedly the embryo of a distinct peasant party [brackets in original]" (*CW*, Vol. 15, 1909, p. 374).

(It's ironic that Mandel, more than three decades after the Chinese revolution, should still be defending the view that there cannot be peasant parties and peasant organizations and that a peasant revolution cannot play any independent role in a social revolution. In China a peasant army headed by a peasant party and with a petty-bourgeois Stalinist leadership made a revolution that opened the door to historic conquests, however badly deformed, of the Chinese proletariat—that is, the establishment of the Chinese workers state.)

The practical political consequences of Trotsky's pre-1917 position can be demonstrated by the scant attention he paid to the question of peasant organizations in his principal pre-1917 writings on the perspectives of the Russian revolution, *1905*[2] and *Results and Prospects*. Trotsky has little to say about the need to establish peasant committees or other organizations of the rural toilers. Nor does he say much about those that the peasants did form in 1905, the role these organizations played, and what they showed about how the worker-peasant alliance could be built in practice.

This was a decisive point of contention between the Bolsheviks and Mensheviks. Lenin, writing about the 1905 Bolshevik and Menshevik conventions, points out: "The 'peasant question' was presented in entirely different ways by the [Bolshevik] Party Congress and the [Menshevik] Conference. The [Bolshevik] Congress drew up a resolution on the 'attitude to the peasant movement'; the [Menshevik] Conference—on 'work among the peasants.'

"In the one case prominence is given to the task of guiding the entire revolutionary-democratic movement in the general national interests of the struggle against tsarism," Lenin said. "In the other case the question is reduced to mere 'work' among a particular section of society. In the one case, a central practical slogan for our agitation is advanced calling for the immediate organization of revolutionary peasant committees in order to carry out all democratic changes. In the other, a 'demand for the organization of committees' is to be presented to a constituent assembly" (*Two Tactics*, 1905, p. 75–76).

Trotsky certainly never held the Menshevik position that the formation of peasant committees should be put off to a decision of a constituent assembly. Nevertheless, he placed little emphasis on them. This is not surprising, given his view that an independent peasant movement was impossible.

Whereas Lenin's articles are peppered with phrases about the proletariat "leading" the peasantry, carrying out "joint actions" with it, and forming "alliances" and "coalitions" with peasant organizations, Trotsky's writings during this period focus on the proletariat "emancipating the peasantry," "winning support" from the peasantry, and establishing its "dominance" and "hegemony." Behind what might seem simply to be a difference of vocabulary or style was a more profound

2. The 1971 English-language edition of *1905* by Vintage includes the major part of a German edition of *1905* that was written in 1908–09. It also includes the following: "The Proletariat and the Russian Revolution" (1908); "Our Differences" (1909); "The Struggle for Power" (1915); "On the Special Features of Russia's Historical Development" (1922). In addition, it includes Trotsky's speech on the relationship of social democracy to the bourgeois parties at the 1907 congress of the Russian Social Democratic Labor Party.

divergence over the proletariat's political *approach* toward the peasant masses and the role and weight of the peasant revolution in the struggle to bring down tsarism and open the socialist revolution.

In 1909 Trotsky defended his position in an article entitled, "Our Differences," which appeared in a Polish Social Democratic journal. He charged the Bolsheviks with favoring "self-limitation" by the working class after a revolutionary victory. (By the way, Mandel's quotation marks around "self-limitation," which the reader would logically assume is quoted from Lenin, is in fact taken from this article by Trotsky. It is not and never was Lenin's term. It's a charge—and a false one—by Trotsky.)

Trotsky wrote, "the objection might be raised that I am imagining a situation in which the dictatorship of the workers is unlimited, whereas in fact what we are talking about is the dictatorship of a coalition between the proletariat and the peasantry. Very well, let us take this objection into account.

"We have just seen how the proletariat, despite the best intentions of its theoreticians, must in practice ignore the logical boundary line which should confine it to a democratic dictatorship. Lenin now proposes that the proletariat's political self-limitation should be supplemented with an objective antisocialist 'safeguard' in the form of the muzhik [peasant] as collaborator or co-dictator.

"If this means that the peasant party, which shares power with the social-democrats, will not allow the unemployed and the strikers to be maintained at state cost and will oppose the state's opening of factories and plants closed down by the capitalists," Trotsky said, "then it also means that on the first day of the coalition, that is, long before the fulfillment of its tasks, the proletariat will enter into the conflict with the revolutionary government. This conflict can end either in the repression of the workers by the peasant party, or in the removal of that party from power. Neither solution has much to do with a 'democratic' dictatorship by a coalition" ("Our Differences" in *1905*, p. 315–316).

The Russian revolution itself proved Trotsky wrong on this point. As described earlier in this article, the Soviet government, established in October 1917, was a two-class government, a coalition of the Bolsheviks and the Left SRs. Trotsky's 1933 article, mentioned earlier, affirmed this.

Rather than suppressing or limiting the demands of the working class, this government was the instrument used by the workers and poor peasants for carrying through the expropriation of the capitalists and deepening the class struggle between the exploiters and the exploited in the countryside.

In the process, the Bolsheviks strengthened their own base among the rural proletariat and poor farmers and divided the Left SRs between those committed to traveling the socialist course being charted by the exploited and those who recoiled from this course and deserted to the camp of the exploiters, the camp of the counterrevolution. The Russian working class would have had a much weaker and more tenuous alliance with the peasantry at the outset of the civil war had the Bolsheviks tried to *skip over* rather than *go through* this coalition with a party initially much more firmly based in the countryside.

Trotsky missed this transitional character of the alliance of the working class and the revolutionary peasantry. While he, like Lenin, correctly saw the class lines within the peasantry that would inevitably surface as the revolution deepened, Trotsky lacked a transitional strategy capable of simultaneously galvanizing the broadest layers for the democratic revolution against the old order, while preparing the proletariat to maintain the strongest possible alliance with the rural poor and middle peasants to open the road to the socialist revolution.

The dispute in 1915–17

The outbreak of World War I in August 1914 accelerated the crisis of the imperialist system and opened the road to proletarian revolutions and wars of national liberation. It raised all the stakes for the working class and its vanguard organizations and intensified the conflicts between the revolutionary and opportunist wings of social democracy organized in the Second International.

In a series of 1915 articles in the Paris-based *Nashe Slovo*, which he coedited with Martov, Trotsky drew the opposite conclusion from Lenin's as to the effect on the peasantry of World War I and the economic changes in Russia since 1905. In the process, Trotsky deepened his error on the role of the peasantry in the Russian revolution. Trotsky stated:

"The experience of the Russian revolution and of the reaction tells us that now, to an *even smaller* extent than in 1905, can we hope for an independent, and *still less* decisive role to be played by *the peasantry*. In so far as the peasantry has remained in the grip of 'estate' and feudal slavery, it continues to show in its elemental opposition to the old regime all those features of economic and ideological disunity and political immaturity, cultural backwardness and helplessness, which always and in every movement paralyze its social energy and oblige it to come to a standstill at the point where really revolutionary action begins. (emphasis added)

"In so far as the peasantry has made economic and cultural progress in this period," Trotsky argued, "such progress has proceeded entirely along the line of bourgeois development and is therefore associated with a further development of class contradictions within the peasantry itself.

"This means that for the industrial proletariat it is now—immeasurably more so than in 1905—a question of attracting to its side the proletarian and semi-proletarian elements of the countryside, rather than the peasantry as an 'estate.' The revolutionary movement thus necessarily acquires, in these circumstances, a very much less 'national,' very much more 'class' character than it had even in 1905" ("The Military Catastrophe and the Political Prospects," to be included in a forthcoming Pathfinder Press collection of Trotsky's writings during World War I).

Trotsky, here, has gone further than in *Results and Prospects*. While in the 1906 article he correctly recognized that "the fate of the most elementary revolutionary interests of . . . the peasantry *as a whole*, as an estate, is bound up with the fate of the entire revolution, i.e., with the fate of the proletariat" (*Results and Prospects*, p. 179), nine years later he explicitly rejected an orientation based on an alliance of the working class and the *peasantry as a whole*.

Yet it was precisely this strategy, advocated and carried out by the Bolsheviks, that was borne out by the October Revolution, as Lenin explained time and again after 1917.

Lenin read Trotsky's *Nashe Slovo* articles and was quite sharp in his criticism of them. In his article "On the Two Lines in the Revolution," Lenin wrote:

"To bring clarity into the alignment of classes in the impending revolution is the main task of a revolutionary party. . . . This task is being wrongly tackled in *Nashe Slovo* by Trotsky," Lenin said, "who is repeating his 'original' 1905 theory and refuses to give some thought to the reason why, in the course of ten years, life has been bypassing this splendid theory."

Lenin continued:

"The peasantry, [Trotsky] asserts, are divided into strata, have become differentiated; their potential revolutionary role has dwindled more and more; in Russia a 'national' revolution is impossible; 'we are living in the era of imperialism,' says Trotsky, and 'imperialism does not contrapose the bourgeois nation to the old regime, but the proletariat to the bourgeois nation.'"

Lenin drew quite different conclusions from Trotsky's about the changes in Russian politics since 1905. He stressed not only the growing class differentiations inside the peasantry, but also the growing potential for a general peasant revolution against tsarism and landlordism.

"The differentiation of the peasantry has enhanced the class struggle within them; it has aroused very many hitherto politically dormant elements," Lenin wrote. "It has drawn the rural proletariat closer to the urban proletariat." On this, Lenin had no fundamental disagreement with Trotsky's *Nashe Slovo* articles. But Trotsky was blind to the other side of the Russian political reality, which would be critical to the next necessary stage of revolutionary development.

"However, the antagonism between the peasantry, on the one hand, and the [old order], on the other, has become stronger and more acute," Lenin pointed out. "This is such an obvious truth that not *even* the thousands of phrases in scores of Trotsky's Paris articles will 'refute' it."

In fact, Lenin said, by insisting that the peasantry *won't* play a decisive role as a revolutionary force, Trotsky ended up giving aid and comfort to the petty-bourgeois misleaders of the workers and peasants who sought *to ensure* that the peasants remained quiescent. "Trotsky is in fact helping the liberal-labor politicians in Russia," Lenin wrote, "who by 'repudiation' of the role of the peasantry understand a *'refusal'* to raise up the peasants for the revolution!" (*CW*, Vol. 21, 1915, p. 419–420).

By dismissing this alliance between the working class and the peasantry *as a whole*, Trotsky tended to dissolve the democratic-peasant revolution into the class struggle of the working class against the capitalists. Far from promoting the prospects of socialist revolution, however, Trotsky's lack of a transitional approach actually left the proletariat without a guide as to how to advance along their historic line of march toward the expropriation of the exploiters.

Lenin had pointed to this error in 1909 when he wrote that "Trotsky's major mistake is that he ignores the bourgeois character of the revolution and has no clear conception of the transition from this revolution to the socialist revolution" (*CW*, Vol. 15, 1909, p. 371).

Lenin's 1915 answer to Trotsky's *Nashe Slovo* articles, however, did present a clear strategy for this transition.

"The proletariat," Lenin wrote, "are fighting, and will fight valiantly, to win power, for a republic, for the confiscation of the land, i.e., to win over the peasantry, make *full* use of their revolutionary powers, and get the *'non*-proletarian masses of the people' to take part in liberating *bourgeois* Russia from *military-feudal* 'imperialism' (tsarism).

"The proletariat will at once utilize this ridding of bourgeois Russia of tsarism and the rule of the landowners," Lenin said, "not to aid the rich peasants in their struggle against the rural workers, but to bring about the socialist revolution in alliance with the proletarians of Europe" (*CW*, Vol.21, 1915, p. 420).

Trotsky was not convinced by Lenin on this question, however. Their differences on the role that a peasant revolution would play as an ally of the proletariat widened, if anything, right up to the eve of the Febuary 1917 revolution. Here, for example, is what Trotsky had to say on January 9, 1917, in an article published in New York commemorating the twelfth anniversary of the 1905 revolution:

"If a 'national' revolution was a failure twelve years ago, there is still less hope for it at present. It is true in the last years that the cultural and political level of the peasantry has become higher. However, there is less hope now for a revolutionary uprising of the peasantry as a whole than there was twelve years ago. The only ally of the urban proletariat may be the proletarian and half-proletarian strata of the village" ("The Lessons of the Great Year," *Our Revolution*, Trotsky, 1918, p. 176–7).

Two lines of the revolution

Mandel opens his article by stating that his aim is to demonstrate that "there were three—and not two—strategies proposed by Russian socialists" prior to 1917: those of the Bolsheviks, the Mensheviks, and Trotsky.

A correct and more useful approach to this question was presented by Lenin in his 1915 article, "On the Two Lines of the Revolution," where he took up Trotsky's *Nashe Slovo* articles. Lenin anchored the disputes in the Russian workers movement not in the clash of divergent *conceptions* or *theories* but of *social classes*.

"The experience of the 1905 Revolution and of the subsequent counter-revolutionary period in Russia teaches us that in our country *two* lines of revolution could be observed," Lenin wrote, "in the sense that there was a struggle between two classes—the proletariat and the liberal bourgeoisie—for leadership of the masses."

Lenin continued: "The Bolsheviks helped the proletariat consciously to follow the first line, to fight with supreme courage and to lead the peasants. The Mensheviks were constantly slipping into the second line; they demoralized the proletariat by adapting its movement to the liberals . . ." (*CW*, Vol. 21, 1915, p. 416).

There were two class lines: 1) organize the proletariat, in alliance with the peasantry, to take power, or 2) support the liberal bourgeoisie. The Bolsheviks followed the former course, the Mensheviks the latter.

"Only these trends—the Bolshevik and the Menshevik," Lenin continued, "manifested themselves in the politics of the *masses* in 1904–08, and later in 1908–14. Why was that? It was because only these trends had firm class roots—the former in the proletariat, the latter in the liberal bourgeoisie."

Trotsky's "new and original position" was not one of the trends reflected in the Russian *masses*. Why was that?

"From the Bolsheviks, Trotsky's original theory

has borrowed their call for a decisive proletarian revolutionary struggle and for the conquest of political power by the proletariat," Lenin explained, "while from the Mensheviks it has borrowed 'repudiation' of the peasantry's role" (*CW*, Vol. 21, 1915, p. 419).

Trotsky's perspectives didn't represent a trend rooted in one of the fundamental classes. Rather, it was a centrist amalgamation of the positions of the two principal trends. In relation to these two class lines of the revolution, Trotsky stood closer to the Bolsheviks than to the Mensheviks on the key question of the vanguard role of the working class and opposition to the liberal bourgeoisie.

During the 1905 revolution and its immediate aftermath, Trotsky was drawn closer to the Bolsheviks; there was a convergence in action. Trotsky collaborated with the Bolsheviks in the soviets and made a bloc with them against the Mensheviks on the defense policy for the October 1906 trial of the workers deputies to the Soviet, in which Trotsky was the leading defendant.

In November 1905, when the bourgeois liberal journal *Nasha Zhizn* (Our Life) attempted to pit Trotsky's view of the Russian revolution against that of the Bolsheviks, the Bolsheviks' organ, *Novaya Zhizn* (New Life), defended him. It argued that the *Nasha Zhizn* report "is of course sheer nonsense. Comrade Trotsky said that the proletarian revolution, without standing still at the first stage, by pressing hard upon the exploiters, can continue on its road, while Lenin pointed out that the political revolution is only the first step. The publicist of *Nasha Zhizn* would like to perceive a contradiction there. . . .

"The whole misunderstanding comes, first, from the fear with which the name alone of the socialist revolution fills *Nasha Zhizn*" the Bolshevik paper pointed out, "secondly, out of the desire of this paper to discover some sort of sharp and piquant difference of opinion among the social democrats and, thirdly, in the metaphorical expression of Comrade Trotsky: 'at one fell swoop.'

"In No. 10 of *Nachalo* [The Beginning], Comrade Trotsky explains his ideas quite unequivocally: 'The complete victory of the revolution signifies the victory of the proletariat,' writes Comrade Trotsky. 'But this victory in turn signifies the further uninterruptedness of the revolution. The proletariat realizes the fundamental tasks of democracy and the logic of its immediate struggle for the safeguarding of political domination causes purely socialist problems to arise at the given moment. Between the minimum and maximum program of the social democracy, a revolutionary continuity is established. This is not one 'blow,' it is not one day and not a month, it is a whole historical epoch. It would be absurd to want to determine its duration in advance'" (*The Stalin School of Falsification*, Trotsky (Pathfinder Press, 1937, 2004), pp. 386–387 [2021 printing]).

At the united congress of the RSDLP in London in 1907, Lenin also noted a convergence in Trotsky's position with that of the Bolsheviks.

"I shall only note," Lenin told the delegates, "that in his book *In Defense of the Party* Trotsky expressed, in print, his solidarity with Kautsky [while Kautsky was still a revolutionist], who wrote about the economic community of interests between the proletariat and the peasantry in the present revolution in Russia. Trotsky acknowledged the permissibility and usefulness of a Left bloc [with the peasants] against the liberal bourgeoisie. These facts are sufficient for me to acknowledge that Trotsky has come closer to our views. Quite apart from the question of 'uninterrupted revolution', we have here solidarity on fundamental points in the question of the attitude towards bourgeois parties" (*CW*, Vol. 12, 1907, p. 470).

On at least one occasion following this 1907 convention, Lenin seriously probed the possibility of a political rapprochement with Trotsky. Trotsky rebuffed this 1909 probe, however, and moved toward establishing his own faction in the RSDLP. Political differences between Trotsky and the Bolsheviks remained from this time up to the eve of the February 1917 revolution.

Trotsky not only disagreed with the Bolsheviks on the role of the peasant movement, he also differed with Lenin's view that the political differences between the Bolsheviks and Mensheviks were a genuine reflection of different class forces.

In 1910 Trotsky and Martov wrote articles for Kautsky's paper, *Die Neue Zeit,* explaining their views of the differences in the Russian social democracy to their German cothinkers. Trotsky argued that the Russian working class was still politically immature compared to Western Europe and that the conflicts in the Russian social democracy were a result of the adaptation of the Marxist intelligentsia to this backwardness. Neither the Mensheviks nor Bolsheviks "have struck deep roots in the proletariat," he contended. These factors, Trotsky said, offered the explanation for the "sectarianism, intellectualist individualism, ideological fetishism" allegedly racking Russian Social Democracy.

Lenin responded with an article that Kautsky did not publish. Lenin pointed out that:

"The crux of the matter is not whether the theoretical formulations of the differences [in Russian social democracy] have penetrated 'deeply' into this or that stratum of the proletariat, but the fact that the economic conditions of the Revolution of 1905 *brought* the proletariat into hostile relations with the liberal bourgeoisie—not only over the question of improving the conditions of daily life of the workers, but also over the agrarian question, over all the political questions of the revolution, etc.

"To speak of the struggle of trends in the Russian revolution," Lenin said, "distributing labels such as 'sectarianism', 'lack of culture', etc., and not to say a word about the fundamental economic interests of the proletariat, of the liberal bourgeoisie and of the democratic peasantry, means stooping to the level of cheap journalists" (*CW*, Vol. 16, 1910, p. 375).

Standing on the political middle ground between the Mensheviks and Bolsheviks, Trotsky attempted to build political and organizational bridges between these two opposing organizations, to unite these conflicting expressions of the class struggle. The most serious attempt at this took the form of the so-called August Bloc formed in 1912 by conciliationists such as Trotsky and a few dissident Mensheviks and Bolsheviks.

Trotsky's failure to recognize the need to build the Bolshevik Party in this period was not only or primarily a weakness on the "organizational question" narrowly construed. Though closer politically to the Bolsheviks, Trotsky's conciliationism toward the Mensheviks reflected his *political* differences with Bolshevism. Trotsky didn't join the Bolsheviks because he *didn't agree* with the Bolsheviks.

Defeatism in World War I

The outbreak of World War I drew an unbridgeable gulf between Trotsky and social-patriots of all stripes. It also brought to the fore further differences between the Bolsheviks and Trotsky. The war accelerated the pressures on the toiling classes, initially retarding but before long heightening the prospects for revolution in Russia. Lenin pointed to the effects of the war on the peasants, particularly on those in uniform fighting and dying on the front.

A central axis of the Bolsheviks' proletarian internationalist position against the war was to call on the working class in all imperialist countries, including Russia, to turn the imperialist war into a civil war. Depending on the particular circumstances, the Bolsheviks said, the working class should do everything possible to carry out revolutionary work aimed at overthrowing their own government and bringing the workers and peasants to power.

The military defeat of the imperialist government in one's own country, Lenin argued, would facilitate such a social revolution. That had been shown in life by the defeat of the tsarist army in the war with Japan, which helped spark the 1905 revolution.

"Wartime revolutionary action against one's own government indubitably means, not only desiring its defeat," Lenin wrote in 1915, "but really facilitating such a defeat." Lenin added the following clarification: "('Discerning reader': note that this does not mean 'blowing up bridges,' organizing unsuccessful strikes in the war industries, and in general helping the government defeat the revolutionaries)" (*CW*, Vol. 21, 1915, p. 275).

This has remained the position of proletarian revolutionists in imperialist countries toward wars waged by "their" governments from that time to today.

Lenin's revolutionary defeatism was part and parcel of the Bolsheviks' general strategy for the Russian revolution; it was interconnected with their view of the peasant question and the weight and place of the democratic revolution. The military defeats of the tsarist army in World War I, which led to the February revolution and the overthrow of the tsar, confirmed the Bolsheviks' course.

Trotsky, however, had a different approach, an incorrect one. While he fought the chauvinist capitulation of the majority of the Second International, he also polemicized against the Bolsheviks' defeatist position. Trotsky dealt with this question at length in the same 1915 articles where he explained the diminishing prospects of the peasants playing a role as an ally of the working class in the Russian revolution. He made several points:

- "To the same extent that defeat, all other things being equal, shatters a given state structure, so does the victory of the other side, which is implied by this defeat, strengthen the state organization of that other side. And we do not know of any European social and state organism which it is in the interest of the European proletariat to strengthen, nor do we assign to Russia the role of the state chosen to have its interests subordinated to those of the development of other European peoples."
- "Defeats disorganize and demoralize the ruling reaction, but at the same time war disorganizes the whole of social life, and above all the working class."
- "A revolution which grows out of a defeat inherits an economy disordered to the utmost by war, exhausted state finances, and extremely strained international relations."
- . . . while war may give an impetus to revolution, it may at the same time create a situation such as will make extremely difficult the social and political utilization of a victorious revolution" ("The Military Catastrophe and the Political Prospects," Trotsky, 1915).

In another 1915 article, Trotsky went so far as to label the Bolsheviks' defeatist position "a fundamental connivance with the political methodology of social patriotism." (June 1915 letter to the editorial board of *Kommunist*.)

Trotsky's alternative slogan was, "Neither victory, nor defeat."

Lenin sharply attacked Trotsky for having "completely lost his bearings on a simple issue. It seems to him that to desire Russia's defeat *means* desiring the victory of Germany." But the defeatist demand, Lenin countered, is profoundly internationalist, indeed the only truly proletarian internationalist position, since "in *all* imperialist countries the proletariat must now desire the defeat of its own government" (*CW*, Vol. 21, 1915, p. 276).

Trotsky's opposition to the Bolsheviks' revolutionary strategy against the war was reflected on the international level, where he continued to pursue a course of conciliation toward the opportunists.

There were essentially three currents in the international movement.

One was the outright social patriots, such as the majority of German and French social democratic leaders, who openly supported their own imperialist governments, voted for war credits, and participated in war cabinets. In Russia this was the position of right-wing SR and Menshevik leaders, and it became the position of a big majority of the leaderships of these parties following the February 1917 revolution.

The second trend was represented by the opportunists, most prominent of whom was Kautsky. They opposed the war, voted against war credits, and called for international solidarity of the working class. However, they refused to break with the Second International or link up the antiwar struggle with the revolutionary struggle in their own countries. Martov and other "Menshevik-Internationalists" represented this current in Russia.

The third trend converged around the revolutionary communist policy put forward most consistently by Lenin and the Bolsheviks. From the very outset Lenin called for the formation of a new, third international, and he attacked not only the social patriots, but the opportunists who gave them cover.

From the beginning of the war, Trotsky strongly opposed the social patriots. He differed with the Bolsheviks not only on the question of defeatism, however, but also on the necessity of breaking with the Kautskyists in order to move toward a new revolutionary international. Trotsky held a centrist position between the Bolsheviks and the Kautskyists.

As the imperialist slaughter dragged on, the internationalist position won increasing support among socialists. This laid the basis for the conference in Zimmerwald, Switzerland, in September 1915, that brought together social-democratic opponents of the war. It was attended by 38 delegates from 11 European countries.

Two principal political currents waged a political struggle at this conference—the proletarian communists led by Lenin and the "vacillating, near Kautskyites" (as Lenin characterized the right wing at the conference).

The Bolsheviks, represented by Lenin and Zinoviev, and a handful of international supporters fought for a resolution, drafted by Lenin, that explicitly attacked both the social patriots and the opportunists, favored defeatism, and called for turning the imperialist war into a civil war (See *CW*, Vol. 21, 1915, p. 345–348). The right wing strongly disagreed with these points.

Trotsky, whose *Nashe Slovo* articles opposing defeatism had appeared only a few weeks before the conference, also disagreed with the Left Zimmerwaldists on other points. He also disagreed with the Zimmerwald right, however. Holding the middle ground, Trotsky was designated to draft a compromise manifesto, which was adopted unanimously. It has become widely known as the Zimmerwald Manifesto, despite the fact that it had, according to Lenin, "inconsistency, timidity and a failure to say everything that ought to be said."

"Our non-agreement, the non-agreement, not only of our Central Committee but of the entire *international* Left-wing section of the Conference, which stands by the principles of *revolutionary Marxism,* is openly expressed in a special resolution, a separate draft manifesto, and a separate declaration on the vote for a compromise manifesto," Lenin stated. "We did not conceal a jot of our views, slogans, or tactics.

"A German edition of our pamphlet, *Socialism and War* [written by Lenin and Zinoviev in preparation for the conference—see *CW,* Vol. 21, p. 295–338], was handed out at the Conference. We have spread, are spreading, and shall continue to spread our views with no less energy than the manifesto will.

"It is a fact that this manifesto is a *step forward* towards a real struggle against opportunism, towards a rupture with it," Lenin said. "It would be sectarianism to refuse to take this step forward together with the minority of German, French, Swedish, Norwegian, and Swiss socialists, when we retain full freedom and full opportunity to criticize inconsistency and to work for greater things" ("The First Step," *CW,* Vol. 21, 1915, p. 387).

The Zimmerwald Left remained an organized international current. It distributed the Zimmerwald Left Manifesto and other resolutions as widely as possible and briefly published its own organ. It continued to participate in the Zimmerwald organization, and at the April 1916 conference held in Kienthal, Switzerland, the Zimmerwaldists—under the impetus of the Bolshevik-led left wing—took an even bigger step in breaking with the opportunists. It was the work done by the Zimmerwald Left that assembled the first nuclei of the Third International, which was formally established in early 1919.

Why Trotsky didn't join the Bolsheviks

Despite Trotsky's agreement with many of the Bolsheviks' positions, his differences on key questions of strategy for the Russian revolution prevented him from joining. This was not an error, in the sense that simply out of mistaken *organizational* conceptions Trotsky did not join a party that *politically* he should have been part of. To the contrary, Trotsky's centrist position on the organizational level reflected his political centrism.

But the clear logic of Mandel's article is that since Trotsky was correct on the basic political strategy for the revolution, he should have been inside the organization that was assembling the cadres capable of leading the workers to power, fighting there to win it to his program and away from that fought for by Lenin.

Mandel actually makes this explicit in a recent article, "The Need for a Revolutionary International," coauthored with John Ross in the Spring 1982 *International Marxist Review,* a magazine published in Britain.

Mandel and Ross declare that Trotsky made a "disastrous mistake" when "not merely did he not join the Bolsheviks, which was the biggest mistake of his entire life, but when he did not build up a serious force in Russia of any major dimensions.

"In consequence Trotsky entered the Russian Revolution with an excellent programme, and some brilliant cadres, but with an organization (the *Mezhrayontsi*) so small that it could never have built even in the revolutionary conditions of Russia a party capable of taking power in 1917" (Spring 1982, *International Marxist Review,* p. 50).

The point is unambiguous. Trotsky's error was not that he didn't become a Leninist, but that he didn't join the Bolshevik Party in order to fight for his "excellent program," or in the words of Mandel's *ISR* article, his "entirely new and original position."

But adjectives like "excellent," "new," or "original" shouldn't weigh heavily in the balance for Marxists. The decisive question is whether or not a position is correct, whether or not it serves to chart a course for the working class and its allies to take and hold political power. Trotsky's pre-1917 strategy, insofar as it differed from the Bolsheviks', was wrong.

What if Trotsky *had* joined the Bolshevik Party and won major parts of it away from Lenin's strategy to his own political perspectives? That would have greatly increased the likelihood that the party would have failed to take power in October 1917, and that the Russian workers and peasants would have gone down to defeat. It was Lenin's strategy that built the party that led the workers to victory.

Mandel argues that Lenin came over to Trotsky's pre-1917 strategy for the Russian revolution, while Trotsky came over to Lenin's view of party organization. But this is not true. In fact, it makes no sense at all. How can a historical materialist explain this supposed complete dichotomy between program and strategy, on the one hand, and their organizational expression, on the other?

When Trotsky joined the Bolshevik Party in the summer of 1917, he became a Leninist and remained one for the rest of his life.

Mandel tends to artificially separate the "excellent program," i.e., Trotsky's, from the excellent organization, i.e., the Bolsheviks', as if the Bolsheviks' revolutionary proletarian strategy was not what ultimately determined the organizational character of their party. This is the opposite of Lenin's view.

The Bolsheviks' strategy for the revolution can't be divorced from the kind of party they built, any more than Trotsky's "new and original position" can be separated from his organizational conciliationism toward the opportunists and his other errors on the organization question.

The differences between Lenin and Trotsky on the question of the Russian revolution cannot be divorced from the overall living process of building a proletarian revolutionary party. They cannot be reduced to a conflict between two "theories" of the revolution. To understand the differences, it is necessary to descend from the realm of ideas and "brilliant cadres" to that of classes and their alignment, conflicts, and relations. That's where both strategies and organizations *come from*, not vice versa.

Lenin's strategy was not the idea of one individual, but the generalized lessons from the collective revolutionary activity of a party that was part of the Russian working class, as well as from the previous historical experiences summed up by the Marxist movement. The positions of the Bolsheviks were continually being tested, modified, and retested in the class struggle by worker-Bolsheviks. The collective determination and testing of positions was directed toward leading the day-to-day work of the party—its fractions in the factories, its Duma fractions, its underground cells, its exile organizations, its blocs with peasant organizations, its defense cases, its election campaigns, and its press.

The party was a "single great . . . mechanism," as Lenin put it. Party literature "must become *part* of the common cause of the proletariat, 'a cog and a screw'" of this mechanism, Lenin said. This was the Bolshevik approach to all party activity (*CW*, Vol. 10, 1905, p. 45).

The activity of the party was directed toward advancing the political consciousness of the working class, of helping to lead it from one stage of the class struggle to the next. It was preeminently a transitional approach to party building. And nothing shows this more clearly than the approach that the Bolsheviks developed to the relationship between the democratic and socialist revolutions.

The historical record clearly shows that it was the strategy of Bolshevism that was confirmed in the Russian revolution, and that became the programmatic basis of the Communist International. It was not a fusion of one part Bolshevism with one part Trotsky's pre-1917 centrism.

'Discovering' a new law

Mandel claims that the view of the Russian revolution that Trotsky began developing in 1904 "flowed from his discovery of the law of uneven and combined development, undoubtedly his fundamental contribution to Marxism." Later Mandel states that this law "implied that the proletariat could take power in a backward country before it did so in the most advanced countries."

The biggest problem with this is that no fact or action "flows from" or "is implied by" any law of historical materialism.

Mandel argues that *a fact*—that is, that the working class could take power in a backward country before it did in an advanced country—was "implied" by the law of uneven and combined development. If things should be called by their proper names, then this statement should be labeled a serious concession to idealism and antimaterialism. Historical laws and theories can be applied to political situations to help analyze them and to anticipate the contours of future development. But no facts are implied by historical laws. None at all.

In 1847, when the petty bourgeois socialist Pierre Joseph Proudhon argued that economic competition at a particular historical stage is the necessary result of "the theory of the reduction of general expenses," Marx retorted: "For M. Proudhon, the circulation of the blood must be a consequence of Harvey's theory." (William Harvey was a British physician who first sought to explain the circulation of blood in the human body) (*MECW*, Vol. 6, p. 194).

Both Trotsky and Lenin examined the economic and social relations in Russia and the world from the standpoint of Marxism and historical materialism, and they drew certain conclusions about strategy. But nothing could be deduced from the law of uneven and combined development to prove that Lenin or Trotsky was correct. Before 1917 Trotsky did not describe or generalize the law of uneven and combined development any differently than Lenin. Trotsky did not use the name "uneven and combined development" to describe this basic law of historical materialism until 1930 in the first chapter of his *History of the Russian Revolution*.

While it is true that Trotsky was the first Marxist to give the law of uneven and combined development its name and to elaborate it as a fundamental law of historical evolution, Trotsky, unlike Mandel, claimed no more in using this tool than to be scientifically systematizing one law on the basis of the historical materialist method that he had learned from the study of Marx and Engels's writings.

Trotsky would have been the first to ridicule the notion that he discovered the law of uneven and combined development. He considered this to be an integral part of historical materialism as developed by Marx and Engels. "The unevenness of capitalist development . . . were as well known to Marx and Engels as they are to us," he said in 1926 ("Speech to the Fifteenth Congress," *The Challenge of the Left Opposition 1926–27* (Pathfinder Press, 1980), p. 208 [2019 printing]).

If Marx and Engels did not recognize unevenness in historical development and the combined character of social formations, then what *was* historical materialism before Trotsky's "discovery"? A theory of unvarying, uniform, and strictly sequential development? A scheme *imposed* on human history, rather than a scientific generalization of its laws of development drawn from the dialectic of its concrete unfolding? That's what bourgeois opponents and social-democratic revisionists of scientific socialism have claimed, but never Marxists.

How could Marx and Engels, at the very beginning of their political lives, have understood the class struggle in their own native Germany otherwise? Despite its low level of industrial development and small industrial proletariat compared to other major Western European nations, they nonetheless predicted in the *Communist Manifesto* that Germany had the greatest revolutionary potential in the late 1840s—precisely because of the social contradictions created by its backwardness in the context of an expanding world capitalist system.

Moreover, Marx and Engels explained the theoretical basis for such a conclusion one year earlier in 1846 in their very first work outlining much of historical materialism, *The German Ideology:*

"It is evident that large-scale industry does not reach the same level of development in all districts of a country," Marx and Engels wrote. "This does not, however, retard the class movement of the proletariat, because the proletarians created by large-scale industry assume leadership of this movement and carry the whole mass along with them, and because the workers excluded from large-scale industry are placed by it in a still worse situation than the workers in large-scale industry itself."

Applying this to capitalist development on a world scale, they continued:

"The countries in which large-scale industry is developed act in a similar manner upon the more or less non-industrial countries, insofar as the latter are swept by world intercourse [economic trade and social relations] into the universal competitive struggle. . . .

"Thus all collisions in history have their origin, according to our view, in the contradiction between the productive forces and the form of intercourse. Incidentally, to lead to collisions in a country, this contradiction need not have necessarily reached its extreme limit in that particular country," Marx and Engels wrote. "The competition with industrially more advanced countries, brought about by the expansion of international intercourse, is sufficient to produce a similar contradiction in countries with a less advanced industry (e.g., the latent proletariat in Germany brought into more prominence by the competition of English industry)" (*Marx and Engels Collected Works* (MECW), Vol. 5, p. 74–5).

Of course, the massive expansion of world capitalism and the emergence of imperialism since the *German Ideology* was written have greatly magnified and transformed the processes that Marx and Engels were pointing to. Can it be denied, however, that they took the uneven and combined development of the world capitalist system into account from the outset in developing their historical materialist outlook and its programmatic and strategic conclusions?

Lenin, too, discerned unevenness and combination in historical and political developments, and examples have already been cited in this article.

It is ludicrous to believe that a Marxist committed to building a proletarian party and making a socialist revolution in a country such as Russia could have been oblivious to its contradictory social and economic conditions—the most backward political forms and agrarian relations, combined with industrialization and a growing modern proletariat. Lenin analyzed these aspects of Russian society at great length, and integrated them into his strategy for the Russian revolution.

In the late 1920s, when Stalin, in an attempt to deify Lenin and to justify his own personality cult, developed the notion that Leninism is a superior kind of Marxism peculiar to the imperialist epoch, Trotsky responded:

"In essence the singling out of Leninism as a special kind of Marxism peculiar to the age of imperialism was necessary for the revision of Marxism, something Lenin in fact fought against throughout his life. Inasmuch as the central idea of this latest revision of Marxism was the reactionary idea of national socialism (the theory of building socialism in one country), it was necessary to demonstrate or at least proclaim that Leninism had taken a new position on this central question of Marxist theory and politics in opposition to the Marxism of the preimperialist era."

Trotsky continued: "We have already heard [from Stalin] that *Lenin supposedly discovered the law of uneven development, that there could have been no question of such a thing in the time of Marx and Engels*. That is precisely the absurdity that the Thomas Aquinases of our day call on us to have faith in" (emphasis added, *The Challenge of the Left Opposition 1928–29*, Trotsky (Pathfinder Press, 1981), pp. 506–507 [2019 printing]).

Finally, Mandel asserts that discovering the law of uneven and combined development was Trotsky's "fundamental contribution" to Marxism. Regardless of how one weighs this contribution, would it be greater than other important contributions such as applying, defending, or passing Bolshevism on to a new generation after Lenin's death?

In the face of the massive use of state power by the Stalinist bureaucracy to break the revolutionary continuity of Marxism, Trotsky taught us to be Bolsheviks and to read Lenin, Marx, and Engels. During this struggle against the reversal of Bolshevism, he analyzed the degeneration of the Soviet workers state. He taught us what was progressive and required defending—state property, planning and the monopoly of foreign trade—and what was reactionary and needed to be removed—the parasitic bureaucratic caste that had usurped governmental power from the workers and farmers.

Marx, Engels, and Lenin did not live to see this new phenomenon, but Trotsky did. His analysis built on the Marxist theory of the state and of government, enriched it, and made an indispensable contribution to the transitional program and the communist strategy for the world socialist revolution in all three of its sectors. It has been incorporated into the revolutionary continuity of Marxism.

In the 1920s and 1930s, Trotsky developed and enriched the transitional method and Leninist strategy of party building that he had learned as a Bolshevik. He also made important contributions to the Marxist understanding of fascism, the colonial revolution, and of the national question, including its application to the oppression of Blacks in the United States.

Trotsky's principal contributions to the Marxist movement, to the working-class movement, were made *after* he had become a Leninist. They were made *because* he had dumped the worst of his pre-1917 positions, not in continuity with them. After the death of Lenin, Trotsky became the foremost proponent of the revolutionary continuity of Marxism and of Leninism and helped build an international organization of cadres to defend and apply that continuity in the developing class struggle.

The proletariat's line of march

As indicated at the beginning of this article, the question of what strategy helped lead the Russian workers to power is of decisive importance, since it determines where proletarian revolutionists today should look for our own continuity—with the pre-1917 Trotsky, or with Lenin and the Bolsheviks.

It is Bolshevism, it is Leninism that represents our continuity with Marxism. The Leninist strategy for the revolutionary workers party in Russia was firmly rooted in the generalizations drawn by Marx and Engels in their writings from the experience of the working class. The basic rudiments of the Bolsheviks' strategy for the Russian revolution, in fact, come straight from the *Communist Manifesto*, written by Marx and Engels in December–January 1847–48. If we substitute "Russia" for "Germany" in the last section of the *Manifesto*, it reads as follows:

"In Russia they [the Communists] fight with the bourgeoisie whenever it acts in a revolutionary way, against the absolute monarchy, the feudal squirearchy, and the petty bourgeoisie.[3]

"But they never cease, for a single instant, to instill into the working class the clearest possible recognition of the hostile antagonism between bourgeoisie and proletariat in order that the Russian workers may straightaway use, as so many weapons against the bourgeoisie, the social and political conditions that the bourgeoisie must necessarily introduce along with its supremacy, and in order that, after the fall of the reactionary classes in Russia, the fight against the bourgeoisie itself may immediately begin.

"The Communists turn their attention chiefly to Russia, because that country is on the eve of a bourgeois revolution that is bound to be carried out under more advanced conditions of European civilization, and with a much more developed proletariat, than that of England was in the seventeenth, and of France in the eighteenth century, and because the bourgeois revolution in Russia will be but the prelude to an immediately following proletarian revolution" (*MECW*, Vol. 1, p. 137).

This was the general approach of the Bolsheviks in Russia. It wasn't new or original, but it did the job.

3. By "petty bourgeoisie," Marx and Engels are not referring here to the peasantry, but to what Engels describes in another 1847 article as "the poor burghers, especially those of the small provincial towns," who as a layer "clings to the existing state of things and supports the nobility with the whole weight of its inertia." He distinguished explicitly between them and "the peasants and the propertyless classes" in Germany. ("The Constitutional Question in Germany," *MECW*, Vol. 6, p. 82–3.)

In other writings in 1847, Marx and Engels also differentiated between this layer, primarily a hangover from the feudal period, and the more modern urban middle class—small artisans, shopkeepers, etc.—which they considered an ally of the workers in the democratic revolution, although an inconsistent and vacillating one. For example, Engels writes that a key "task of the German democratic press" is "to reveal the oppression of the proletarians, small peasants and urban petty bourgeoisie, for in Germany these constitute the 'people', by the bureaucracy, the nobility, and the bourgeoisie." The democratic press should also show "how not only political but above all social oppression has come about, and by what means it can be eliminated," Engels wrote, and "that the conquest of political power by the proletarians, small peasants and urban petty bourgeoisie is the first condition for the application of these means." ("The Communists and Karl Heinzen," *MECW*, Vol. 6, p. 294.)

IN DEFENSE OF PERMANENT REVOLUTION

A reply by Ernest Mandel to Doug Jenness

EDITOR'S INTRODUCTION

The following article, "In Defense of Permanent Revolution," by Ernest Mandel, is part of a continuing public debate on the continuity of communist strategy from 1848 to today. At the heart of this discussion is the question of the dictatorship of the proletariat—the touchstone of Marxist strategy.

The debate began following the publication of an article in the *International Socialist Review* (a magazine supplement to the U.S. weekly *Militant*, which reflects the views of the Socialist Workers Party) in November 1981, celebrating the 64th anniversary of the Russian Revolution. On that occasion the *International Socialist Review* featured Lenin's 1921 article, "On the Fourth Anniversary of the October Revolution." This was the first time it had been published in the *Militant* or the *International Socialist Review*. A brief commentary by *Militant* editor Doug Jenness accompanied Lenin's article.

Ernest Mandel, like Jenness a member of the United Secretariat of the Fourth International, took issue with this article describing the Bolsheviks' strategy. Mandel's polemic, entitled "The Debate Over the Character and Goals of the Russian Revolution," appeared in the April 1982 *International Socialist Review*.

Jenness responded in "Our Political Continuity with Bolshevism," published in the June 1982 *International Socialist Review*.

This unfolding discussion has also been appearing publicly in French in *Inprecor* and *Quatrième Internationale*.

For those who may not have read the earlier articles in this discussion, it is useful to review briefly the key issues under debate.

Four years of Russian revolution

Lenin's 1921 anniversary article reviewed the stages in the development of the Russian revolution since the workers and peasants established their rule in October 1917. He explained, "The direct and immediate object of the revolution in Russia was a bourgeois-democratic one, namely, to destroy the survivals of medievalism and sweep them away completely, to purge Russia of this barbarism, of this shame, and to remove this immense obstacle to all culture and progress in our country."

Lenin pointed out that once the workers and peasants republic had consummated this task "as nobody had done before," it advanced "towards the socialist revolution consciously, firmly and unswervingly, knowing that it is not separated from the bourgeois-democratic revolution by a Chinese Wall, and knowing too that (in the last analysis) *struggle alone* will determine how far we shall advance, what part of this immense and lofty task we shall accomplish, and to what extent we shall succeed in consolidating our victories" (emphasis in original for all quotations).

Lenin stated that four years of experience of the revolution "have proved to the hilt that our interpretation of Marxism on this point, and our estimate of the experience of former revolutions were correct."

Lenin also noted that all of the Bolsheviks' opponents in the working-class movement during the First World War had "derided our slogan 'convert

---

This editor's introduction and article by Ernest Mandel first appeared in *Intercontinental Press,* August 8, 1983 (Vol. 21, No. 15).

the imperialist war into a civil war.' But that slogan proved to be the *truth*—it was the only truth, unpleasant, blunt, naked and brutal, but nevertheless the *truth*, as against the host of most refined jingoist and pacifist lies."

It is impossible for working people to escape the inferno of imperialist war, Lenin explained, *"except by a Bolshevik struggle and a Bolshevik revolution."*

Jenness' accompanying article pointed to the historic importance of the Russian revolution for working people. It altered the relationship of class forces internationally between the imperialist rulers and the toiling masses in favor of the latter, he said. And it offered the world working class its richest experience yet in applying communist strategy.

Jenness observed that "Lenin was the central leader of the Bolshevik party and of the Soviet workers state in its early revolutionary years. The best place to learn the lessons of Bolshevism—to understand how the Bolshevik party was trained, carried through the October revolution, and led the organization of the world's first workers state—is Lenin's writings and speeches."

Democratic and socialist revolution in Russia

Jenness commented on and amplified the points in Lenin's article regarding the relation between the democratic and socialist revolutions in Russia. He referred readers to *The Proletarian Revolution and the Renegade Kautsky*, a polemic written by Lenin in 1918 against Karl Kautsky's condemnation of the dictatorship of the proletariat in Soviet Russia. Kautsky was a prominent leader of the Second International.

Jenness quoted Lenin's brief summary of the principal contending strategies in the Russian labor movement before the Russian revolution:

"The Russian revolution is a bourgeois revolution, said all the Marxists of Russia before 1905. The Mensheviks, substituting liberalism for Marxism, drew the conclusion from this that, hence, the proletariat must not go beyond what was acceptable to the bourgeoisie and must pursue a policy of compromise with it. The Bolsheviks said that this was a bourgeois-liberal theory. The bourgeoisie, they said, was trying to bring about the reform of the state on bourgeois, *reformist*, not revolutionary lines, while preserving the monarchy, landlordism, etc., as far as possible. The proletariat must carry through the bourgeois-democratic revolution to the end, not allowing itself to be 'bound' by the reformism of the bourgeoisie. The Bolsheviks formulated the relation of *class* forces in the bourgeois revolution as follows: the proletariat, joining to itself the peasantry, will neutralize the liberal bourgeoisie and utterly destroy the monarchy, medievalism, and landlordism.

"The alliance between the proletariat and the peasantry *in general* reveals the bourgeois character of the revolution, for the peasantry in general are small producers who stand on the basis of commodity production. Further, the Bolsheviks then added, the proletariat will join to itself *the entire semi-proletariat* (all the toilers and exploited), will neutralize the middle peasantry and *overthrow* the bourgeoisie; this will be a Socialist revolution, as distinct from a bourgeois-democratic revolution (see my pamphlet *Two Tactics*, published in 1905 and reprinted in *Twelve Years*, St. Petersburg, 1907)."

Jenness then turned to *Two Tactics* to show the continuity between the Bolsheviks' pre-1917 strategic orientation and Lenin's evaluation of the revolution after 1917. In this work Lenin explained that the working class should forge an alliance with the peasantry *as a whole*, that is, with capitalist farmers as well as with exploited and semiproletarian peasants with small land holdings, to overturn the monarchy and landlordism.

"Such a victory will assume the form of a dictatorship," Jenness quoted Lenin from *Two Tactics*, "i.e. it is inevitably bound to rely on military force, on the arming of the masses, on an uprising, and not on institutions established by 'lawful' or 'peaceful' means. It can only be a dictatorship, for the introduction of the reforms which are urgently needed and absolutely necessary for the proletariat and the peasantry will call forth the desperate resistance of the landlords, the big bourgeoisie and tsarism. Without a dictatorship it will be impossible to break down that resistance and to repel the counterrevolutionary attempts. But of course it will be a democratic, not a socialist dictatorship."

Jenness cited Lenin's explanation that the workers and peasants dictatorship, after carrying out the democratic revolution, "shall at once, and precisely in accordance with the measure of our strength, the strength of the class-conscious and organized proletariat, begin to pass to the socialist revolution. We stand for uninterrupted revolution. We shall not stop half-way."

Jenness noted that Lenin's assessment of the popular mass committees and delegated bodies, called soviets, that arose during the 1905 revolution "gave a glimpse of how the revolutionary-democratic dictatorship might emerge."

He pointed out that when the soviets were established again in February 1917, on a much more extensive basis, Lenin recognized and promoted them as the basis of a new government based on the workers and peasants. Through these organs, the workers established their rule in October 1917 and proceeded to carry through, at first with the peasantry as a whole, the democratic revolution. When the semiproletarian and poor peasants launched a struggle against the capitalist farmers (kulaks) in the spring and summer of 1918, the Soviet republic advanced toward the socialist revolution.

Jenness concluded that the course projected by the Bolsheviks before 1917 "gave an accurate portrayal of the line of march the Russian workers would follow and how the revolution would unfold. It armed them to participate effectively in the class struggle and to assume a leadership role in the revolution."

Marx and Engels on Russia

Mandel, in his article "The Debate Over the Character and Goals of the Russian Revolution," began by presenting his view of Marx and Engels' positions on Russia and their relations to the Russian narodniks (populists) in the latter part of the 19th century.

Mandel argued that "after some hesitation," Marx—in correspondence with populist leader Vera Zasulich in 1881—"arrived at an unambiguous position: Russia could 'leap over the stage of capitalism.'" "Through this analysis," Mandel said, "Marx provided support" to the narodniks against a current led by Georgi Plekhanov, evolving toward proletarian communism away from populist positions.

In the late 1880s and early 1890s, following Marx's death, according to Mandel, Engels drew the conclusion that history was not bearing out Marx's 1881 hypothesis. Only then did Engels give "his full support to the first nucleus of Russian Marxists around Plekhanov."

In "Our Political Continuity with Bolshevism," Jenness responded, "From Mandel's description of this debate . . . one might draw the incorrect impression that Marx and Engels, in the 1870s and 1880s, adapted to populism. It is important to be clear on this, since Lenin consciously and explicitly rooted himself in the continuity of Marx and Engels's writings."

Jenness pointed out, "Marx and Engels's views on the development of Russian society and their relations with the emerging movement there were quite a bit richer and more complex," than indicated by Mandel. "In fact, they provide a model both of a materialist analysis of a concrete social and economic situation and of how proletarian revolutionists approach fighters struggling against oppression who show potential to evolve toward scientific communism."

Mandel, in his latest contribution, does not return to this issue.

In his April 1982 article, Mandel sharply disagreed with Jenness' evaluation of the Bolsheviks' strategy and offered his own interpretation. He argued that the Bolsheviks were correct against the Mensheviks in rejecting a political bloc with the bourgeois parties in order to carry out the bourgeois-democratic revolution. However, Mandel said, the Bolsheviks made many serious errors in their strategy that were not reversed until April 1917.

Lenin's strategy

These mistakes included Lenin's "erroneous dogma" of dividing the Russian revolution into two distinct stages—the democratic revolution and the social revolution. In Lenin's strategy, Mandel argued, "the goal of the democratic revolution was to be *the unfettered development of capitalism.*"

The Bolsheviks were educated by Lenin in the "spirit of limiting the 'first stage' of the revolution to purely democratic tasks." Lenin favored the "'self-limitation of the proletariat,' that is the refusal to move beyond the realization of the most radical bourgeois-democratic demands."

For Lenin, he said, "The capacity of the Russian proletariat *to begin* to resolve the socialist tasks of the revolution . . . did not exist."

As a result of Lenin's errors, Mandel concluded, the Bolshevik party found itself disarmed following the February 1917 revolution. "When *all* the Bolshevik leaders and *all* the Bolshevik cadres favored 'critical' support to and even collaboration with the provisional coalition government."

Mandel said, "Unlike the Mensheviks, Lenin, in line with his own position, called for Social Democratic participation in a revolutionary insurrectional government, and even for an insurrectional process culminating in a revolutionary government under Social Democratic leadership. . . ."

But Lenin's view of an "insurrectional government," Mandel stated, did not include advancing to the socialist revolution following the consummation of the democratic revolution. Lenin, according to Mandel, believed this government "will have to give up or lose power later on, given the bourgeois character of the revolution."

In conjunction with this, Mandel added that Lenin radically rejected "any notion of 'revolutionary communes,' any notion of a state (in contrast to an insurrection) based on soviets. . . ."

Mandel said that Lenin explicitly corrected himself in his April Theses of 1917 and "now in fact stood for the same positions Trotsky had defended since 1904–1906. . . ."

Trotsky's pre-1917 position

Leon Trotsky, before the 1917 revolution, was one of the leading Russian Social Democrats who stood outside both the Bolshevik and Menshevik factions. Shortly after his return to Russia from exile in May 1917, Trotsky joined the Bolshevik party. He remained a Bolshevik, defending the principles of revolutionary communism until his assassination in 1940.

Mandel stated, "Beginning in 1904, Trotsky developed an entirely new and original position on [the] character and perspectives of the Russian revolution. He and his supporters alone defended that position against both the Mensheviks and the Bolsheviks."

Trotsky correctly agreed with the Bolsheviks, Mandel said, in opposing the Mensheviks' practice of supporting the liberal bourgeoisie. He was also correct in opposing the Bolsheviks' "erroneous dogma" of a prolonged capitalist stage, during which Russia would undergo modernization and industrialization through a "rapid development of capitalism."

Trotsky was also right, according to Mandel, in defending "the impossibility for the peasantry to constitute a political party or force that would be independent both of the bourgeoisie and the working class," while Lenin "was certain that the revolutionary peasantry had to *take political power.*"

Jenness responded in "Our Political Continuity with Bolshevism" that Mandel's article "is an erroneous presentation of the Bolshevik strategy and a distorted picture of the differences in the Russian workers movement leading up to the 1917 revolution."

Jenness rejected Mandel's statement that Lenin saw the "goal of the democratic revolution" in Russia to be a "prolonged" period of "unfettered development of capitalism."

Lenin, Jenness said, often explained the elementary historical materialist precept that the "complete elimination of the remnants of medievalism and serfdom, together with the overturn of the autocracy, would create the best conditions for the development of capitalism, especially in agriculture." However, Jenness added, this "neither meant that the bourgeoisie would lead it or support it, nor that the government issuing from it would put the bourgeoisie in power."

Jenness argued that Lenin, following the 1917 revolution, saw the fundamental outlines of the question in the same way as he did before. He quoted Lenin in 1918 on the import of nationalizing the land immediately following the October Revolution. "This laid the foundation, the most perfect from the point of view of the development of capitalism (Kautsky cannot deny this without breaking with Marx), and at the same time created an agrarian system which is the *most flexible* from the point of view of the transition to socialism."

Relationship of class forces is key

Jenness also took issue with Mandel's statement that the Bolsheviks' strategy was to "self-limit" a revolutionary upheaval in order to confine it to accomplishing bourgeois-democratic measures, thus assuring an inevitable capitalist takeover of the government. Rather, he argued, the Bolsheviks favored establishing a revolutionary dictatorship of the workers and peasants that would forcibly repress the big capitalists and landlords, carry through the democratic revolution, and advance the socialist revolution as rapidly as the class relationship of forces would permit.

Jenness quoted Lenin in 1905 that "to try to calculate *now* what the combination of forces will be within the peasantry 'on the day after' the revolution (the democratic revolution) is empty utopianism. . . . We shall bend every effort to help the entire peasantry achieve the democratic revolution, *in order thereby to make it easier* for us, the party of the proletariat, to pass on as quickly as possible to the new and higher task—the socialist revolution."

Rejecting Mandel's statement that Lenin did not have any notion before 1917 of a state based on soviets, Jenness pointed to a 1906 polemic with the Mensheviks where Lenin wrote, "The organs of authority that we have described [Soviets of Workers', Soldiers', Railwaymen's and Peasants' Deputies] represented a dictatorship in embryo, for they recognized *no* other authority, *no* law and *no* standards, no matter by whom established."

Jenness also pointed to the theses adopted by the Bolsheviks in October 1915, which specified the initial moves a workers and peasants dictatorship under Bolshevik leadership would take to remove Russia from the war. These theses ruled out participation in a government with "revolutionary chauvinists" (Mensheviks and Socialist Revolutionaries) who were supporting the imperialist war aims.

Sharply differing with Mandel, Jenness argued that it was not the Bolsheviks' strategic perspective that disoriented some Bolshevik leaders in Russia after the February 1917 revolution. To the contrary, the actions of the Bolshevik conciliationists who politically supported the capitalist provisional government "had nothing in common with the positions adopted by the Bolshevik party congresses and carried in its press since 1903. In particular, it would be hard to find any questions that the Bolsheviks were better armed against than conciliationism toward the Mensheviks and opposition to defending the imperialist government's war."

Jenness argued that "the fact that some Bolshevik leaders accepted a conciliationist course and abandoned the Bolshevik line on the war testifies to the profound pressures on the party, especially on those sectors most removed from the working class."

Did Lenin adopt Trotsky's view?

Jenness also took issue with Mandel's argument that Lenin came over to Trotsky's pre-1917 political perspectives on the revolution and that Trotsky came over to Lenin's view of party organization. "The Bolsheviks' strategy for the revolution can't be divorced from the kind of party they built," Jenness said, "any more than Trotsky's 'new and original position' can be separated from his organizational conciliationism toward the opportunists and his other errors on the organizational question."

Jenness pointed to the importance of Trotsky's difference with the Bolsheviks on the place of the peasantry in the Russian revolution. Trotsky dismissed the "alliance between the working class and the peasantry *as a whole*," Jenness said.

He pointed out that Trotsky's difference with the Bolsheviks on this question widened during the First World War. He cited what Trotsky had to say in January 1917 on the eve of the February revolution. "There is less hope now," Trotsky wrote, "for a revolutionary uprising of the peasantry as a whole than there was twelve years ago. The only ally of the urban proletariat may be the proletarian and half-proletarian strata of the village."

Unlike Lenin, Trotsky "tended to dissolve the democratic-peasant revolution into the class struggle of the working class against the capitalists," Jenness concluded.

Jenness argued that Trotsky's differences with the Bolsheviks on the alliance of the working class and the peasantry as a whole in the democratic-peasant revolution were part and parcel of other fundamental differences he had with the Bolsheviks, including those on the war question.

The Bolsheviks argued that a military defeat of the imperialist government would facilitate a social revolution. Trotsky countered that "while war may give an impetus to revolution, it may at the same time create a situation such as will make extremely difficult the social and political utilization of a victorious revolution." His alternative slogan was "Neither victory, nor defeat."

"The historical record clearly shows," Jenness concluded, "that it was the strategy of Bolshevism that was confirmed in the Russian revolution, and that became the programmatic basis of the Communist International. It was not a fusion of one part Bolshevism with one part Trotsky's pre-1917 centrism."

Mandel's article in this issue of *Intercontinental Press* has extended the debate by challenging the view that the continuity of revolutionary Marxism on the strategy for establishing soviet power in the semicolonial countries is rooted in the resolutions and reports prepared by Lenin and adopted by the Bolshevik-led Communist International. "More than Lenin's writings is . . . needed to find one's way around" on this question, Mandel writes.

Differences go back before 1963

Finally, it should be noted that Mandel says that "for more than two decades we [the reference is unclear] systematically warned the comrades leading the SWP of the dangers" in its "sectarian and dogmatic position" on the dictatorship of the proletariat.

Mandel thus dates the continuity of his differences with the SWP leadership on such questions as Cuba and the workers and farmers government to before the reunification of the Fourth International in 1963. These positions were presented primarily in the writings of Joseph Hansen, and in resolutions of the SWP over two decades, including most recently those on Nicaragua and Grenada. In 1977 Hansen explained that both the Cuban revolution and a review of all the overturns of capitalism since World War II made clear that a workers and farmers government is the "first form of government that can be expected to appear as the result of a successful anticapitalist revolution." (See Hansen's introduction to the SWP educational bulletin, *Workers and Farmers Governments Since the Second World War*, by Robert Chester.)

These SWP positions, according to Mandel, are a "simplistic and mechanistic . . . conception of the leadership of a revolutionary process that ended with the establishment of the dictatorship of the proletariat."

Mandel's article also refers to another public debate taking place in the Fourth International, a debate that also relates to the question of the dictatorship of the proletariat, and one that is converging with the discussion thus far described. This other debate began in 1979 following the overthrow of the murderous Pol Pot tyranny in Kampuchea and Peking's invasion of Vietnam.

Vietnam and Kampuchea

Some leaders of the Fourth International, including Mandel, condemned the use of Vietnamese troops in Kampuchea and called for their immediate, unconditional withdrawal.

Others, including leaders of the SWP, supported the actions of the Vietnamese government, which allied itself with revolutionary workers and peasants in Kampuchea to overthrow the Pol Pot regime. They said it was a big step forward for the class struggle in Indochina and a blow against imperialism.

Mandel argued that a socialist revolution took place in Kampuchea in 1975 and a workers state was established by the Pol Pot regime.

The SWP leadership, on the other hand, rejected the idea that a workers state or workers and peasants government had come into being in Kampuchea. Instead, the Kampuchean workers and peasants had been murderously crushed by a regime that instituted policies that in no sense marked an historic advance in the interests of the Kampuchean toilers.

The main documents in this debate are "Behind Differences on Military Conflicts in Southeast Asia," by Ernest Mandel (see *Intercontinental Press*, April 9, 1979); the majority and minority resolutions presented to the November 1979 World Congress of the Fourth International (see *Intercontinental Press*, June 4, 1979); "War and Revolution in Indochina—What Policy for Revolutionists?" a reply to Ernest Mandel by Steve Clark, Fred Feldman, Gus Horowitz, and Mary-Alice Waters (see *Intercontinental Press*, July 16, 1979); and "The 21 Theoretical Errors of Comrades Clark, Feldman, Horowitz, and Waters," by Ernest Mandel (see *Intercontinental Press*, May 4, 1981).

BY ERNEST MANDEL

Comrade Doug Jenness' article "Our Political Continuity with Bolshevism" (*International Socialist Review*, April 1982) opens a new stage in the debate on revolutionary strategy for the less developed countries. In his first contribution,[1] Comrade Jenness limited himself to coming up with a "new reading" of Lenin's writings. Now, he has moved to a direct attack on Trotsky and the theory of permanent revolution—often explicitly, sometimes by feigning a polemic with me.

A false method

Comrade Jenness' article examines the vital problem of revolutionary strategy for the less developed capitalist countries by means of a thoroughly false method. Instead of looking at *real revolutionary processes* as they developed from the Russian revolution of 1917 until today, studying the way social classes acted during all these revolutions, the strategies followed by the various parties and political currents that influenced or led these revolutions, the results of these strategies—the victories or defeats that ensued—he essentially concentrates on *a study of the texts*, an examination of what Lenin, Trotsky, Marx and other authors wrote on the question. This method is not materialist. It is dogmatic.

The error in Comrade Jenness' method is not just dogmatic. His dogmatism is also scholastic—he selects quotations to try and demonstrate a preconceived thesis. He can't be bothered with reading these works to find out what the authors really thought on a given topic. This is obvious from a large number of cases.

1. Basing himself on a quotation taken out of context from a polemical article written by Trotsky in 1933, *The Class Character of the Soviet State*, Comrade Jenness attributes to Trotsky (on page 50 of his article) the idea that the workers state, the dictatorship of the proletariat, was not created in Russia starting from the 1917 October revolution, but only from autumn 1918, or even 1921, or later still. There is no basis for such a supposition.

In that article, Trotsky was in fact polemicizing against those who want to apply absolute (and therefore false) norms to the definition of the dictatorship of the proletariat so as to deny the existence of a workers state in the USSR in 1933. With fine irony, he shows how such arguments lead to absurd conclusions. He tells them: if we were to follow your use of absolute norms, then the dictatorship of the proletariat would not have existed after October 1917, it would not have existed in 1918, nor in 1920, and it would not even have existed during the NEP. In other words, since you deny that it exists under Stalin, it never could have existed. But Trotsky unravels this argument to its absurd conclusion, *not because he agrees with it, but because he rejects it*. For the very paragraph Doug Jenness took the quote from ends with these words, which Comrade Jenness omitted to quote:

"To these gentlemen, the dictatorship of the proletariat is simply an imponderable concept, an ideal norm not to be realized upon our sinful planet" (Leon Trotsky, *Writings 1933–1934*, p. 140).

In the same article, Trotsky explicitly states:

"The dictatorship of the proletariat was established by means of a political overturn and a civil war of three years."

And:

"So long as the forms of property that have been *created by the October revolution* are not overthrown, the proletariat remains the ruling class" (op. cit., p. 138—our emphasis).

He defended without fail, until the end of his life, the idea that the dictatorship of the proletariat was indeed achieved by the socialist revolution of October 1917.

2. Comrade Doug Jenness states (p. 50):

"using the scientific criteria for a workers state that Marxists have used since the 1930s, based on our analysis of the bureaucratic degeneration of the Soviet workers state—a workers state did not come into existence in Russia until at least the autumn of 1918, as Trotsky explained in the 1933 article."

Comrade Doug Jenness does not produce the shadow of a proof that Trotsky or other revolutionary Marxist authors have supposedly modified, "since the 1930s," the definition of the October revolution as establishing the dictatorship of the proletariat. On the other hand, we could quote numerous documents written after the 1933 article which state exactly the opposite:

- In *The Workers State, Thermidor, and Bonapartism*, written in 1934, Trotsky stated:

"October 1917 completed the democratic revolution and began the socialist revolution. . . ."

- *The Revolution Betrayed*, written in 1936, starts with the following sentence:

1. It appeared in the *International Socialist Review* inserted in the *Militant*, Vol. 45, No. 42, November 13, 1981.

"Owing to the insignificance of the Russian bourgeoisie, the democratic tasks of backward Russia—such as the liquidation of the monarchy and the semifeudal slavery of the peasants—could be achieved only through a dictatorship of the proletariat."

- In *Ninety Years of the Communist Manifesto* (October 1937), he wrote:

"Marx later counterposed the state of the Commune type to the capitalist state. This 'type' later took the very much more graphic form of the Soviets."

- In the *Transitional Program*, written in 1938, Trotsky wrote:

"The power of the soviets, that is, the dictatorship of the proletariat."

- In his article *From a Scratch to the Danger of Gangrene*, dated January 24, 1940, Trotsky spoke of "the social foundations (of the USSR) established by the October revolution."

- Many authors who are members of the SWP hardly express things differently. In his preface to *The Transitional Program for Socialist Revolution*, published in 1973, Joseph Hansen wrote this, concerning the conception of the Russian revolution defended by Trotsky:

"He [Trotsky] did this in his theory of the permanent revolution, which correctly predicted, twelve years in advance, the course taken by the October 1917 revolution."

- Comrade Dick Roberts wrote in the September 1973 issue of *International Socialist Review*:

"In October, after the Bolsheviks won a majority inside the Soviets, Trotsky and Lenin led a socialist revolution against the provisional government, overthrowing it and establishing a proletarian dictatorship."

- And Comrade Doug Jenness himself, writing in 1970, stated:

"Although Lenin was in total accord with Trotsky's analysis that the capitalist class could not lead the Russian Revolution, before 1917 he believed that the revolution would be 'democratic' rather than socialist, i.e., that it would not go beyond the bounds of bourgeois democracy. In addition, his justified emphasis on the importance of the peasantry in the Russian Revolution led him, in describing the dynamics of the revolution, to put forward an intermediate formula ascribing to the peasant allies of labor a joint leadership role they were unable to assume. He called for a 'democratic dictatorship of the working class and peasantry' and not in *Trotsky's correct formulation, a dictatorship of the working class supported by the peasantry*" (Doug Jenness, "Introduction" to *Leon Trotsky on the Paris Commune*, N.Y.: Pathfinder, 1970).

3. On Pages 52–53 of his article, Comrade Doug Jenness suggests that Lenin in his polemic with Kautsky (*The Proletarian Revolution and the Renegade Kautsky*) had implied, or even explicitly stated ("Things have turned out just as we said they would"), that the proletariat marched alongside the peasantry as a whole in the democratic revolution, and *then with the poor peasants alone*, in the socialist revolution. But Lenin does not at all say that in his 1918 pamphlet. In fact, he states the contrary. For he is referring to the alliance between the proletariat and the peasantry *after the conquest of power by the proletariat* in October 1917, that is, *after the establishment of the dictatorship of the proletariat*, and not at all in the course of a so-called democratic revolution in February–March 1917, or some time prior to the October socialist revolution. Comrade Doug Jenness seems to have forgotten even the title of Lenin's pamphlet, which is *The PROLETARIAN* [proletarian and not bourgeois-democratic!) *Revolution and the Renegade Kautsky*. But here are some exact quotes:

Page 413: "Finally, between August and September 1917, that is *before the proletarian revolution in Russia (October 25/ November 7, 1917). . . .*"

Page 430: ". . . *the power of the soviets, that is the dictatorship of the proletariat in its given form.*"

Page 437: "He [Kautsky] does not say that in these theses (of December 26, 1917, on the Constituent Assembly) the question was treated . . . in relation to the break which emerged in our revolution *between the Constituent Assembly and the dictatorship of the proletariat.*"

Page 480: "However, a state of the Commune type, the soviet state, tells the truth openly and without ambiguity to the people, and explains to them that it is the dictatorship of the proletariat and poor peasantry" (our emphasis in all these quotations; translated from the French).

The list of quotations could be extended further. But what would be the use?

4. Furthermore, Comrade Jenness suggests in

his article (p. 53) that Lenin maintained after April 1917 that his 1905 positions were confirmed by the course of the Russian revolution of 1917. Apart from the fact that the quotations transcribed by Doug Jenness do not say that at all, but refer only to particular aspects of Lenin's position of 1905 and not to the "democratic dictatorship of the workers and peasants," Comrade Doug Jenness eliminates a little detail throughout this passage. In 1905, Lenin said: "But of course it will be a democratic, not a socialist dictatorship" (Lenin, *Collected Works*, Vol. 9, p. 56).

By contrast, after his April 1917 Theses, Lenin never again used the formula "democratic dictatorship of the workers and peasants," (why?) but referred many times to the Russian revolution as establishing (or having established) the dictatorship of the proletariat (the power of the soviets). His entire book *State and Revolution* is given over to this issue.

The Declaration of the Rights of the Working and Exploited People, written by Lenin on January 4, 1918, and submitted by the Bolshevik fraction to the Constituent Assembly—a document which, for the Bolsheviks, had an historical importance, since it was meant to be the proletarian "counterpart" to the *Declaration of the Rights of Man and the Citizen* of the great French bourgeois revolution—begins with the following words:

"Russia is hereby proclaimed a Republic of Soviets of Workers', Soldiers', and Peasants' Deputies. All power centrally and locally is vested in these Soviets" (Lenin, *CW*, Vol. 26, p. 423). We already know that for Lenin, Trotsky and the Bolsheviks, soviet power was synonymous with the dictatorship of the proletariat. Further on, point 5 of this *Declaration* states:

"To insure the sovereign power of the working people, and to eliminate all possibility of the re-establishment of the power of the exploiters, the arming of the working people, the creation of a socialist Red Army of workers and peasants, and the complete disarming of the propertied classes are hereby decreed," (Idem, p. 424).

Is there any other state than a workers state, the state of the dictatorship of the proletariat, that can decree the disarmament of the bourgeoisie, the arming of the workers, the formation of a socialist army?

The Soviet Constitution adopted in July 1918, before the nationalizations of the factories, established preferential voting rights specifically for the proletariat, and stipulated in article 23:

"*In the interests of the working class*, the Soviet Socialist Federal Republic shall deprive of their rights individuals and groups of individuals who use them to the detriment of the socialist revolution."

The program of the Bolshevik party, adopted in 1919, begins with the following words:

"The October revolution in Russia established the dictatorship of the proletariat."

The A.B.C. of Communism, a popular presentation of this program, written by Bukharin and Preobrazhensky, stated:

"The proletariat, which took power in October 1917. . . ."

The first congress of the Communist International, which met in 1919, adopted Lenin's theses on "Bourgeois Democracy and the Dictatorship of the Proletariat," which state:

"The form of the dictatorship of the proletariat which is already being practically worked out, that is the power of the soviets. . . ."

". . . what defines the power of the soviets is that all soviet state power, the whole state apparatus has a single and permanent basis, the mass organization of the classes that were oppressed by capitalism, that is the workers and semiproletarians. . . ."

The point is clear: Comrade Doug Jenness can only establish an alleged "continuity" with the 1905 positions of Bolshevism on strategy for the Russian revolution by first junking the whole continuity of the positions of Lenin, the Bolshevik Party, the Communist International, Trotsky, the Left Opposition, and the Fourth International, from April 1917 until today.

5. Comrade Doug Jenness protests against my statement (although it is taken literally from Trotsky) that one of the reasons for the differences between Lenin and Trotsky from 1905 to 1916 was the fact that Lenin expected that a victory of the Russian revolution under "the democratic dictatorship of the workers and peasants" would inaugurate a long period of *capitalist* development in Russia, the economic and social prerequisite for the later victory of the socialist revolution (the old thesis of the whole Russian Social-Democracy

first formulated by Plekhanov and reasserted in the Party program drafted jointly by Lenin and Plekhanov, which only Trotsky had challenged in 1905–1906).

To support his point, Doug Jenness quotes the famous sentence from Lenin's 1905 pamphlet *Two Tactics of Social-Democracy in the Democratic Revolution*, a sentence in which Lenin asserts that one should not erect a Chinese wall between the democratic and socialist revolutions. In our opinion, this sentence refers not to the *victory* of the socialist revolution (i.e., the seizure of power by the proletariat) but to the *beginning of the struggle* for the seizure of power. The whole context demonstrates this. At any rate, Comrade Doug Jenness' quote is selective to the point of being scandalous. For the fact is that in the same pamphlet, Lenin writes exactly what Mandel (and Trotsky before him) claimed he did concerning the possibility of *a capitalist development of Russia* as a result of the victory of the democratic revolution:

". . . under the present social and economic order this democratic revolution in Russia will not weaken but strengthen the domination of the bourgeoisie . . ." (Lenin, *CW*, Vol. 9, p. 23).

"Finally, we will note that the resolution, by making implementation of the minimum programme the provisional revolutionary government's task, eliminates the absurd and semi-anarchist ideas of giving immediate effect to the maximum programme, and the conquest of power for a socialist revolution. *The degree of Russia's economic development (an objective condition), and the degree of class-consciousness and organisation of the broad masses of the proletariat (a subjective condition inseparably bound up with the objective condition)* make the immediate and complete emancipation of the working class impossible" (Idem, p. 28, emphasis added).

We should add that this "maximum programme" scarcely mentions classless society and gives the "complete emancipation of the proletariat" the meaning of the establishment of . . . the dictatorship of the proletariat.

"Marxists are absolutely convinced of the bourgeois character of the Russian revolution. What does that mean? It means that the democratic reforms in the political system, and the social and economic reforms that have become a necessity for Russia, do not in themselves imply the undermining of capitalism, the undermining of bourgeois rule; on the contrary, they will, for the first time, really clear the ground *for a wide and rapid European, and not Asiatic, development of capitalism*" (Idem, p. 48—emphasis added).

"In countries like Russia the working class suffers not so much from capitalism as from the insufficient development of capitalism. The working class is, therefore, *most certainly interested* in the broadest, freest, and most rapid development of capitalism. . . ."

"That is why a *bourgeois* revolution is *in the highest degree advantageous to the proletariat*" (Idem, p. 45–50—emphasis in original).

A few months later, Lenin wrote *Socialism and the Peasantry* and stated even more clearly:

"Bourgeois in its social and economic essence, the democratic revolution cannot but express the needs of all bourgeois society" (Idem, p 307).

"The mass of the peasants do not and cannot realise that the fullest 'freedom' and the 'justest' distribution even of all the land, far from destroying capitalism will, on the contrary, create the conditions for a *particularly extensive and powerful development of capitalism*" (Idem, p. 309—emphasis added).

Similarly, in his 1905 article entitled "The Petty-Bourgeoisie and Proletarian Socialism," he stated:

"In Russia, just as was the case in other countries, it is a necessary concomitant of the democratic revolution, which is bourgeois in its social and economic content. It is not in the least directed against the foundations of the bourgeois order, against commodity production or against capital. . . . *Consequently, full victory of this peasant movement will not abolish capitalism: on the contrary, it will create a broader foundation for its development, and will hasten and intensify purely capitalist development.* Full victory of the peasant uprising can only create a stronghold for a *democratic bourgeois republic* within which a proletarian struggle against the bourgeoisie will for the first time develop in its purest form" (Idem, p. 440—emphasis added).

Lenin's article on "The aim of the struggle of the proletariat in our revolution," written March 9–21, 1909, is sometimes quoted to make the opposite point: it does discuss the proletariat as "the guide," "the leader" of the revolution, "drawing the peasantry in behind it." The same article gives an important role to soviets along with participation in the revolutionary government (Lenin, *CW*, Vol. 15).

But an objective review of the context clearly shows that what is being discussed is still the role of soviets in a *democratic, non-socialist, non-permanent revolution*, that is, in a situation in which the social and economic foundations of capitalism have not been shattered but rather are being intentionally *fostered*.

This follows clearly from a comparison of the stated article with another one Lenin wrote, a few months later, and entitled *Some Sources of the Present Ideological Discord* (November 28, 1909). This article states with no possible uncertainty or misunderstanding:

". . . the bourgeois development of Russia is now a foregone conclusion but it is possible in two forms—the so-called 'Prussian' form (the retention of the monarchy and landlordism, the creation of a strong, i.e., bourgeois, peasantry on the given historical basis, etc.) and the so-called 'American' form (a bourgeois republic, the abolition of landlordism, the creation of a farmer class, i.e., of a free bourgeois peasantry, by means of a marked change of the given historical situation). The proletariat must fight for the second path as offering the greatest degree of freedom and speed of development of the productive forces of capitalist Russia, and *victory in this struggle* is possible only with a revolutionary alliance between the proletariat and the peasantry" (Lenin, *CW*, Vol. 16. pp. 87–88—emphasis added).

"The proletariat must put its stake on democracy, without exaggerating the latter's strength and without limiting itself to merely 'pinning hopes' on it, but steadily developing the work of propaganda, agitation and organisation, mobilising all the democratic forces—the peasants above all and before all—calling upon them to ally themselves with the leading class, *to achieve the 'dictatorship of the proletariat and the peasantry' for the purpose of a full democratic victory and the creation of the best conditions for the quickest and freest development of capitalism*" (Idem, p. 94—emphasis added).

Unless one assumes Lenin contradicted himself not only between March and December 1909, but also inside the very article he wrote in March 1909 (which contains formulations of the same type as that of December 1909), there is no room for doubt. The revolutionary government he speaks of, as well as the soviets, are in his eyes formations akin to those of the Jacobins of 1792–93, and of the *Jacobin clubs*, i.e., bodies meant to carry out a bourgeois-democratic revolution, to open the road not to expropriations, but to the take-off of capitalism.

In light of all these quotes—and many others could be added both from 1905 and from the period stretching to 1916[2]—it is a genuine falsification of Lenin's positions to claim that the great Russian revolutionary did not, in 1905, foresee a lengthy capitalist development in Russia (as occurred in other countries which underwent a bourgeois revolution, i.e., Great Britain, the United States, France, etc.) or only foresaw it in agriculture. Lenin says: a purely capitalist development, the rule of Capital; how could they possibly exist if capital was destroyed in industry and banking?

6. No doubt, the algebraic formulas of the Bolsheviks in 1905 allowed for interpretations that imply support for the bourgeois provisional government of February–March 1917, although other interpretations were also possible. Hence the need for rearming the party after the outbreak of the February 1917 revolution. Hence the historically decisive function of Lenin's April Theses, which we emphasized in our first article.[3]

Comrade Doug Jenness systematically plays down the importance of the turn represented by the April Theses. He even goes so far as to deny that there was a real turn, and heavily emphasizes instead the continuity. He quotes a passage from Marcel Liebman's book *Leninism Under Lenin* dealing with the allegedly correct position of

2. "The international proletariat undermines capital in two ways: by transforming Octobrist capital into democratic capital, and by transplanting it among the savages—by chasing Octobrist capital from its home. This broadens the basis of capital and brings it closer to its doom. In Western Europe, there is already almost no Octobrist capital left because all capital is democratic. Octobrist capital migrated from England and France towards Russia and Asia. *The Russian revolution and the revolutions in Asia are the struggle to chase Octobrist capital and replace it with democratic capital*" ("Letter from Lenin to Gorky," January 3, 1911, in Lenin, *CW*, vol. 34, p. 439; translated from the French).

3. Ernest Mandel, "Nature and Perspectives of the Russian Revolution", *International Socialist Review*, inserted in the *Militant*, April 1982.

Shliapnikov and other Bolshevik leaders prior to Lenin's return to Russia. It so happens Jenness is mistaken even in this minor detail. But that is not the main point.

The main point, once more, is that Jenness has Liebman say exactly the opposite of what he actually said. Here is what Liebman actually writes on the "turn" of the April Theses:

"Thus the difference between Lenin and the Bolshevik leadership in Russia was deep-going and wide-ranging. . . . In the last analysis, all these political disagreements were derived from a more important cause. Lenin saw differently from his chief supporters the fundamental problem that faced the Russian labour movement in 1917, and which was bound up with the very nature of the revolution in progress. The entire tactic adopted by the Bolshevik leaders in Russia, with its caution, moderation and concern for unity with the Mensheviks, reflected a belief that the Bolshevik leaders shared with the Right-wing Socialists. As they saw it, the fall of Tsarism was the first victory in the bourgeois revolution, which must be followed up by other successes, and in this way consolidated, without there being any question of going beyond the limits of such a revolution and undertaking socialist tasks. . . . This was an opinion Lenin had held for a long time and that only the 1905 revolution led him to question albeit without replacing it with a sufficiently elaborated new perspective" (Liebman, *Leninism Under Lenin*, London, Merlin Press, 1975, p. 127).

7. Because he systematically downplays the turn represented by the April Theses, Doug Jenness must distort the facts, the historical truth. He keeps mum about the first vote of the St. Petersburg party committee which rejected the April Theses 13 to 2 with one abstention,[4] and of the Moscow and Kiev party committees which did likewise. Nor does Doug Jenness mention that Lenin himself proclaimed: *"Old Bolshevism must be abandoned!"* (Lenin, *CW*, Vol. 24). "Old Bolshevism" obviously meant the 1905 positions on the nature of the revolution and revolutionary strategy—positions Doug Jenness now wants to uphold *against* Lenin's advice, rather than abandoning them. Nor does he utter a word about the fact that all the interpretations of the April Theses until the mid-20s, that is, until the victory of counterrevolutionary Stalinist monolithism, unanimously considered the Theses represented a decisive turn.

Here is what Stalin himself—who scarcely needed additional attention drawn to the event, since he was among its main instigators—wrote as late as 1926:

"[The party] adopted a policy of Soviet pressure on the provisional government on the question of peace, and did not immediately decide to take the step that would have carried it from the old slogan of dictatorship of the proletariat and peasantry, to the new slogan of power to the soviets . . . this was a profoundly mistaken position" (*On the Opposition*).

8. Comrade Doug Jenness reproaches us with having stated that Trotsky discovered the law of uneven and combined development, which he claims is intrinsic to historical materialism (pp. 66–67). But the quote he produces to back up his contention refers to the law of uneven development, that Marx obviously knew. The law of uneven *and combined* development is a *second* law. It was, indeed, discovered by Trotsky. Let us examine the following quote and ask ourselves whether Marx, Plekhanov, or Lenin, ever wrote anything of the kind (at least Lenin before 1917):

"Russia *entered the road of proletarian revolution not because its economy was the ripest for socialist transformation, but because that economy could no longer develop on capitalist foundations.* The socialization of the means of production had become the necessary condition above all to lift the country out of barbarism: *such is the law of combined development for backward countries*" (*The Revolution Betrayed*; translated from the French—emphasis added).

"Russia's evolution is characterized above all by its lateness. A historical lag does not mean, however, a mere repetition of the evolution of advanced countries, with a delay of one or two hundred years, *but gives birth to an entirely new, 'combined,' social formation* in which the latest achievements of capitalist technology and structure take root in the social relations of feudal and prefeudal barbarism, transform them and subordinate them, *thereby cre-*

4. This figure is quoted by the very official *History of the USSR*, by Aragon, Vol. 1, p. 51. Liebman mentions three votes in favor of Lenin's Theses.

ating an original relationship between classes" (*Three Conceptions of the Russian Revolution*; translated from the French—emphasis added).

Moreover, we would like to know whether Comrade Doug Jenness will reject the testimony of the following witness, as well as what the witness himself now thinks of his rather definitive assertions of 1973:

"Trotsky himself made *prodigious theoretical contributions to Marxism* in his celebrated theory of the permanent revolution, *in his formulation of the law of uneven and combined development*, and in his program for the regeneration of workers democracy in an unhealthy workers state" (George Novack, "Introduction" to *The Transitional Program for Socialist Revolution*, New York: Pathfinder Press, 1973—our emphasis).

9. Doug Jenness protests against Mandel's assertion (which is really Trotsky's) that Lenin went over to Trotsky's pre-1917 position on the strategy of permanent revolution (p. 65). But he keeps mum about the fact that, as early as the April Theses, Lenin speaks of the need for *a workers government* in Russia. He keeps mum about Joffe's testament which states Lenin explicitly told Joffe that Trotsky had been right on the question of permanent revolution. Did Joffe lie about this on the eve of his suicide?

Jenness remains silent on Trotsky's 1927 statement that:

"Upon our group's arrival in Petrograd, comrade Fedorov, then a member of the Bolshevik Central Committee, welcomed us in its name at the Finland station and in his speech of welcome posed sharply the question of the next stages of the revolution, *the dictatorship of the proletariat and the socialist course of development.* The reply I gave was in full accord with Lenin's April Theses which, for me, flowed unfailingly from the theory of the permanent revolution. As comrade Fedorov told subsequently, the fundamental point of his speech had been formulated by him in agreement with Lenin, or, more accurately, at Lenin's direction" (Leon Trotsky, *The Stalin School of Falsification*, p. 29—emphasis added).

Did Trotsky lie? Moreover, where did Comrade Doug Jenness fetch the assertion that Trotsky had become "Leninist" on the question of revolutionary strategy for Russia the moment he joined the Bolshevik Party in 1917? Doug Jenness produces not the slightest shred of evidence, not a single document, not a single quote, to support his contention, which is false from A to Z. The truth is that from 1904 to his death in 1940 Trotsky did not change his position one iota on the applicability of the theory of the permanent revolution to Russia. He only extended it, subsequently, beginning in 1927, to other less developed capitalist countries—as did the Fourth International, and as did the SWP (that is, its founding nucleus, the Communist League of America, when it joined the International Left Opposition).[5]

The nub of the issue

On this question of the theory of the permanent revolution, Doug Jenness manages to pile confusion upon contradiction upon deplorable mistake. Yet it revolves around a single and central problem: *under what government, in what state, could the bourgeois-democratic tasks of the revolution on the agenda in Russia, be accomplished*? What flowed from this in terms of the inevitable dynamic of the revolution?

The Mensheviks said: because the tasks of the revolution are bourgeois-democratic, only a bourgeois government and a bourgeois state can accomplish them. Any attempt by the working class to take power "prematurely" would lead to a revolutionary setback and a catastrophe for the revolution.

Trotsky answered: in the imperialist epoch, given the extent of capitalist development in Russia and the weight of the proletariat on the one hand, and the close intertwining of land ownership and capitalist property on the other, the bourgeoisie will inevitably go over to the camp of counterrevolution. If the bourgeoisie maintains its hegemony within the revolution, the revolution will be defeated.

---

5. The first programmatic document of the International Left Opposition, of which the Communist League of America led by James P. Cannon was part and parcel, stated: "Rejection of the democratic dictatorship of the proletariat and peasantry formula as a specific regime different from the dictatorship of the proletariat drawing the peasant masses, and the oppressed masses in general, behind it. Rejection of the anti-Marxist theory of the peaceful transformation of the democratic dictatorship into a socialist dictatorship" ("The International Left Opposition, its tasks, its methods, February 1933," *The Congresses of the Fourth International*, Vol. 1, p. 62; translated from the French).

The only class capable of leading the revolutionary process is the proletariat. To do so, it must ally with the poor peasantry, and win the support of the majority of the peasantry (the majority of the nation). But it can do so only by destroying the bourgeois state and dominating the government. In this endeavor, lest it demoralize itself and thereby cause a defeat of the revolution, it cannot limit itself solely to implementing the revolutionary-democratic tasks of the revolution; it must simultaneously *begin* to resolve the socialist tasks (not all of them, and not instantly, of course, but at least some of them).[6] By the same token, any notion of a "two-class" government, not to mention a "two-class state," is a complete utopia. *The tasks of the national-democratic revolution will be accomplished by the establishment of the dictatorship of the proletariat allied to the poor peasantry*, that is, by the destruction of the bourgeois state and the creation of a new type of state, the state of the Commune, the state of the Soviets, the state of the dictatorship of the proletariat. Only the proletariat and its *decisive predominance* within the government can guarantee the revolution will move forward to victory. Every other strategic line of march will lead the revolution to defeat.

Prior to 1917, Lenin had adopted an intermediate position in between these two clearly counterposed positions. His outlook fluctuated over the years. Trotsky was therefore right to characterize it as based on an *algebraic formula*. Like Trotsky, Lenin rejected any notion that the bourgeoisie, or a coalition government with the bourgeoisie, could realize the tasks of the national-democratic revolution in Russia. Like Trotsky, he held that these tasks could only be accomplished against the bourgeoisie. But, unlike Trotsky, he did not specify, prior to April 1917, that their accomplishment also required the destruction of the bourgeois state apparatus, that is, not the establishment of a bourgeois-democratic republic (see the 1905 quotations mentioned above), but the dictatorship of the proletariat, the rule of the soviets. The reason for his hesitation was that he did not exclude the hypothesis of a revolutionary government in which the proletariat would not be hegemonic, in which the proletariat and peasantry would have equal weight, or even one with a peasant majority.

True, Lenin, under the direct impact of the 1905 revolution—especially in 1906—shifted his position closer to Trotsky's, even spoke of the proletariat with the poor peasantry alone,[7] and mentioned a rapid transition to the "socialist phase" of the revolution. But, following the victory of the counterrevolution, he basically reverted to the 1905 formulations: *bourgeois*-democratic republic; development of capitalism in Russia; shift of the workers party into the opposition as soon as the democratic revolution triumphed.

What was the nub of this difference? It had nothing to do with any "underestimation" of the peasantry by Trotsky. That is a legend of the Thermidorians, the epigones of Lenin, passed on and amplified by the various anti-Trotskyist Stalinist and post-Stalinist factions (including the Maoists), a legend which Comrade Doug Jenness now suddenly wants to make his own, although the SWP

6. The Cuban leaders themselves clearly state that the national-democratic tasks overlapped and intertwined with the anti-capitalist tasks in the twentieth-century Cuban revolution. They are therefore more "Trotskyist" than Comrade Doug Jenness:

"The content of our revolution which, in the colonial period, could not go beyond the limits of a national liberation movement based on the liberal principles of the last century, necessarily had to shift, by virtue of the capitalist development of our country and the emergence of the working class, towards a revolution that was also social. To the task of freeing the nation from imperialist domination, was added inevitably, thenceforth, the task of liquidating the exploitation of man by man in our society. These two objectives were already part of our historical process since the capitalist system that oppressed us from the outside as a nation, oppressed us and exploited us from the inside as workers, and since the social forces that could free the country from the inside from oppression, that is to say the workers themselves, were the only forces that, on the external plane, could support us against the imperialist power that was oppressing the nation" (Fidel Castro, *Balance Sheet of the Cuban Revolution*. Report to the First Congress of the Cuban Communist Party, December 1975; translated from the French—our emphasis).

7. See Lenin, "The crisis of Menshevism," *CW*, Vol. 11, December 1906: "Larin states that the disturbances in the countryside cannot be stopped. Did he prove it? No. He took no account whatsoever of the role of the peasant bourgeoisie which is systematically corrupted by the government. He gave little attention to the fact that the 'reliefs' obtained by the peasantry . . . intensify the break among the rural population between the counterrevolutionary rich and the poor masses" (translated from the French).

combated it all along the fifty years of its existence. Trotsky always emphasized the decisive role of the peasants in the Russian revolution, given the predominant weight of the peasantry in the active population. Like Lenin, he rejected the putschist, "Blanquist," notion of a revolution supported only by a minority of the masses of the people (the working-class minority). Like Lenin, he emphasized the need for *a broad soviet organization of the peasantry*.

The real difference lay elsewhere. Trotsky rejected the idea that the peasantry could form *a political party, a political force, that was truly independent*, both of the bourgeoisie and proletariat. Yet, willy nilly, a government must be composed of political parties, or of groups acting as de facto parties. For Trotsky, "a coalition government" of workers and peasants parties could only lead to the victory of the revolution if the latter *followed the leadership of the proletariat in moving towards the smashing of the bourgeois state apparatus*, that is, if they were not bourgeois peasant parties but peasant "parties" or "groups" that were satellites of the proletariat. For Lenin until 1916, the possibility of genuine peasant parties, independent of both the bourgeoisie and proletariat, was not excluded. Hence the imprecise nature of his formulas *on the government and the state* that would lead the revolution to victory.

But beginning in 1917, Lenin resolved this question *in the same way as Trotsky*. We see the following:

"A mass Social-Democratic movement has existed in Russia for twenty years (if one takes the great 1896 strikes as its beginning). One can see over this great time period, through two powerful revolutions, through the whole political history of Russia, that the same essential question was raised: will the working class lead the peasants forward, towards socialism, or will the liberal bourgeois take them backwards towards a reconciliation with capitalism?" (V.I. Lenin, *CW*, Vol. 25, September 11, 1917, p. 303; translated from the French).

"Our experience taught us—and this is confirmed *by the development of all the revolutions of the world*, if one considers the present epoch, that is, the last one hundred and fifty years—that this was so everywhere and always; all attempts by the petty-bourgeoisie in general, and by the peasants in particular, to become aware of their own strength, to lead the economy and politics in their fashion, led to a failure. Either they were placed under the leadership of the proletariat, or under that of the capitalists. There is no middle ground. Those who dream of a middle term are but dreamers, empty-dreamers" ("Speech to the Congress of Transport Workers," March 29–30, 1921; translated from the French—our emphasis).

Dictatorship of the proletariat or 'two-class government': the historical balance sheet

The real criterion for judging the problem of permanent revolution is not, of course, what Trotsky, or Lenin, or whoever, wrote in 1905, 1906, 1909, 1917, or 1921. It is what actually happened in history. The balance sheet, here, is clear and illuminating. Wherever the historical tasks of the national-democratic revolution as a whole—above all the agrarian question—were accomplished, this was due to the fact that the proletariat, with the support of the poor peasantry, had previously taken power, smashed the bourgeois state, and built a state of a new type, that is to say, the dictatorship of the proletariat, even though this may have taken place in a highly bureaucratized form and under the leadership of an extremely bureaucratized workers party (except in Cuba). Wherever the bourgeois state was preserved, the solution of the national-democratic tasks of the revolution remained in abeyance. In fact, the counterrevolution eventually won out, even though sometimes in a "diluted" form, as in Algeria. But it often was not that diluted: remember Iraq, Egypt, Bolivia at the end of the 1950s and in 1971. And many times it meant counterrevolutionary bloodbaths: China in 1927, Indonesia, Iran after Mossadegh, Brazil, Chile, Uruguay, Turkey, to mention only a few instances.

But nowhere, in no historical case, was there something in between a country that would have experienced a broad popular revolution in which millions of workers and peasants actively participated, which led neither to the establishment of the dictatorship of the proletariat nor to a victory of the counterrevolution, but to the implementation of a thoroughgoing land reform under a "two-class" regime or government in which the working class and peasantry would have shared roughly equal power, that is, with no clear and definite proletarian hegemony.

Is this what happened in the Yugoslav revolution? Then, where was the "independent peasant party" or "independent mass organization" in the 1945 Yugoslav government? Is this what happened in the Vietnamese revolution? Then when and where did we see such "independent" peasant formations appear in the Vietnamese revolutionary government, formations comparable in weight to the VCP? Did it happen in the Cuban revolution? Where and when were such "peasant formations" comparable in weight to the July 26 Movement, part of the Cuban governments of 1958, of 1960, or 1961? Has this happened even in the Nicaraguan revolution? Where can we find such "representatives of the peasantry" in the Revolutionary Directorate or governments that have ruled since Somoza was overthrown, to say nothing of representatives comparable in weight to the Sandinistas?

Comrade Doug Jenness refers to the case of the coalition government which existed in Soviet Russia between December 1917 and March 1918. He considers the Bolshevik-Left SR government was the very model of the "workers and farmers government" without clear proletarian hegemony, that is, without the dictatorship of the proletariat. This gets him entangled in some chronological problems. According to him, the dictatorship of the proletariat was only established in October 1918.

Yet the Left-SRs only left the government in March 1918. What then was the purely Bolshevik government from March to October 1918? A "workers and peasants government" without peasants? Or could the "governmental representatives of the peasantry" have infiltrated the very ranks of the Bolshevik Party itself?

The real problems are far more serious. First of all, the Left-SRs never had equivalent weight with the Bolsheviks, whether in the government or the Executive Committee of the Soviets. Bolshevik hegemony was clearly established everywhere. Moreover, the Left-SRs never represented "the peasantry as a whole." Otherwise, how could one explain the *split* within the SRs? What would the Right-SRs, who had an absolute majority of peasant votes in the Constituent Assembly, have represented? Finally, one has to resort to extraordinary acrobatics to portray the Left-SRs as a "peasant party." This was a party which advanced the dictatorship of the proletariat, the rule of the soviets, the elimination of capitalist private property (including in the countryside) and wage slavery (including in the countryside). Can Comrade Doug Jenness produce a single other instance, anywhere in the world, where a "peasant party" had a program and an orientation of that kind?

In order to fit the real historical process into his preconceived schema, Comrade Doug Jenness is forced to uncover "representatives of the peasantry" inside . . . the workers parties (or the bureaucratized and petty-bourgeoisified workers parties) themselves, that is, to move from the revisionist formula of "two-class government" to the even more revisionist formula of "two-class parties." This emerges clearly from his reference to the Chinese revolution:

"(It's ironic that Mandel, more than three decades after the Chinese revolution, should still be defending the view that there cannot be peasant parties and peasant organizations and that a peasant revolution cannot play any independent role in a social revolution. In China a peasant army headed by a peasant party and with a petty-bourgeois Stalinist leadership made a revolution that opened the door to historic conquests, however badly deformed, of the Chinese proletariat—that is, the establishment of the Chinese workers state.)"

A social revolution means that state power passes from one class to another amidst tumultuous events including the smashing of the state apparatus of the old ruling class and the formation of a new state that serves as the instrument for the rule of another class. Comrade Jenness would have us believe that this event did not take place in 1949, in full view of the entire world, but only in 1953 or 1954, when no one noticed, except a few Trotskyist theoreticians. He would have us believe that the People's Republic of China, established in 1949 by a revolutionary government, was a bourgeois state led by a "peasant government" (or in the best of cases, by a "workers and peasants government under peasant hegemony," since the army was "peasant").

But he runs into a slight problem: it was *this state and this government* that, without any break in continuity, destroyed not only capitalist private property but even peasant private property! When, then, was there a change in the Chinese Communist Party, or in the Chinese army, between 1949 and 1954? Is not the idea of a "peasant" party and a "peasant" army that destroy peasant property, pushing things a bit far from the standpoint of Marxism? Is this not turning dialectics into gross sophistry?

Moreover, if we moved, *without a new revolution*, from the bourgeois state of 1949 to the "dictatorship of the proletariat" of 1953, does not this mean that we can pass from the one to the other by peaceful, gradual means? Are we not then beginning to rerun the whole "reformist scenario," to borrow a formula from Trotsky? Does not that mean abandoning the whole Marxist theory of revolution after abandoning that of the state?

Comrade Doug Jenness' error obviously arises from the fact that he confuses the largest social component of a party or an army with its actual structure, including its command structure, the objective role it plays in society, and the class interests it serves historically. If we look at the class composition of an imperialist army, it is mainly proletarian. Yet no one can seriously doubt that it is a bourgeois army, because of its command structure, because of the role it has played and still plays as an instrument that defends the bourgeois state and the interests of the bourgeoisie, even when there are "bourgeois workers parties" in the government, as in Great Britain under the Labour government or in France under the Mitterrand-Mauroy regime. Likewise, despite its predominantly working-class social composition, the Peronist party of Argentina is a bourgeois party. Likewise also, the Chinese People's Liberation Army, not to mention the Chinese Communist Party, which have been the historical instruments of the destruction of capitalist property and peasant property, can only be considered a "peasant" army or party by emptying Marxist class analysis of all its substance.

Thus the case of China confirms most resoundingly Trotsky's prediction and the verdict of the Russian revolution. The peasantry, although capable of mobilizing by the millions, and by the tens of millions, in the course of a revolutionary process such as the Chinese, is incapable of playing, at least on a national level, a political role independent of both the proletariat and the bourgeoisie. Its colossal revolutionary forces are centralized either under bourgeois leadership—in which case the revolution heads for certain defeat—or under proletarian leadership (even though it may be extremely bureaucratized, as in China) and in that case, and that case only, the victory of the revolution is possible.

In China, it was the Chinese CP, a bureaucratized proletarian party, a petty-bourgeoisified workers party if you wish (we decidedly prefer the first formula over the second), a party that had inscribed the dictatorship of the proletariat in its program and that had charted a course towards establishing the dictatorship of the proletariat *in fact* if not in theory,[8] a party that was able to centralize and unify under its command—and not under the command of some "independent peasant force" or other—the immense revolutionary potential of the peasantry. This is what allowed the Chinese revolution to be victorious through the establishment of the dictatorship of the proletariat.

Why is the question of the dictatorship of the proletariat, of the smashing of the bourgeois state apparatus, of the seizure of political power, so decisive for the future of a people's revolution in a less developed capitalist country? From the intertwining of the interests of landowners and capitalists, of the "national" bourgeoisie and imperialism, of the *compradore* bourgeoisie and the industrial bourgeoisie, of usurers, bankers, and finance capital, which is characteristic of the less developed capitalist countries' economy, there follows that, as the popular revolution unfolds, as the mass mobilizations extend, as their anger deepens and their militancy sharpens, the masses threaten "to take their destiny into their own hands," that is, to implement *themselves* the expropriation of landowners, usurers, imperialist properties, and even some "national bourgeois" sectors.

8. At the time, the Chinese CP wanted to defend at all cost Mao Tse-tung's erroneous theory on "new democracy" and persisted in denying what it had done in 1949, that is, establish the dictatorship of the proletariat with the support of the peasantry. Later on, it rectified its theoretical position, and now states that from October 1949 onwards, the dictatorship of the proletariat has existed in the People's Republic of China. See the new Statutes adopted at the 1977 Congress: "The state established after victory in the new-democratic revolution was a People's Republic under the dictatorship of the proletariat."

The bourgeoisie is perfectly aware of this. It strives, doubtless through all sorts of maneuvers, including alliances with opportunist workers parties (sometimes disguised as "peasant parties"), to postpone the time of reckoning. But the moment *of the beginning of its expropriation* gets inexorably closer, *because of the very logic of the mass movement*, whatever learned (that is, hemming and hawing) tactic the conciliationist leaders of the workers movement may use.

This is why the entire fundamental strategic orientation of the bourgeoisie in the revolution is to prepare a counterrevolutionary coup to disarm, or to smash, the masses. This was the case in France in 1848 and 1871. This was the case in Spain in 1931–37. It was so in China in 1925–27 and in 1946–49. It was so, too, in many other revolutions. It was so in Russia in 1917–18. The fundamental line of the Russian bourgeoisie was not the bourgeois-democratic revolution, not the Constituent Assembly, but Kornilov, Krasov, Denikin, Koltchak, Wrangel.

To foil this strategy, it is necessary to arm the workers and peasants, to centralize their armed power, that is, to establish their political power, that is, to constitute a dictatorship of the proletariat supported by the poor peasantry. *The irony of history makes the survival of the bourgeois state in the epoch of imperialism (and already before then) the main obstacle to the implementation of the tasks of the bourgeois-democratic revolution.*

Comrade Doug Jenness managed the feat of writing 35,000 words on the problem of the permanent revolution *without saying a single word to answer this burning question in all twentieth century revolutions.* We have entered this debate in defense of the theory of the permanent revolution with passion, neither out of some filial piety towards Comrade Trotsky, nor out of some "obstinate traditionalism" toward the program of the Fourth International, but *because one hundred years of historical experience confirms that the real revolutionary processes of our century actually are permanent revolution processes.*

It follows that one cannot cast the lessons of the theory of permanent revolution overboard without causing the defeat of millions and tens of millions of workers and peasants. We discuss this question with passion because it concerns the life and blood of our class, not just some written formulas in books. The sharpest clarity is needed on this question lest the proletariat, the poor peasants, and their vanguards, be drawn into a bloody trap, under the guise of apparently confused formulas that actually spell doom for the revolution.

What we are speaking of is *the strategic orientation* that revolutionaries must adopt to move towards smashing the bourgeoisie's power and state, that is, towards the dictatorship of the proletariat, and not of the agitational slogans to be used on the road to power. That kind of confusion was promoted by the Thermidorian epigones of Lenin after 1923, and revived by the various Stalinist and post-Stalinist factions, until, alas, Comrade Doug Jenness took his turn at it.

No sensible person, beginning with Trotsky, ever said that one could establish the dictatorship of the proletariat, that is, take power, by mobilizing the masses under *the slogan* of "dictatorship of the proletariat" or "workers government," independently of the concrete social, economic, political, and military situation of a given country at a given moment.

The famous slogan "Down with the tsar; for a workers government" never was Trotsky's slogan, neither in 1905 nor in 1917. By contrast, opportunist leaderships, on the grounds that slogans should be flexible and appropriate to carefully analyzed concrete situations, have led innumerable revolutions to their doom, by refusing to chart a course towards the conquest of power and the destruction of the bourgeois state when this was possible.

The pretext of the "stage" of "the coalition with the peasantry as a whole," *without the previous destruction of the bourgeois state*, was also used on innumerable occasions, including by the opportunist leadership of the Sri Lankan LSSP, which claimed to be Trotskyist, when it presented its alliance with the bourgeois SLFP as an alliance "with the peasantry." This is the deadly opportunism to which the vacillations of Comrade Doug Jenness on the dictatorship of the proletariat have now opened the way.

There is no state that is neither a bourgeois nor a workers state, and there cannot be. The revisionist Kautsky believed that between the dictatorship of the bourgeoisie and the dictatorship of the proletariat there stood a coalition between the two. For revolutionary Marxism, between the dictatorship of the bourgeoisie and the dictatorship of the proletariat, there is a phase of dual power, that is, of struggle to the death between the old ruling class and the new class aspiring to rule.

This dual power can take the most diverse and unforeseen forms. Each new living revolution generally reveals another variant, as is the case with the current revolution in Nicaragua. This struggle to the death does not stop with the establishment of the dictatorship of the proletariat. It may continue with a civil war despite the existence of the power of a workers state. The dictatorship of the proletariat, once established, may even subsequently be overthrown, as was the case in Hungary in 1919. But in all of these cases we are dealing with *antagonistic forms of state power pitted one against the other,* not property forms pitted one against the other. Dual power ends either when the organs of proletarian power, or when the remains of bourgeois political power, have disappeared *on the level of the state* (the army, police, judiciary, constitution, law and administration). Moreover, this does not exclude the possibility that they may later revive; but "reviving" is precisely different from "surviving." The former implies that they previously *disappeared.*

Any revolutionary Marxist knows this since 1917. It was definitively clarified in Lenin's *State and Revolution* and the documents of the first four congresses of the C.I. But Doug Jenness has now smeared a thick layer of confusion over it. He writes:

"Lenin and other Bolsheviks at this time used many different formulations to characterize the soviet government: 'workers and peasants government,' 'socialist republic of soviets,' 'dictatorship of the proletariat,' 'dictatorship of the proletariat and poor peasantry,' 'people's government,' and so on" (p. 48).

We should stress that *we are not dealing with different formulations.* If one leaves out the formula "government of the people," which is never found in any document of the slightest programmatic importance, *all these formulas are synonymous.* The Transitional Program explicitly asserts: "For the Bolsheviks, the workers and peasants' government formula was used prior to the October revolution as a synonym for dictatorship of the proletariat." Will Comrade Doug Jenness claim that Comrade Trotsky was deliberately or unconsciously falsifying history when he asserted this in 1938?

We do not challenge the fact that if one goes through Lenin's writings, *one can* find in 1917–1918 ambiguous and even contradictory formulas. But only a sophist would rip one or two paragraphs in a polemical text out of their context and place them on an equal footing, or even above, *the dozens* of quotations from programmatic texts and theoretical writings that assert exactly the opposite. The correct method is to reinterpret these few slips of the pen in the light of the *theoretical continuity* embodied by *all* the Communist programmatic documents from 1917 to 1923, and the revolutionary Marxist ones from 1917 until today.

We know of many revolutions that were *lost* because a counterposition was deliberately created between, on the one hand, the need to mobilize the peasantry, the importance of democratic demands, the "bourgeois-democratic nature of the tasks of the revolution," and, on the other hand, the need to orient towards the seizure of power by the proletariat allied to the poor peasantry. Doug Jenness' ambiguous formulas reintroduce this counterposition, albeit only in undertones, into the ranks of our movement, which until now had been most effectively armed on the programmatic level against the danger of turning democratic demands, or "the democratic stage of the revolution," into a "noose tied around the neck of the proletariat," as the Transitional Program put it. We know of *no revolution* that was lost because it prematurely entered on the road to the dictatorship of the proletariat.

Lenin, of course, cannot be made to bear the least responsibility for any policy of revolution by stages that implies an alliance with the bourgeoisie, or with bourgeois parties, or with bourgeois parties coming forth as "representatives of the peasantry as a whole" during the course of a broad popular revolution. The historical continuity is rather that of the Mensheviks, of Martynov, of the Thermidorian epigones of Lenin (Stalin-Bukharin), and then of the various Stalinist and post-Stalinist factions of the "international Communist movement." Nevertheless, Lenin's algebraic formulas of 1905, and 1906–1916, did leave the door ajar to erroneous interpretations of that type. Trotsky had resoundingly slammed that door shut; Doug Jenness is tugging it open again. It is a sad business, a sorry business.

At the same time, while the utmost clarity on the question of the theory of the permanent revolution, especially on the need for the conquest of power by the proletariat allied to the poor peasantry, is *indispensable* for a revolution to be victorious in a less developed capitalist country, it is by no means *sufficient* to that end. You still need a favorable relationship of forces: a sufficient weakening and decomposition of the ruling classes, a sufficient revolt and mobilization of the popular masses. You need a revolutionary vanguard, that is, a party, with sufficient strength, with sufficient roots in the masses, with already some sufficient level of political authority—gained in the period before the revolution—with a sufficiently concrete and rich analysis of *all* the objective conditions of the country, of *all* the social and political forces at hand, with sufficiently refined tactics, to succeed in bringing the majority of the nation together around the goal of conquering power. At any rate, no one, beginning with Marx and Lenin, ever tried to enumerate the conditions *guaranteeing* a revolutionary victory. That was not the point; the point was to reject the strategies that guaranteed defeat in light of the rich and tragic revolutionary experience.

Finally, when we say that between 1905 and the April Theses of 1917 Trotsky was right over Lenin on the question of the dictatorship of the proletariat, that is, of the theory of the permanent revolution, we are by no means saying that Trotsky was a better revolutionary than Lenin, or that we are Trotskyists rather than Leninists. Trotsky was wrong against Lenin on many questions prior to the Russian revolution of 1917: not only on the question of organization, which was essential, but on that of electoral tactics, on that of unity with the Mensheviks beginning with the second split, on revolutionary defeatism during the First World War. Today no revolutionary Marxism exists, and no revolutionary Marxism can exist, based solely on the continuity of the political and strategic positions of a single source, be it Trotsky or the Bolsheviks of 1905.

Revolutionary Marxism today integrates what was essential in Marx and Engels, a good number of the advances made by the Second International, the theory of organization and most of the tactical choices and theoretical contributions of Lenin and the Bolsheviks prior to 1917 (e.g., his theory of imperialism and his theory of the state), the theory of the permanent revolution of Trotsky, a good deal of the political contributions (not all of course) of Rosa Luxemburg and the German Socialist Left, the main documents of the first four congresses of the Communist International, some of the theoretical advances of other non-Russian Communist leaders between 1919 and 1923, some of the main theoretical conclusions to be drawn from the victories (Yugoslavia, China, Vietnam, Cuba) and defeats of the world revolution since 1918, the Trotskyist theory of the bureaucratic degeneration of the USSR and of the necessary antibureaucratic political revolution, the Trotskyist theory of fascism.

How could it be otherwise? How could a supporter of historical materialism think that revolutionary strategy had already been entirely worked out in 1905–1906, that is, even before the first revolutionary victory had been consolidated and without any knowledge of the three dozens of revolutions that have occurred since 1905?

Comrade Doug Jenness asks a rhetorical question: "Mandel argues that Lenin came over to Trotsky's pre-1917 strategy for the Russian revolution, while Trotsky came over to Lenin's view of party organization. But this is not true. In fact, it makes no sense at all. How can a historical materialist explain this supposed complete dichotomy between program and strategy, on the one hand, and their organizational expression, on the other?"

This is rather strange: historical materialism, according to Doug Jenness, would entail a correspondence between an organization's strategy and program on the one hand, and the organization itself on the other. We always thought rather that historical materialism asserted a correspondence between an organization's links with a given class (or fraction of class), i.e., *the social interests in which it is rooted objectively on the one hand*, and its program and strategy on the other. What is distinctively Lenin's, his main contribution to Marxism, is *his conception of the organization, his organizational theory and practice* that have become part of the revolutionary Marxist program. This was the decisive question on which Lenin was right against Trotsky.

But, in 1905, at the time Lenin formulated his theory of the "democratic dictatorship of the workers and peasants," the "organizational expression" of that conception was a tiny group of 2,000 revolutionaries. It is precisely the excessive narrowness of this group, its lack of real experience in a popular revolution, that was one of the factors (not the only one of course) that made for the ambiguous and algebraic character of his strategic conception. In 1905, *the building of the party had begun; it was far from completed*. To complete it, not only was the historic experience of the revolution of February 1917 necessary. There also had to be the mobilization, self-activity, and self-organization of the Russian proletariat on a qualitatively higher level than occurred in 1905. Above all, there had to be a *massive influx of militant vanguard workers into the Bolshevik Party*, which jumped, in the course of a few weeks, from 15,000 to nearly 100,000 members (the figure most commonly mentioned is 80,000). In many ways it was a new organization, in which the proletarian component weighed incomparably more than in 1905, that helped Lenin in the highly charged aura of the revolution to overcome the errors and reticence of the old Bolshevik cadres who were products of 1905 and not 1917. Their correct organizational conception and the education of the intermediate cadres in uncompromising class independence finished the job. That is the materialist, Marxist, nonhagiographic explanation of what happened to the Bolshevik Party in April 1917.

We obviously never spoke of a "total dichotomy" between the Bolshevik program and the Leninist conception of the organization. We did speak of that program's lack of clarity on *one single* question: the nature of the state and government that could lead the Russian revolution to victory. The program was correct on all other questions, particularly in its rejection of any class collaboration with the bourgeoisie. It was the source of generally correct tactics. What was involved was therefore a partial, not a total, dichotomy. It is neither surprising nor unique in history.

Engels and Lenin completely endorsed—aside for a few details—German Social-Democracy's Erfurt program. They endorsed even more wholeheartedly that party's conception of organization; Lenin explicitly drew his inspiration from it. And yet, by 1908, the party's strategic conception of power was *completely* deficient—infinitely more so than the Bolsheviks' in 1905—to say nothing of its clear failings on the question of the dictatorship of the proletariat. We know the price humanity had to pay in 1914 and 1918–1919 for this "partial deficiency." History thus delivered its scathing answer to the simplistic and mechanistic theses on the automatic "correspondence" between the general program, the general education of the cadre, the organizational conceptions, and the current tactics on the one hand, and the ability to orient correctly in a revolutionary situation, that is, the precise strategy for power, on the other.

Dictatorship of the proletariat and peasant war

Comrade Doug Jenness further weakens his case by referring to the problems of "peasant war," that is, to *the concrete fashion in which the worker-peasant alliance was achieved in the course of the Russian revolution* (and later in the course of the Yugoslav, Chinese, Vietnamese, Cuban, and Nicaraguan revolutions, with the inevitable variations in each case, variations that, on balance, turned out to be minor). This set of problems involves several distinct questions:

1. When did the peasant risings that led to the takeover of the land by the peasants actually take place?
2. What layers of the peasantry participated in them?
3. What social class wielded political power when the agrarian revolution was implemented?
4. What was the concrete political form of the worker and peasant alliance?

There were peasant risings before the October revolution. One could, perhaps, characterize these risings as "risings of the peasantry as a whole." These risings were obviously supported by the Bolshevik Party although it played only a minor, if not a negligible, practical role in them. But these were scattered risings that, while they prepared the ground for the October revolution, while they undermined the social and political bases of the Provisional Government's power, of the bourgeoisie's power, and of the landowners' power, which had the support of the Mensheviks and Right-SRs, neither attacked it nor overthrew it. Only indirectly, through the soldiers' soviets, did the peasants participate in preparing and carrying out the October 1917 revolution. It would be difficult to contend that the majority of soldiers' soviets represented "the peasantry as a whole." How then could one account for the minority, yet rather important, segments of these soviets that continued to support the Right-SRs before, during, and after October?

The real peasant risings, the real "peasant war," the real conquest of the land by the peasants, took place after the October revolution, under the military and political protection, and with the active aid and collaboration of the soviet power, of the dictatorship of the proletariat. *This is the concrete way in which the worker and peasant alliance was achieved in Russia.*

The Bolsheviks, the dictatorship of the proletariat, the power of the soviets, were able to conquer power because they promised the peasants the land. They were able to stay in power because they kept their promise. With the support of the working class alone, that is, of a small minority of the toiling population, it was impossible ("putschist") to conquer and stay in power in Russia. *Trotsky never advocated such nonsense*, contrary to the die-hard Stalinist slander to which Comrade Jenness is beginning to make concessions.

At the November–December 1917 All-Russian Congress of Peasant Soviets, a very significant minority emerged that *opposed* transferring power to the soviets and the October revolution, a minority based mainly among the Right-SRs.

Was this merely a political difference, or did this division also reflect divergent social interests, namely roughly the difference of interests between the rich peasants, the *kulaks*, the rural bourgeoisie, the more prosperous middle peasants, on the one hand, and the agricultural workers, the poor peasants, and the most impoverished middle peasants, on the other? We staunchly subscribe to the second interpretation, which is also supported by Marcel Liebman's book to which Comrade Doug Jenness refers, once again very "selectively."

In the Ukraine (where a large fraction of Tsarist Russia's peasantry lived), in Georgia and elsewhere, the question of the peasants' attitude was closely tied, *from the outset*, to the national question. This applied even more to Finland and Poland. It is beyond doubt that in all these regions, the majority of the peasantry, that is, the whole rich peasantry and a good share of the middle peasantry *opposed the October revolution*, albeit for nationalist reasons, and at first supported counterrevolutionary governments often directly backed by imperialism (German in most cases, British and French in the others). (It *later* changed positions, but that is another story.)

The kulak uprisings took place prior to the nationalization of industry and were not mainly the result of "fear" of seeing "their land collectivized." They were class reactions to the measures taken by the soviets to confiscate their food stocks *in the immediate economic interest* not only of the workers and toilers of the cities, but also of the poor peasants who were often threatened by famine as a result of the disorganization of transportation especially.

We have now arrived at the heart of the matter. The differentiation between poor peasants and rich peasants does not occur after "a prolonged development of capitalism in the countryside" supposedly set off by the victory of the revolution. This differentiation occurs roughly *prior to the revolutionary victory itself.* It is written *into the particular pattern in which capitalist, semi-capitalist, and precapitalist relations of production and exchange interconnect* in the villages of the countries affected by permanent revolution.

In Russia in 1917 the opposition between the rich and the poor, between the exploiters and the exploited, no longer pitted semi-feudal landowners against "the peasantry as a whole." Rather, it pitted landowners, substantial traders-usurers, rural bourgeois and rich peasants against poor peasants and the less-well-to-do middle peasants. Recognizing that there were many *remains*, vestiges, of precapitalist exploitation, including serfdom, in Russia, which the rich peasants were interested in fighting as much as the poor peasants, is one thing. But it is another to claim that it was possible for the poor peasants to rise, without *simultaneously* rising both against these various forms of serfdom, against the bloodsucking usurers, and against the capitalist exploiters who were all driving them to starvation, to claim that the poor peasants were in a position to "distinguish" stages: first with the usurers (since they are capitalist) against the semi-feudal nobility; then with the agricultural and industrial workers against the rural bourgeoisie.

Such "peasant wars," drawn from an abstract theoretical schema that does not take the law of uneven and combined development into account, have never existed since World War I, with the possible exception of extremely backward countries. At any rate there were no such wars in Russia, Yugoslavia, China, Vietnam, Cuba, nor in the innumerable cases of popular revolutions that ended in defeat. In every single one of these cases, the differentiation and latent and sometimes open civil war within the village, erupted in the first stage, from the onset, of the revolutionary process. *They were rooted in the social and economic reality of the village produced by the imperialist epoch* (let us repeat, except in the most backward countries, but, as Trotsky specified, the theory of the permanent revolution does not apply there anyway due to the nearly total lack of an industrial proletariat).

Let us take a typical case from today's world, that of India. At this time, there is no revolutionary situation in that country. The political rule of the Indian bourgeoisie appears to be stable at the national level. The workers movement is going through a temporary ebb rather than an impetuous rise. And yet, at the level of the Indian village, a latent and sometimes open civil war is slowly and inexorably rising with the underground force of a mighty volcano, and pitting the poor peasants (many of whom belong to the *pariah* castes) against the rich peasants who are organizing genuine terrorist armed groups to prevent the poor peasants from defending their immediate class interests. Will Comrade Doug Jenness, mechanically aping Lenin in 1905–1906, claim that the Indian proletariat should first march together "with the peasantry as a whole"? Or will he claim that Indian capitalism is today much more highly developed than Russian capitalism was in 1917, and that that is the reason why "the situation has changed"?

But if the differentiation between poor peasants and rich peasants is not the result of a learned political strategy of "revolution by stage," but the product of *the social and economic reality* of the village in the most important semi-colonial countries, not to mention the less developed imperialist countries, then any attempt to *compel* the poor peasants and agricultural workers, their natural allies, *to limit themselves* to a struggle for "democratic, anti-feudal, and anti-imperialist" goals, at any "stage" of the revolutionary process will mean in practice *compelling them to trample underfoot their own immediate material interests.*

The difference between such a "strategy" and that of the permanent revolution is therefore by no means that the advocates of the latter "underestimate the peasantry." Quite the contrary, it is that its opponents refuse, in practice, to mobilize the poor peasants and the majority of the laboring peasants, and to encourage their self-organization in soviet-type organs, because they fear that such a mobilization will substitute for the utopian and unrealistic alliance of the working class with "the whole peasantry," the real and feasible alliance of the working class with the poor peasantry, an alliance that is sealed on the backs not only of imperialism and the semi-feudal forces, but also of the urban and rural bourgeoisie including the rich peasantry.

Only if one *limits* the goals of the national-democratic revolution *to purely political goals*, as the Mensheviks did in 1905–1906, can one hope for any kind of "political alliance" with the peasantry as a whole. As soon as one broaches the problem of achieving the historical goals of the national-democratic revolution *as a whole*—and that is what the theory of the permanent revolution is about; it never claimed that *none* of the goals of the national-bourgeois revolution could be achieved without a dictatorship of the proletariat; it only asserts that they cannot be achieved *as a whole, overall—one has to* grant the agrarian revolution the *highest priority* among the goals of the revolution, and *one has to* conclude that in the imperialist epoch, such a revolution can no longer be achieved by a mobilization of the peasantry as a whole, but requires a spontaneous development of the class struggle between rich and poor in the countryside, which does not mean, obviously, a class struggle for or against socialism in the countryside, or for or against the collectivization of the land. Indeed, it matters little to a rich peasant-trader-usurer whether the poor peasant wants to cancel his debts because he is a "supporter of socialism," or "simply" to escape from unbearable poverty. What does matter to him is the danger of losing his property, his fortune, and even his life. This is the basis on which he will react.

We say that we are here at the very heart of the debate around the theory of the permanent revolution. For it is around this problem of the prior, inevitable, social and economic, differentiation within the peasantry that the question of the organized political forces and of the nature of the state set up by the revolution is posed from the Marxist, materialist, point of view. The vacillations of the petty-bourgeoisie, the petty commodity producers, i.e., of the peasantry, that Lenin so often refers to, are reflected in concrete events by two diametrically opposed types of political behavior.

Either the "peasant parties" (which are, at any rate, in nine cases out of ten, bourgeois parties with bourgeois leaderships), and especially the peasant mass organizations, follow the rural and urban bourgeoisie and, as soon as the poor peasants mobilize and organize for their own class goals, they will turn to counterrevolutionary behavior on the same pattern as the urban bourgeoisie. In this case, the counterrevolution is victorious (the victory of the counterrevolution in Bolivia, after the 1952 revolution, was due in great part to the alliance of the peasant organizations with the MNR). Or else, the class struggle deeply penetrates the countryside; the poor and less well-off middle peasants mobilize and organize to defend *their own immediate interests*, in which case the worker and peasant alliance *can* march forward towards victory. But it can only get there if the exploiters of the cities and country are unable to drown the "peasant war" in blood, that is, if their army is unhinged, cut to pieces, beaten back, that is, if the proletariat and poor peasants are armed, that is, if the state is a state of the dictatorship of the proletariat (or, what amounts to the same thing, if the civil war between the decomposing bourgeois state and the newly developing workers state has reached the stage where the latter is able to effectively protect the poor peasants against the bloodthirsty repression of the ruling classes).

When the parties that lead the workers refuse to take power, they are displaying not some "more profound understanding of the peasant question," but *a lack of understanding* of the social and economic reality of the village which leads to the "peasant war" being smashed. *The peasant war can only win under the protection of the dictatorship of the proletariat.*

In the light of this analysis, it is now possible to tackle the question of "stages" within the process of permanent revolution. These "stages," to which Trotsky refers in his *Permanent Revolution*, have to do with the sequence in which the concrete goals of mass mobilizations emerge. This is a practical question, a matter of "concrete analysis of a concrete situation."

The revolutionary process (the stormy mobilization of the masses) may *be triggered* by an issue arising in the struggle against imperialism, by the question of national independence, by one of the particular aspects of the agrarian question, by a "national minority" question, by an issue in the struggle against dictatorship (release of political prisoners), or even by the problem of famine, of sharing existing supplies (after all, that is how the February revolution began in Russia in 1917). Any attempt to establish, in advance, a political hierarchy of issues of this type and to deduce it from a general definition of the "stage of development" of these countries, would be totally inoperative. In this field, events will *always* bring forth unforeseen variants.

Moreover, although it may tremendously upset the schematic thinkers, it is perfectly possible for a permanent revolution process to be triggered in an already partly industrialized underdeveloped country by the spark of a "typically" working-class demand. The question of the nationalization of the mines played no small role in setting off the Bolivian revolution of 1952. It was not a "purely" anti-imperialist demand; the same is probably true of the nationalization of the Suez canal in Egypt.

But what sets these "stages" within the permanent revolution process apart from the stages so dear to the Menshevik-Stalinists and their imitators, *is that at no stage* of the process do the political demands rule out of the struggle and mobilizations and self-organization of the masses of workers *and peasants*, their immediate material and historic social and economic interests. These masses can only be forced into such a schema by blocking, by smothering, and by repressing their own mobilizations, that is, let us repeat it once again, those of the workers *as well as of the exploited peasants*. These are the stakes of the real political choice.

Political alliance, "class" alliances, "anti-imperialist united fronts," yes, occasionally, punctually, for well-defined goals *to be struggled for*, and with strict compliance to the rule "march separately, strike together," we do not exclude these. But not at any price. Not at the price of putting a brake on the mobilization of the workers and poor peasants for their own interests, and on their self-organization to this end, even if this means that in real life the "anti-imperialist united front" will fall apart, because the "national" and (or) rural bourgeoisie prefers to capitulate to imperialism, to dictatorships, to "semi-feudalists," etc., rather than allowing itself to be surrounded by the surging flames of the peasant war and workers strikes with factory occupations, which are a deadly threat to it.

We are now in a position to answer another sarcastic remark of Comrade Doug Jenness which demonstrates once more that he often does not even realize what the discussion is about. He writes:

"The October revolution, Lenin says, created the foundation for the 'most perfect' development of capitalism in the countryside. (Mandel cannot deny this without breaking with Marx *and* Lenin.)"

Let Marx and Lenin rest in peace. Let us rather examine the problem both in light of the facts, that is, of historical experience, and from the theoretical point of view.

The facts show that there was not "the most perfect development of capitalism in the countryside" (remember that Lenin is speaking of a development "on the American pattern"), neither after the October revolution, nor after the victory of the Yugoslav revolution, nor after the victory of the Chinese revolution, nor after the victory of the Cuban revolution, let alone the Vietnamese. In all these cases what occurred was mainly a development of *petty commodity production* with an embryo of capitalist agriculture, and not "the most perfect *development of capitalism* in agriculture." Whoever does not understand that "the most perfect development of capitalism" implies a massive development of farm machinery and a massive development of the agricultural proletariat, has not understood much about capitalism according to Marx.

Where was there a private accumulation of capital in the hands of the Russian, Chinese, Yugoslav, or Cuban kulaks after the revolution on a scale that would have allowed them to massively purchase agricultural machinery which was, at any rate, not available in those countries? Lenin, who understood Marx, obviously meant to say: the nationalization of the land could serve as the point of departure for the most perfect development of capitalism, provided that a whole series of *additional* conditions were fulfilled, at the top of which the condition that the dictatorship of the proletariat not exist, would have a prominent place. Doug Jenness' simplistic shortcut transforms that correct observation into utter nonsense.

In fact, because we understand the law of uneven and combined development, we understand that the nationalization of the land under the regime of the dictatorship of the proletariat could lead to "the most perfect development of capitalism in the countryside" (to agribusiness, because that is what we are talking about), only on condition that the workers state had supplied the kulaks with massive deliveries of farm machinery and authorized them to hire millions of farm hands to be exploited by them. But long before such a process could have come to fruition, it would have dealt a deadly blow to the dictatorship of the proletariat, it would have destroyed it. This would have been verified in the economic field (because the private accumulation of capital would have gotten the upper hand over "socialist primitive accumulation," and the law of value would have prevailed in Russia as a result of the links between the world market and the kulaks), and in the social field: the proletarianized and pauperized poor peasants would have revolted against the kulaks, and if the state had not supported them, the worker-peasant alliance would have been shattered.

This is why Lenin could peremptorily proclaim as early as 1917: "Do the SRs fool themselves, do they fool the peasants when they admit and spread around the idea that transformations of that magnitude are possible without overthrowing the dominance of capitalism, without placing all state power in the hands of the proletariat, without the peasants' supporting the most vigorous measures of the proletarian power against the capitalists. . . . The transition of political power to the proletariat, that is the main thing" ("Workers and Peasant," September 1917, *CW* Vol. 25, p. 308; translated from the French).

What a far cry from the "democratic republic" and "the rapid development of capitalism in the European-style" of 1905! The person who persists today, against all the evidence, in placing a "continuity" sign between the two sets of analyses, suffers from the worst kind of blindness, the blindness of those who *refuse* to see.

Paradoxically, even in a bourgeois state, the "most perfect development of capitalism in the countryside" can no longer be reproduced in the imperialist epoch in the less developed countries despite many more or less consistent, and more or less limited, land reforms. Here too, the cause lies in the law of uneven and combined development: the inextricable overlap of agriculture and industry, of agriculture and credit, of usurious and banking capital and finance capital, of national and international capital, of the bourgeois state and capitalist agriculture, of the semi-colonial and (or) dependent bourgeois state and the international imperialist system. At bottom, the problem is that "the most perfect development of capitalism in the countryside" precisely requires an *American-style* overall capitalist development in all its complexity. But, in the epoch of imperialism, "a second America is no longer possible." Doug Jenness started off by accepting this assertion—that only the theory of the permanent revolution can account for in all its dimensions—as a commonplace. But, a minute later, he implicitly rejects it.

This is why even the initial successes of the "green revolution" in the countryside of the most evolved dependent countries (Mexico, South Korea, some parts of India) have not led to "the most perfect development of capitalism in the countryside," but to a partial, hybrid, combined, mongrelized, simultaneous development of development and underdevelopment that keeps these countries far below the conditions of the laggard imperialist countries, not to mention Western Europe, Canada, Australia or the United States.

The question of the self-limitation of the proletariat

In the section of his article which is an open polemic against Comrade Trotsky, Doug Jenness reproaches him with the prediction that a "two-class" government would run the risk of repressing or limiting the struggle of the proletariat for its own objectives (p. 58). He peremptorily asserts that the "two-class government" established in October 1917, far from acting as a brake on the workers demands, including that of seizing the factories and expropriating the capitalists, actually helped the proletariat to achieve them. Trotsky's prediction is therefore allegedly mistaken.

This "refutation" is meaningless. We have already established that according to Lenin and all the programmatic documents of the Bolshevik Party and the C.I., the government that rose to power through the October insurrection was not "a two-class government," but the dictatorship of the proletariat. It was so not only in a "general historic" sense, but also in a concrete and immediate sense.

The workers were armed. The bosses were disarmed. The workers exercised power through their soviets. The bosses were bullied, despised, insulted (read the details in Victor Serge's *The Year One of the Russian Revolution*) and chased from their villas, mansions and apartments by the workers, before being legally expropriated (how "anarchistic" this magnificent workers revolution was, to use an insult Doug Jenness is fond of, but which Comrade Lenin looked upon rather as a compliment in his *State and Revolution*).

Obviously, *under these conditions*, no one in Russia could put a brake on or limit the workers demands. The fact that the Bolsheviks had to revise several times the calendar they had projected for the various nationalizations, under the impact of the battering ram of the spontaneous workers mobilizations, is nowhere mentioned by Doug Jenness although it is a fact recognized by all serious historians. The fact that Lenin and the Bolsheviks complied without the slightest hesitation, cheerfully, that they preferred a thousand times the real revolutionary process to preestablished schemas, testifies to their admirable revolutionary fiber, a fiber we never called into question.

But Comrade Doug Jenness is careful not to ask the question which arises logically from his way of tackling the problem of "class alliances." What happened *in every single case* where the leaders of the revolutionary process actually allowed themselves to be drawn into a "two-class government" that could only be a coalition government *with the bourgeoisie*, since no "peasant party" independent of the bourgeoisie and proletariat ever appeared on the scene of history? What happened even in those cases where the parties leading the revolutionary process, while breaking *in practice* with the bourgeoisie (and its "peasant parties"), tried to express their political orientation through the old formulas of the revolution by stages? *In every single case*, there were attempts, often successful unfortunately, to limit the mobilizations, the self-organization and the self-activity of the *proletariat and poor peasants*, against their will, insofar as these mobilizations did not correspond to the preestablished schemas.

In the worst cases, the result was not only a repression of the masses, but the defeat of the revolution as a consequence of the demoralization caused by that repression. In the best of cases, the result was the emergence of workers states highly bureaucratized *from the outset* as a result of the lack of self-organization of the masses. Disastrous consequences ensued for the solution of the problems, difficulties and conflicts, that inevitably arise on the road to socialism; the transitional society bom under these auspices was "blocked" and unable to move forward towards socialism; this in turn had no less disastrous consequences on the consciousness of the international proletariat and the dynamic of the world revolution, which itself boomeranged back and further worsened the tension and waste afflicting the bureaucratized transitional societies.

About all this. Comrade Doug Jenness keeps mum. Comrade Trotsky had no small merit in perceiving, as early as 1905, most of these problems that, together with those of the permanent revolution, overshadow twentieth century history. That one could reproach him today with such far-sightedness instead of admiring it, is good cause for dismay.

We have already drawn attention to Comrade Doug Jenness' rather selective method of "reading" Lenin. It consists in drawing one or two quotations from a book of 100 to 150 pages in order to "demonstrate" a preconceived thesis, without wondering why the book contains twenty quotations that say the opposite and whether, therefore, one ought not first seek to ascertain the overall opinion of the author as it emerges from the work as a whole. But Doug Jenness attempts to enlist even the works of Marx on behalf of his preestablished thesis. This is only possible thanks to an even more "selective" reading of the works of Marx and Engels.

In this instance, what is alarming and marks a further slippage towards a broader and more complete revision of Marxism, is the fact that he repeats in 1982 one of the last paragraphs of the *Communist Manifesto*, written *before the revolution of 1848*, as if it were still politically valid *today*, as if the Bolsheviks had applied it not only in 1905 but even in 1917, without even explaining what political-strategic thesis is implied in the passage, without asking whether the prediction was borne out by reality in 1848 and whether Marx and Engels continued to uphold it.

What does the passage at hand say? That Germany is on the eve of the bourgeois revolution; that this bourgeois revolution will triumph under the leadership of the bourgeoisie; that it will be the immediate prelude to the proletarian revolution.

Of these three predictions, only the first was verified. The other two were disproved by events. The German revolution was not victorious, and could not be victorious precisely because it remained under the leadership of the bourgeoisie. Nor was it the prelude to the proletarian revolution. The concrete experience of the German and French revolutions of 1848 led Marx and Engels to drastically revamp their revolutionary strategy. In the *Address to the Central Committee of the League of Communists*, written in March 1850, Marx and Engels summarized their balance sheet of the 1848 revolution thus:

"We have already said, in 1848, that the German liberal bourgeoisie would come to power and immediately turn their newly acquired power against the workers. You saw how the business was carried out. The bourgeoisie could not achieve this goal without an alliance with the feudal party that had been brushed aside in March, and even without abandoning power, in the last analysis, to that feudal absolutist party" (Marx-Engels, *Selected Works*; translated from the French).

The historical sequence therefore was not: victory of the bourgeois revolution leading to the beginning of the proletarian revolution, but beginning of the bourgeois revolution leading to a victory of the counterrevolution. The bourgeois' fear of the proletariat got the upper hand over its desire to do away with the semi-feudal remnants.

Marx and Engels drew two strategic conclusions from this which had not been present in the *Communist Manifesto*: firstly, that the proletariat must form itself into an independent political party with its own specific tactics *even before the bourgeois revolution breaks out* and before the "revolutionary" role of the bourgeoisie and democratic petty-bourgeoisie comes to an end, and this *in spite of* the bourgeois character of the revolution; and secondly, the implementation of the strategy known as "permanent revolution," for it is in the *Address to the League of Communists* that this term is used for the first time by the founders of Marxism.

One should not forget that the *Communist Manifesto* calls upon Communists to join workers parties only in Britain and the USA, which remained outside the revolution of 1848. In the two main countries of that revolution, France and Germany, the *Communist Manifesto* explicitly advocates that Communists join petty-bourgeois parties (the party of Louis Blanc in France, the democrats in Germany) and *not* set up independent parties of the working class. Here is the balance sheet of this tactic drawn up by Marx and Engels in the March 1850 *Address*.

"A great part of the members [of the Communist League] directly involved in the revolutionary movement, thought that the time of secret societies had passed and that it was sufficient to operate openly and publicly. The different districts and locals relaxed their relations with the Central Committee and let them gradually come to rest. While the democratic party, the party of the petty-bourgeoisie, organized thus more and more in Germany, the workers party lost its solid basis, remained organized in only a few localities, for purely local purposes, and thereby got in the general movement completely under the domination and leadership of the petty-bourgeois democrats. One must put an end to this situation; the independence of the workers must be established" (Marx-Engels *Werke*, Vol. 7; translated from the French).

Underlying this strategic turn, there also was the experience of the class struggles in France, of the June 1848 insurrection of the French proletariat, of the bloody clash between the bourgeoisie and proletariat *in the very course of the revolution, before* it had completed its tasks, before an institutionalized "democratic republic" had been born. Here also, life, the class struggle, historical experience, demonstrated that the bourgeoisie had become *politically reactionary and counterrevolutionary* long before it had fulfilled its historic economic tasks. To deny this "break" in the thought of Marx and Engels, to proclaim that the Marx and Engels of June 1848, of 1850, of 1871, stood "in the political continuity" of the aforementioned paragraph of the *Communist Manifesto*, and to add on top of that that the Lenin of *State and Revolution* and of the October revolution stood "in continuity" with this paragraph, amounts to turning Marx and Lenin into half-Mensheviks, or even vulgar Mensheviks; it amounts to treating the true history of revolutionary Marxism with intolerable flippancy.

In the course of the German revolution of 1918–1919, a Left Social-Democratic leader (it did not take much to be "to the left" of Noske!) wrote a pamphlet entitled "How to Lose a Revolution." In it, he counterposed the "scientific," balanced, correct, well-thought-out position of the *Communist Manifesto* to the insane, in fact, the "anarcho-Blanquist," position of the Marx who supported the June 1848 insurrection of the Paris proletariat. The latter had no chance of succeeding "since" the bourgeois revolution had not yet been entirely completed, "since" capitalism had not yet "exhausted all its economic potentialities." As a result, the only possible outcome of this "insane" insurrection was to drive the bourgeoisie into the arms of the counterrevolution.

The Menshevik (correction: Left Social-Democratic) author of this pamphlet had not yet understood, seventy years after the event, that the fact that the French bourgeoisie had gone over to the camp of the counterrevolution in France, was not the result of the "insane insurrection" of the Paris proletarians, but quite clearly that of the *inexorable maturation of the class contradictions between Capital and Labor*, given the development of capitalism, of the workers consciousness, and of the workers movement. The workers insurrection was a response to this evolution of the bourgeoisie and not its cause. The name of this genuine supporter of the "self-limitation of the proletariat in the democratic revolution" was Eduard Bernstein. Bernstein: you have heard of him, haven't you? And of the kind of revisionist logic that led Bernstein to his conclusion?

Theoretical roots of the errors of Doug Jenness

How was it that comrades educated for decades in revolutionary Marxist theory and traditions could "founder" and sink towards such deeply erroneous positions? We see essentially three causes, all interrelated, that illustrate yet another time in the history of the Marxist movement the terrible "objective dialectic of ideas," a logic over which Doug Jenness and his cothinkers seem to have lost all conscious control: "Du glaubst du schiebst und wirst geschoben" ("You think you push, and you are pushed"), as was put so neatly by that great dialectician who went by the name of Goethe.

- It all began with the present leaders of the Socialist Workers Party's faulty understanding of the way in which Trotsky and the Fourth International had used the criterion of the nationalization of the means of production as the basic criterion showing the USSR remained a workers state, despite the monstrous bureaucratic dictatorship that held sway over it. For Trotsky, that nationalization was *the decisive residual element*, that is, as he often put it, what *survived* from the October revolution. But he never dreamed of *reducing* the conquests of October, and still less the nature of the October revolution to this nationalization alone, and to consider as "less important," or "less decisive," the destruction of the bourgeoisie's state power and the creation of the new power of the soviets.

For Trotsky, as for Lenin, as for Engels, as for Marx, what is decisive in a social revolution is the transfer of power from one class to another, and not the instant and complete abolition of a given form of property. The *Communist Manifesto* already stated explicitly:

"We've already seen that the first stage of the workers revolution is the formation of the proletariat as the dominant class, the conquest of democracy.

"The proletariat will use its political supremacy to wrest *little by little all capital from the hands of the bourgeoisie*, to centralize all the instruments of production in the hands of the state, that is, of the proletariat organized as the ruling class, and to increase as fast as possible the amount of productive forces" (translated from the French—our emphasis).

The new theoretical problem with which Trotsky and all revolutionary Marxists were confronted beginning in the 1930s was that of a state that was born out of an undeniable victory of the proletarian revolution, but in which "the proletariat organized as a class" no longer wielded political power, no longer enjoyed "political supremacy," and where proletarian democracy no longer existed. Could one still speak of a workers state under those conditions, despite the dictatorship of the bureaucracy? Yes, answered Trotsky, insofar as the nationalization of the means of production and the monopoly of foreign trade born of the October revolution still *survived.* It was a new criterion for a new problem, that of *the class nature of a bureaucratically degenerated workers state.* It was by no stretch of the imagination a new "scientific criterion for the creation of a workers state" to be applied by Marxists to all workers states.

- Driven by the will to "systematize" this wrong criterion for the definition of all workers states—which they had already applied to all the victorious socialist revolutions, including by the absurd denial that the Paris Commune was a dictatorship of the proletariat—the SWP leaders who share Comrade Jenness' current ideas began to revise *the whole* Marxist theory of the state. They began to identify "state" and "society," forgetting that the state is, by its very Marxist definition, *a set of apparati*, of bodies of specialized men (mainly, but not exclusively, "armed men") that take over functions previously exercised by society as a whole, and this in the interest of a ruling class.

The class nature of a state is determined by answering the following question: "what class interests do these special apparati fundamentally serve on the scale of history?" and not by the question: "what property forms are developed or preserved in the immediate period under the rule of this state?" The state of the absolutist monarchy was a semi-feudal state, despite the fact that semi-feudal landed estates may have declined or even disappeared in this or that country, in one or another period. Yet there is no doubt that, on the whole, this state continued to defend the interests of the semi-feudal nobility and upper clergy, and that if it had not existed, or after it had been destroyed by a bourgeois revolution, the fate of these social classes would have qualitatively worsened.

Similarly, in the epoch of capitalism's decline, the bourgeois state can nationalize not unimportant sectors of the means of production (not only under nationalist-populist regimes in the semi-colonial countries, but also in the imperialist countries, both under parliamentary-democratic regimes and under authoritarian and fascist regimes), and still remain a bourgeois state. If it did not exist, the breadth of the nationalizations would be far greater, the interests of the bourgeoisie as a class would be damaged definitively and comprehensively, rather than partially and temporarily.

This theoretical error is especially serious for revolutionaries in semi-colonial countries, because it can lead them to completely false conclusions on the class nature of certain states that seem, at first sight, to have nationalized the means of production as, or more, extensively than the USSR under the NEP, yet remain bourgeois states. This is demonstrated by the entire subsequent evolution of Egypt, Iraq, Algeria, Syria, the People's Republic of the Congo, that belonged in that category; and events will unfortunately confirm that, barring new upheavals, Angola, Mozambique, Zimbabwe and South Yemen should be classified in the same category.

Comrade Doug Jenness uses a strange argument to justify this revision of the Marxist theory of the state: since the October revolution did not "immediately" abolish private property of the large means of production, it allegedly preserved the bourgeois state, since this state (that is, the ruling soviets!) acted to "protect" and even "defend" that property. In other words: if you bring a knife to the throat of a fascist mass murderer who brutally assaulted you after slaughtering several other people, yet do not immediately cut it, in order to check if he has an accomplice who might attack you from behind (you "only" cut it a quarter of an hour "later"), you are "protecting" him, you are "defending" him, you are "saving his life." The knife that cuts the throat becomes a "protecting knife." Truly irresistible "logic!"

Right from the moment they seized power the Bolsheviks proclaimed their intention of socializing the Russian economy. On December 25, 1917, Lenin already wrote in his article "How to Organize Competition":

"The lackeys of the money-banks, the mercenaries of the exploiters, the gentlemen among the bourgeois intellectuals tried to scare the people away from socialism, whilst it is precisely capitalism that condemns them to forced labor, to a barracks-like existence, to excessive and monotonous work, to a life of famine and direst poverty. The first step towards the emancipation of the workers from this forced labor, is to confiscate the estates of the landowners, to introduce workers control, the nationalization of the banks. The next steps will be: the nationalization of factories and enterprises, the compulsory centralization of the whole population in consumers' cooperatives that will serve at the same time as distribution cooperatives, the introduction of state monopoly over trade in wheat and other basic necessities" (*CW*, Vol. 24; translated from the French).

A state that proclaims that intention, *from the moment of its creation*, and carries it out without the slightest new revolution or internal transformation; a state that, a few weeks later, proclaims "the socialist homeland threatened," and ends that February 21, 1918, appeal with the words "Long Live the World Socialist Revolution" (p.312–313), allegedly is a "bourgeois state" led by a "two-class government?" Need we emphasize once again the absurdity of such "conclusions" that provide sufficient ground, in and of themselves, to condemn Comrade Jenness' entire sophistry as devoid of the slightest theoretical and political value?

• The third theoretical error, which is connected to the previous two, was a false, because excessively simplistic and mechanistic, conception of the leadership of a revolutionary process that ended with the establishment of the dictatorship of the proletariat. Comrades who share Doug Jenness' opinion are, by the same token, locked in an antinomy: either the dictatorship of the proletariat was established under the leadership of a party, and then this party *must* be a revolutionary Marxist party; or there is no revolutionary Marxist party and then, either there is no dictatorship of the proletariat or it was established despite and against the leading party, "under the pressure of the masses."

This error first led to a systematically sectarian attitude toward the Yugoslav, Chinese, and Vietnamese CPs that were falsely labelled as "Stalinist parties," which also led to long delays in recognizing the emergence of new workers states. That attitude was associated with a scholastic and dogmatic conception of "Stalinism" that reduced it to "theoretical conceptions," independently of the real links which may have existed with the Soviet bureaucracy, and more importantly, *independently of these parties' real political practice* and objective role in the revolutionary process of the class struggle. All this led to a crassly spontaneist conception of the Yugoslav, Chinese and Vietnamese revolutions, in which the role the CPs of those countries played in preparing and leading the overthrow of capitalism was completely denied (vestiges of these conceptions are still found—but for how long?—in Comrade Doug Jenness' article, with regard to the Chinese CP).

For more than two decades we systematically warned the comrades leading the SWP of the dangers in such a sectarian and dogmatic position that, moreover, had failed the test of history, but to no avail. Black and white are not the only colors just as "counterrevolutionary Stalinism" and "revolutionary Marxism" are not the only alternatives. There are intermediate categories. There was the Paris Commune, established without a "revolutionary Marxist" leadership, under a leadership that included some Marxists (a minority), Proudhonists, Blanquists, and others. There was the dictatorship of the proletariat established in 1919 in Hungary, under a mixed leadership including Left Social-Democrats and Communists. The dictatorship of the proletariat was established in Yugoslavia, China, Vietnam, and Cuba by *pragmatic revolutionary leaderships* that had a revolutionary practice but a theory and program that was adequate neither to their own revolution, nor especially to the world revolution.

The fact that they carried out a socialist revolution—a fact that is infinitely more important than their lack of an adequate theory—means that it would be the height of sectarianism to call them "counterrevolutionaries." To call them "Stalinists" would amount to giving Stalinism entirely new merits. However, the fact that they did not and still do not have an adequate overall program for constructing a socialist world means that calling them "revolutionary Marxists" would be entirely out of place. They are pragmatic revolutionaries, we would say "left centrists" from a theoretical point of view, without giving the slightest pejorative coloration to that term. But the lack of a correct program is not a tiny little wart on a face radiating with beauty. It is a serious deficiency, which has *negative practical consequences* both for their intervention in the world revolution and for the construction of socialism in their own country.

The sectarian-dogmatic position first began to crumble under the hammer blows of the Cuban revolution, then of the Nicaraguan revolution. However, Doug Jenness' cothinkers remained locked in their "black or white" simplistic outlook, and simply reversed their position within the same antinomy they had created. The generalization of the concept of the "workers and farmers government" as something other than the dictatorship of the proletariat, and its extension even to the October 1917 revolution, is the instrument with which the reversal will be "systematized."

The slogan for a "workers government" or for a "workers and farmers government" (in countries where the peasants are still an important part of the working population) is an indispensable *transitional slogan.* It crowns all the transitional demands. Its pedagogic, propaganda, and sometimes agitational function, is to bring the masses through their own experience, and starting from their really given level of consciousness, to pose in practice the question of overthrowing the bourgeois government, to take all the power, and destroy the bourgeois state.

This is why it is an eminently algebraic slogan whose concrete formulation depends on a series of conditions that vary from one country to another and from one conjunctural situation to another: the acuteness of the class struggle; the level of mass mobilization; the seriousness of the bourgeoisie's political crisis; the extent (and precise forms) of self-organization of the masses; the amount of confidence they still retain in their traditional organizations; the emergence, or non-emergence, of genuine revolutionary parties with mass influence, even though still real minorities, etc.

But it is a necessary slogan, *not a necessary stage* in the revolutionary process, not an alleged intermediate stage between the bourgeois state (the dictatorship of the bourgeoisie) and the workers state (the dictatorship of the proletariat). In practice, it turned out not to be necessary, and it turned out that it had no actual concretization (except as synonymous to the dictatorship of the proletariat) in Russia, in Yugoslavia, in Vietnam, or even, in our opinion (but this is no longer controversial inside the FI), in China. When it is concretized as something different from the dictatorship of the proletariat, it is only, as specified both by the Resolution on Tactics of the Fourth Congress of the Communist International and the *Transitional Program*, because the (or one of the) leading parties of the revolutionary process believes that it should not immediately push its break with the bourgeoisie to the end (or else *cannot* immediately push it to the end because of the extremely backward nature of the country).

We are speaking, of course, of a *political* break, of a break with the institutions of the bourgeois state and their destruction, and not of the "immediate and total" elimination of private property that no sensible person, beginning with Marx, Engels, Lenin and Trotsky, ever thought was a precondition for establishing the dictatorship of the proletariat. Moreover such a "total elimination" exists nowhere on earth. Even today in the USSR, 65 years after the October revolution, 6–8% of the means of production, and some 25% of agricultural production are still private.

In the past, all those who were not Trotskyists were counterrevolutionaries. Now, all those who are not counterrevolutionaries are revolutionary Marxists (you can bet that it will not be long before Doug Jenness attributes that virtue first to the Vietnamese CP, and then, who can say, also to the Chinese CP). In the past, getting enthusiastic about the victorious Yugoslav, Chinese, and Vietnamese *revolutions* was "capitulating to Stalinism." Now, expressing the slightest criticism of the Cuban, Nicaraguan, and even Vietnamese *leadership*, has become "sterile sectarianism." Either uncritical support or sectarian rejection: the comrades who agree with Doug Jenness cannot escape this dilemma. Yet its solution is quite simple: *combining* total support for the revolutionary process with justified criticism of its leadership every time it acts against the interests of the ("national" or "international") proletariat.

After accusing us of "opportunism" towards the living revolutions, the comrades who agree with Doug Jenness now accuse us of "sectarianism" towards their leaders. Both accusations are false.

But since the world revolution forms a whole (albeit a whole structured by three deeply interrelated sectors), the increasingly clear adaptation of the comrades who agree with Doug Jenness to the pragmatism of the leaderships that led real revolutions since World War II cannot save them from the pitfall of sectarianism. It is in fact leading them to increased sectarianism towards all sectors of the world revolution and the world mass movement that do not fit into the simplistic schema of "campism" based on states: increasing sectarianism towards *Solidarnosc* militants; increasing sectarianism towards the activists of the *Labour Party* left; increasing sectarianism towards the activists of the mass antiwar movement; increasing sectarianism towards the trade union left struggling against capitalist austerity; increasing sectarianism towards the proletariat confronting so-called "anti-imperialist" bourgeois governments, etc.

The source of this increasing sectarianism (combined with opportunism towards the Fidelista current) is still the same: *the inability to judge a movement above all in relation to the objective consequences of its political practice in the class struggle;* the systematic substitution of a dogmatic-idealist criterion to this Marxist, materialist criterion, namely, the attitude of the leaders of this movement towards a political question determined to be "central" (without the slightest theoretical justification): previously it was the question of "Stalinism"; now it is the question of "the defense of the USSR."

This is not the place for a review of the trajectory of the Nicaraguan revolution. Our movement has already done so in several documents; it will continue to do so at the Twelfth World Congress. But one thing is sure: nothing in the real course of the Nicaraguan revolution confirms the existence of some two-class "power," "government" or "state," or worse yet, of a revolutionary government that would destroy the bourgeois state apparatus while maintaining—a bourgeois state.

There can be dual power between the power of two antagonistic classes in a situation where history has not yet settled the question of which class, which power, has defeated the other. But there cannot be a "two-class government" in the sense that it would be neither under the hegemony of the proletariat, nor under that of the bourgeoisie.

In obfuscating this decisive question, the comrades who agree with Doug Jenness are entering, without being aware of it, the path that leads to justifying some of the main revolutionary defeats of the twentieth century. Precisely the same line of argumentation was used to justify the course that led to defeat in Spain in 1936 and to defeat in Chile in 1973, to mention only two examples. If, at the level of real power, there is an "intermediate solution" between the dictatorship of the bourgeoisie and the dictatorship of the proletariat, pray tell us why workers parties could not exercise *genuine power* in the framework of a "truly weakened" bourgeois state. The whole of Leninism is being poured down the drain despite all the oaths to continuity . . .

From abandoning permanent revolution to abandoning the antibureaucratic political revolution?

Three years ago, in our article on "The Twenty-One Theoretical Errors of Comrades Clark, Feldman, Horowitz, and Waters" (dated September 15, 1979, and published in *Intercontinental Press combined with Inprecor,* Vol. 19, No. 16, p. 456, May 4, 1981), we predicted that the leading comrades of the SWP who agree with Comrade Doug Jenness' ideas would consummate an explicit break with the theory of the permanent revolution. Now that course is appearing more clearly. We still have to find out what its practical political consequences will be; (fortunately!) the SWP leadership has not yet elaborated them fully.

Today, we will be so bold as to venture a second prediction: if Comrade Jenness and his "cothinkers" do not stop in time their advance down this revisionist path, they risk being drawn, unawares and unwillingly, at least at this time, into gradually abandoning the Marxist theory of the Soviet bureaucracy, and especially into abandoning our strategy of antibureaucratic political revolution, in favor of some meek perspective of "gradual democratization" of these states, and worse yet, "democratization from above."

What is the basis for this prediction?

First of all, a fundamental fact of the international workers movement. The Communist movement has only given birth to two fundamental ideological currents that lasted a long time and were present everywhere: the Stalinist current and its byproducts, and the revolutionary Marxist current, that is, mainly the Trotskyist current. Between these two currents, there is no space for a stable, lasting current, not even an "authentically Leninist" one, for the simple reason that Lenin stopped writing in 1923. Over the last sixty years, innumerable phenomena of great historic importance took place for which Lenin's works only provide a few points of reference, but no proposals for overall solutions that can be verified or invalidated in the light of experience.

More than Lenin's writings is therefore needed to find one's way around. Let us mention the following items to be remembered: the question of fascism; the question of the bureaucratic degeneration of the USSR; the question of the relationship between socialist democracy and the economic problems of building socialism; the question of the strategy for power in the semi-colonial countries; the question of nuclear weapons; the place of workers management in the fight against bureaucracy; the question of the connection between the decline of capitalism and the strategy for workers power in the imperialist countries, etc.

Under these circumstances, it is not by chance that, as Trotsky himself wrote:

"We can say that all of Stalinism considered at the theoretical level, issued from a critique of the theory of the permanent revolution as it was formulated in 1905" (*Three Conceptions of the Russian Revolution*).

"A critique of the theory of the permanent revolution," "all of Stalinism": let Comrade Doug Jenness and his cothinkers ponder the fateful meaning of that analysis by Trotsky. Since 1923, in the history of the Communist movement, in the history of the revolutionary movement, every turn against the need for a *direct* seizure of power *by the proletariat* has always begun with an attack on Trotskyism.[9]

9. Let us add that *almost all* the arguments used by Comrade Doug Jenness against Comrade Trotsky come down to us in a straight line from the polemic of the Thermidorian epigones of 1923–1928, from the polemic of neo-Stalinists like Mavrakis (*On Trotskyism*) or can be found in the Soviet bureaucracy's pamphlet written by M. Basmanov, *Contemporary Trotskyism: Its Anti-Revolutionary Nature,* Moscow: Progress Publishers, 1972.

The denial of the theory of "socialism in one country" (that is, the theory that says that the construction of socialism not only can, but must, *begin* in each country where the socialist revolution has already been victorious, but that it cannot be completed there) is part and parcel of the theory of the permanent revolution. As it were, the interconnection between the international revolution and a victorious revolution in one or several countries implies also an interconnection between the process of bureaucratization of these workers states and the defeats of the international revolution, an interconnection which flows from the same source as the theory of the permanent revolution: *a correct judgment on the relationship of forces between social classes* on the eve of, during, and after the revolution, both within the less developed countries and on an international scale. The same lack of understanding of the key role of the proletariat and the dictatorship of the proletariat in insuring the victory of the revolution in those countries lies at the root of the lack of understanding of the key role of the proletariat in clearing the way for the elimination of the obstacle of bureaucratic dictatorship, an obstacle on the path of both the international revolution and the construction of socialism.

Wherever one may look for the solution, be it in the economic, social, political or cultural field, it always involves *a strengthening of the objective and subjective weight of the proletariat in the revolution and in the state* (which is linked to a beginning withering away of the state). International extension of the revolution; accelerated industrialization; the broadening of socialist democracy; the return to genuine soviets; real democracy within the party; soviet party pluralism: all these proposals, this whole strategic line, this whole revolutionary Marxist "counter-project" set against the strategy inspired by the material interests of the bureaucracy, rest on a single internal logic: *the qualitative increase of the weight and power of the proletariat* in the society and the state, establishing, extending, and generalizing the power of the workers councils (soviets).

It must be understood that the socialist revolutions that were victorious after World War II took a particular form, different from that of the October revolution, above all because—aside from the subjective, historical factors—of the fundamental fact that, in the countries where they were victorious, the urban proletariat was not the majority class and did not have sufficient weight to *impose* its own forms of action and specific forms of self-organization and make them hegemonic within the revolutionary process. But this is no longer the case in today's world, in all the imperialist countries, in most of the semi-industrialized dependent countries, and in all the bureaucratized workers states. This is the reason why any proletarian revolution in a large country, and *especially* any victorious proletarian revolution, including an antibureaucratic political revolution, will lead to the formation of workers councils whose rule is the unifying goal that brings together all the various aspects of our world revolutionary strategy.

This is the link between the second and third fundamental theses of the theory of the permanent revolution and the theory of the antibureaucratic political revolution, since a self-reform of the bureaucracy is excluded as all of history has shown since 1923. It is enough to quote Stalin's famous outcry, "These cadres will not be eliminated short of a civil war." Insert "bureaucrats" instead of "cadres" and you have understood the inevitability of the political revolution.

Finally, since the elimination of the bureaucracy, of its monopoly over power, is impossible without a revolution, as confirmed most recently by the Polish events, because for the bureaucracy this monopoly over power ("the leading role of the party") is the source of enormous material privileges which the bureaucrats cherish as the apple of their eye, the question of political revolution now concerns over one-third of humankind, almost one-third of the world proletariat. Any subordination of the political revolution to some alleged "priority" of the "anti-imperialist struggle," associated with a parallel subordination of the uncompromising defense of the proletariat's own interests in the semi-colonial and dependent countries to the same alleged "priority" of the "anti-imperialist objectives," *reduces more than half the world proletariat to the role of auxiliary* (in the best cases), or victim, of the alleged "struggle between the two camps," which are no longer real class camps, but camps made up of states and governments independently of their concrete relations with the real proletariat.[10]

From then on, the unity of the world proletariat, the dialectical unity of the three sectors of the world revolution which expresses this unity, is broken. From then on, the orientation towards the real world revolution which can only be this dialectical unity, is postponed to better days, if not till Doomsday (The day when imperialism will have been defeated? How? Without a victory of the international proletariat?). When one abandons the theory and practice of the permanent revolution, that is the only alternative path which remains open.

Is the problem merely an attempt to "adapt our language" to "facilitate a dialogue" with the Castroist and Sandinist comrades? After all, "workers states," "bureaucratically deformed workers states," "bureaucratically degenerated workers states," "bureaucratized workers states," this is the "jargon of sectarians": no one should be expected to make head or tail of this hokus pokus. Why not use "current language," "common language," when we speak with the "new revolutionary vanguards," and simply say "socialist" states, even if we have to specify that the bureaucracy exists, etc.

But remember that the beginning revision of the theory of permanent revolution had also begun with a simple change in formulas. Then came the revision of the content, and it all ended up with the current rejection of both the formula and the content. This is cause for further thought.

Moreover, the possibility of a regeneration of the CPs is already being raised, albeit (for the moment) only for Central America. But why stop there? What about the CPs of the rest of Latin America? What about those of Africa (the South African ANC, notoriously CP-led, is already projected by some as an emerging "revolutionary leadership")? What about some Arab countries? What about Vietnam? What about Ireland? Are not we slowly evolving towards envisaging the possibility of a regeneration ("democratization") of ruling parties of the bureaucracy in Eastern Europe too?

All moot or even slanderous speculation? Let's hope so. But we noticed that in the *Militant* of October 1, 1982, Comrade Ellen Kratke wrote:

"Many [workers] know there's a struggle going on in the world between two economic systems, capitalism and socialism."

So, an "economic system of socialism" already exists, even if it is a "socialism" with a money economy, a market, large-scale commodity production, wage-labor and many other "niceties" like "socialist" firing of strikers and "socialist" bans on strikes, "socialist" censorship of communist ideas and bookstores, "socialist" internment of oppositionists in psychiatric clinics, etc. So, "socialism in one country" is possible after all?

Just a slip of the pen? Again, let's hope so. But let's note that Comrade Doug Jenness is the editor of the *Militant* and has accustomed us generally to much more "Leninist vigilance."

The reason we are provoking Comrade Jenness in this way is neither because of some hostility nor because of some desire to paint the devil on the wall, as a German proverb puts it. It is because it is the duty of the Fourth International, of all revolutionary Marxist cadres and activists, to pull the alarm signal, to solemnly warn that a scratch is about to turn gangrenous. Our polemic has only one goal: to save the *Socialist Workers Party* for revolutionary Marxism, for the American revolution, for the world revolution. But it will be saved only if it stops the march of some of its leaders towards a break with Trotskyism in time. This is also how the "outside world" that watches us and observes us, has assessed the evolution of Comrade Doug Jenness and his cothinkers, as is obvious from the following quote from the formerly pro-Stalinist and still anti-Trotskyist American weekly, *The Guardian*: "The SWP has been quietly dropping overboard some of its Trotskyist baggage" (July 14, 1982).

DECEMBER 1, 1982

10. The non-Marxist nature of "campism" is revealed most clearly in its assessment of China. During China's military conflict with Vietnam, some campists even called it a "fascist country" or "fascist government." China had become "hegemonic," "reactionary," or even "imperialist" for the apologists of "campism." Yet the relations of production in China and the nature of the state are *identical* to those of the USSR. Does the conjunctural alignment of a state in the game of diplomacy determine its social nature, and not its social and economic foundations? Was not this the erroneous method of the Shachtmanites at the time of the Stalin-Hitler Pact?

Also from Pathfinder

The Communist Manifesto

Karl Marx and Frederick Engels

Communism, say the founding leaders of the revolutionary workers movement, is not a set of ideas or preconceived "principles" but workers' line of march to power, springing from a "movement going on under our very eyes." $5. Also in Spanish, French, Farsi, and Arabic.

Socialism: Utopian and Scientific

Frederick Engels

"To make men the masters of their own form of social organization—to make them free—is the mission of the modern proletariat," writes Engels. A classic guide to the operations of capitalism and struggles of the working class. $10. Also in Farsi.

The Teamster Series

Farrell Dobbs

Four books on the strikes, organizing drives, and political campaigns that transformed the Teamsters across the Midwest in the 1930s into a militant industrial union movement. Written by Farrell Dobbs, the general organizer of these Teamster battles and leader of the Socialist Workers Party.

A tool for workers seeking to use union power in every workplace and advance the fight for an independent labor party. $16 each, series $50. Also in Spanish. *Teamster Rebellion* is also available in French, Farsi, and Greek.

The Jewish Question

A MARXIST INTERPRETATION

Abram Leon

Why is Jew-hatred still raising its ugly head? What are its class roots—from antiquity through feudalism, to capitalism's rise and current crises? Why is there no solution under capitalism? The author, Abram Leon, was killed in the Nazi gas chambers. Revised translation, new introduction, and 40 pages of illustrations and maps. $17. Also in Spanish and French.

EXPAND YOUR REVOLUTIONARY LIBRARY

Cuba and the Coming American Revolution

JACK BARNES

This is a book about the struggles of working people in the imperialist heartland, the youth attracted to them, and the example set by the Cuban people that revolution is not only necessary—it can be made. It is about the class struggle in the US, where the revolutionary capacities of workers and farmers are today as utterly discounted by the ruling powers as were those of the Cuban toilers. And just as wrongly. $10. Also in Spanish, French, and Farsi.

Women's Liberation and the African Freedom Struggle

THOMAS SANKARA

"There is no true social revolution without the liberation of women," explains the leader of the 1983–87 revolution in the West African country of Burkina Faso. $5. Also in Spanish, French, and Farsi.

Women in Cuba: The Making of a Revolution within the Revolution

VILMA ESPÍN
ASELA DE LOS SANTOS
YOLANDA FERRER

The integration of women in the ranks and leadership of the Cuban Revolution was intertwined with the proletarian course of the leadership of the revolution from the start. This is the story of that revolution and how it transformed the women and men who made it. $17. Also in Spanish, Farsi, and Greek.

The Clintons' Anti-Working-Class Record

Why Washington Fears Working People

JACK BARNES

What working people need to know about the profit-driven course of Democrats and Republicans alike over the last three decades. And the political awakening of workers seeking to understand and resist the capitalist rulers' assaults. $10. Also in Spanish, French, Farsi, and Greek.

50 Years of Covert Operations in the US

Washington's Political Police and the American Working Class

LARRY SEIGLE, FARRELL DOBBS
STEVE CLARK

How class-conscious workers have fought against the drive to build the "national security" state essential to maintaining capitalist rule. $10. Also in Spanish and Farsi.

Marianas in Combat

Teté Puebla and the Mariana Grajales Women's Platoon in Cuba's Revolutionary War, 1956–58

TETÉ PUEBLA

Brigadier General Teté Puebla, the highest-ranking woman in Cuba's Revolutionary Armed Forces, joined the struggle to overthrow the US-backed dictatorship of Fulgencio Batista in 1956, when she was fifteen years old. This is her story—from clandestine action in the cities, to serving as an officer in the victorious Rebel Army's first all-women's unit. The fight to transform the social and economic status of women in Cuba remains inseparable from its socialist revolution. $10. Also in Spanish and Farsi.

The History of the Russian Revolution

LEON TROTSKY

How, under Lenin's leadership, the Bolshevik Party led millions of workers and farmers to overthrow the state power of the landlords and capitalists in 1917 and bring to power a government that advanced their class interests at home and worldwide. Unabridged, 3 vols. in one. Written by one of the central leaders of that socialist revolution. $30. Also in French and Russian.

Red Zone

Cuba and the Battle against Ebola in West Africa

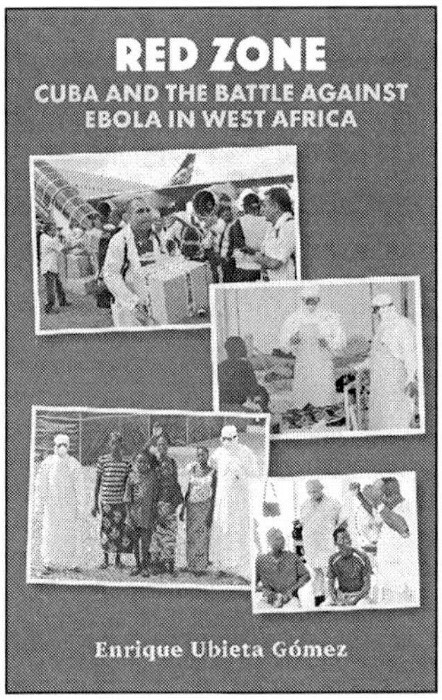

ENRIQUE UBIETA GÓMEZ

When three African countries were hit in 2014–15 by the Ebola epidemic, Cuba's revolutionary government sent what no other country even pretended to provide: more than 250 volunteer doctors, nurses, and other medical workers. This firsthand account of their actions shows the kind of men and women only a socialist revolution can produce. $17. Also in Spanish and French.

Maurice Bishop Speaks

The Grenada Revolution and Its Overthrow, 1979–83

The triumph of the 1979 revolution in the Caribbean island of Grenada under the leadership of Maurice Bishop gave hope to millions throughout the Americas. Invaluable lessons from the workers and farmers government destroyed by a Stalinist-led counterrevolution in 1983. $20

To See the Dawn

Baku, 1920—First Congress of the Peoples of the East

How can peasants and workers in the colonial world achieve freedom from imperialist exploitation? By what means can working people overcome divisions incited by their national ruling classes and act together for their common class interests? These questions were addressed by 2,000 delegates to the 1920 Congress of the Peoples of the East. $17

Cosmetics, Fashions, and the Exploitation of Women

JOSEPH HANSEN, EVELYN REED
MARY-ALICE WATERS

How big business reinforces women's second-class status and uses it to rake in profits. Where does women's oppression come from? How has the entry of millions of women into the workforce strengthened the battle for emancipation, still to be won? $12. Also in Spanish, Farsi, and Greek.

Lenin's Struggle for a Revolutionary International

Documents, 1907–1916; The Preparatory Years

The debate among revolutionary working-class leaders, including V.I. Lenin and Leon Trotsky, on a socialist response to World War I. $30

Socialism on Trial

Testimony at Minneapolis Sedition Trial

JAMES P. CANNON

The revolutionary program of the working class, presented in response to frame-up charges of "seditious conspiracy" in 1941, on the eve of US entry into World War II. The defendants were leaders of the Minneapolis labor movement and the Socialist Workers Party. $15. Also in Spanish, French, and Farsi.

Capitalism and the Transformation of Africa

Reports from Equatorial Guinea

MARY-ALICE WATERS
MARTÍN KOPPEL

Describes how, as Equatorial Guinea is pulled into the world market, both a capitalist class and a working class are being born. Also documents the work of volunteer Cuban health-care workers there—an expression of the living example of Cuba's socialist revolution. $10. Also in Spanish and Farsi.

By Any Means Necessary

MALCOLM X

"The imperialists know the only way you will voluntarily turn to the fox is to show you a wolf." In eleven speeches and interviews, Malcolm X presents a revolutionary alternative to this reformist trap, taking up political alliances, women's rights, US intervention in the Congo and Vietnam, capitalism and socialism, and more. $15

Are They Rich Because They're Smart?

Class, Privilege, and Learning under Capitalism

JACK BARNES

In battles forced on us by the capitalists, workers will begin to transform our attitudes toward life, work, and each other. We'll discover our worth, denied by the rulers and upper middle classes who insist they're rich because they're smart. We'll learn in struggle what we're capable of becoming. $10. Also in Spanish, French, Farsi, and Arabic.

Labor's Giant Step

The First Twenty Years of the CIO: 1936–55

ART PREIS

The story of the explosive labor struggles and political battles in the 1930s that built the industrial unions. And how those unions became the vanguard of a mass social movement that began transforming US society. $27

Problems of Everyday Life

LEON TROTSKY

Articles from the early Soviet press on social and cultural issues in the struggle to forge new social relations. The advance of culture, Trotsky notes, requires an increasing level of scientific, technological, and industrial development to "free humanity from a dependence upon nature that is degrading"—a goal that can only be completed when social relationships are "free from mystery and do not oppress people." $20

The Revolution Betrayed

What Is the Soviet Union and Where Is It Going?

LEON TROTSKY

In 1917 workers and peasants of Russia were the motor force for one of the deepest revolutions in history. Yet within ten years a political counterrevolution by a privileged social layer, whose chief spokesperson was Joseph Stalin, was being consolidated. The classic study of the Soviet workers state and its degeneration. $17. Also in Spanish, Farsi, and Greek.

We Are Heirs of the World's Revolutions

Speeches from the Burkina Faso Revolution, 1983–87

THOMAS SANKARA

How peasants and workers in this West African country established a popular revolutionary government and began to fight hunger, illiteracy, and economic backwardness imposed by imperialist domination. They set an example not only for workers and small farmers in Africa, but their class brothers and sisters the world over. $10. Also in Spanish, French, and Farsi.